Anonymous

Compilation of the tariff act, of the Confederate States of America, approved May 21st, 1861,

Showing the rates of duties payable on imported goods, wares and merchandise, from and after September 1st, 1861, alphabetically arranged

Anonymous

Compilation of the tariff act, of the Confederate States of America, approved May 21st, 1861,
Showing the rates of duties payable on imported goods, wares and merchandise, from and after September 1st, 1861, alphabetically arranged

ISBN/EAN: 9783337714994

Printed in Europe, USA, Canada, Australia, Japan

Cover: Foto ©ninafisch / pixelio.de

More available books at **www.hansebooks.com**

COMPILATION

OF THE

TARIFF ACT

OF THE

CONFEDERATE STATES OF AMERICA,

APPROVED MAY 21st, 1861,

SHOWING THE

Rates of Duties Payable on Imported Goods, Wares and Merchandise,

FROM AND AFTER SEPTEMBER 1st, 1861,

ALPHABETICALLY ARRANGED;

ALSO CONTAINING

RECENT ACTS OF CONGRESS

AND CIRCULARS OF THE TREASURY DEPARTMENT,

RELATIVE TO

COMMERCE, NAVIGATION AND THE REVENUE;

TOGETHER WITH THE

WAREHOUSE SYSTEM,

FORMS OF CUSTOM HOUSE BLANKS; PROTESTS AND APPEALS; TABLES OF FOREIGN WEIGHTS, MEASURES AND CURRENCIES, REDUCED TO THE STANDARD OF THE CONFEDERATE STATES; RULES FOR ADMEASUREMENT OF VESSELS FOR TONNAGE, &c.

Arranged by P. E. WALDEN,

DEPUTY COLLECTOR, CUSTOM HOUSE, PORT OF NEW ORLEANS.

NEW ORLEANS:
PRINTED AND PUBLISHED BY CORSON & ARMSTRONG, 50 CAMP STREET.
1861.

Entered according to the act of Congress, in the year 1861, by Corson & Armstrong, in the Clerk's Office of the Eastern District of Louisiana.

INDEX.

A

	PAGE
Abatement of Duty for Damage	242
Act to Provide Revenue from Imports	1
Act to Amend Tariff Act of 21st May, 1861	16
Act to Continue certain Laws of the United States in force	105
Act to Define the Limits of the Port of New Orleans	105
Act to Prohibit Exportation of Cotton, except through Seaports	106
Act Declaring the Free Navigation of the Mississippi River	107
Act to Modify Navigation Laws and Repeal Discriminating Duties	110
Act Authorizing Additional Ports of Entry, etc	110
Act Providing for Export Duty on Cotton	111
Act Removing Prohibitions on certain Importations	111
Act Providing for Registration of Vessels	112
Act to Regulate Foreign Coins	112
Act to Provide for Light Money	114
Act to Exempt from Duty certain Articles	114
Act to Authorize the Transit of Merchandise	115
Additional Duty	239
Admeasurement of Vessels	229
Admeasurement of Coal in Flatboats	229
Allowances	210
Amsterdam Pounds, Reduction of	86
Antwerp Pounds, Reduction of	82
Appeals—See Protest and Appeals	208
Applications for Damage Allowance	217
Arrobas, Spanish, Reduction of	86
Arrobas, Portuguese, Reduction of	88
Austrian Pounds, Reduction of	82

B

Bremen Rix Dollar, Reduction of	78
Bonded Warehouses	159
Bonded Yards and Sheds	164

ii INDEX.

C

	PAGE
Charges for Storage, etc.	170
Change of Master of Registered Vessels	249
Claims for Refunding	248
Clearances for Foreign Ports	221
Clearances Coastwise	222
Clearance, Form of	227
Certificate of Payment of Light Money	157
Circular Instructions	116 to 158
Cotton Press Rates at New Orleans	259
Cotton, Exportation of—See Act of Congress	106
Cotton, Export Duty on—See Act of Congress	111
Coal, how Measured in Flatboats	229
Commissions—See Dutiable Value of Imports	235
Commissions on Sales, Rates of at New Orleans	253
Compensation of Merchant Appraisers	246
Commercial and Port Rates at New Orleans	253
Currencies, Tables of	71 to 81
Currencies, Foreign, Rates of, by Law	89
Currencies, Rates of, by Usage	90
Custom House Blanks	224
Cwts. Reduced to Pounds	84

D

Damage on Voyage of Importation	242
Damage, etc., on Goods in Bond	243
Deficiencies, etc	239
Delivery of Appraised Packages	216
Discounts	236
Discriminating Duties Repealed—See Act of Congress	110
Dockage, Rates of at New Orleans	256
Duties, Allowances, Deficiencies, etc	239
Dutiable Value of Imports	235

E

Entrance and Clearance of Vessels	219
Extracts	247
Express Carriers—See Treasury Circulars	145, 155
Entries, persons authorized to make	233
Exportation of Cotton—See Act of Congress	106

INDEX.

	PAGE
Export Duty on Cotton—See Act of Congress	111
Export from Warehouse	195
Exportations in Bond Inland to Mexico	203
Export Bonds, how Cancelled	198
Equalization of Foreign Vessels	248
Entry of Goods in Bond	174
Entry for Warehousing	175
Entry for Withdrawal for Consumption	178
Entry for Withdrawal for Transportation	180
Entry for Re-warehousing	183
Entry for Warehouse and Transportation	192
Entry for Exportation	195
Entry for Consumption	212
Entry by Appraisement	217
Entry of Manufactures, etc., of the U. S., exported and brought back	237

F

Francs, Reduction of	76
Fees, List of	230
French Killogrammes, Reduction of	87
French Litres, Reduction of	87
French Feet, Reduction of	88
Freights, Rates of at New Orleans	258
Foreign Currencies, Rates of	89
Foreign Coins, Rates of	91
Foreign Coins, Act Regulating	112
Foreign Weights and Measures, Tables of	92 to 101
Form of Protest	208
Form of Appeal	210
Form of Consumption Entry	213

H

Harbor Masters' Fees at New Orleans	280

I

Inland Exportation to Mexico in Bond	203
Inland Manifest	205
Importations by Mississippi and other Rivers—See Treasury Circular	116, 126
Importation Bond, Form of	139
Importations by Railroad and Inland Routes—See Treasury Circular	131

	PAGE
Imports, Dutiable Value of	235
Information for Shipmasters and Others	248

K

Killogrammes, French, Table of	87

L

Levee Dues at New Orleans	280
List of Fees	230
List of Tares	102
Litres, French, Table of	87
Light Money—See Act of Congress and Treasury Circular	114, 157
Light Money	248
Liquors Invoiced and Entered by the Package	241
Louis D'or, Thaler, Table of	78

M

Manifests, Forms of	226
Manner of Transacting Business at the Custom House	212
Mexico, Inland Exportation to	203
Merchant Appraisers, Compensation of	246
Miscellaneous Valuable Information	224
Mississippi River, Free Navigation of—See Act	107
Mississippi River, Importations by—See Treasury Circulars	116, 126
Mobile, Port Charges at	281
Moving Vessels	275

N

Navigation Laws Modified—See Act of Congress	110
New Orleans Levee and Wharfage Dues	280
New Orleans, Limits of the Port of—See Act of Congress	105
Notice of Dissatisfaction or Protest, etc	209

P

Persons Authorized to Make Entries	233
Printing of Silks in Bond	200
Protests and Appeals	208
Port of New Orleans, Limits Defined	105
Ports and Places of Entry and Delivery, Additional ones authorized	110
Portuguese Arrobas, Tables of	88

INDEX.

	PAGE
Port Charges at Mobile............................	281
Port Wardens' Fees at New Orleans...................	279
Pounds Spanish, Table of............................	81
Pounds Austrian, Table of...........................	82
Pounds of Amsterdam and Netherlands, Table of.......	86
Pounds of Antwerp, Table of.........................	82
Pounds Sterling, Table of............................	71
Power of Attorney, Form of..........................	227
Prussian Rix Dollars, Table of.......................	80

Q

Qrs. Reduced to Pounds, Table of....................	85
Quarantine Charges at New Orleans...................	279

R

Rates of Foreign Money or Currencies, by Law........	89
Rates of Foreign Currencies, by Usage................	90
Rates of the New Orleans Tow Boats...........261 to	275
Rates for Pilotage in and out of the Mississippi Passes...	277
Rates of Towage on Dog River Bar, Mobile............	281
Registration of Vessels—See Act and Circular......112,	129
Receiving and Forwarding Merchandise, Rates of at New Orleans.	254
Re-warehouse Entry..................................	183
Re-warehousing and Withdrawal Entry................	185
Re-warehouse and Withdrawal Entry for Export.......	187
Re-warehouse Withdrawal Entry for Consumption.....	190
Re-warehouse Withdrawal Entry for Transportation...	191
Re-warehouse Withdrawal Entry for Exportation......	191
Re-appraisement.....................................	245
Report and Entrance.................................	251
Rix Dollar of Bremen, Table of.......................	78
Rix Dollar of Prussia, Table of.......................	80

S

Spanish Pounds, Table of.............................	81
Spanish Arrobas, Table of............................	86
Sterling Money, Table of.............................	71
Shipmasters, Information for.........................	218
Storage and Labor, Rates of at New Orleans..........	257

T

	PAGE
Table of Sterling Money	71
" Francs	76
" Bremen Rix Dollars	78
" Prussian Rix Dollars	80
" Tons Reduced to Pounds	83
" Spanish Pounds	81
" Austrian Pounds	82
" Antwerp Pounds	82
" Cwts. Reduced to Pounds	84
" Qrs. Reduced to Pounds	85
" Amsterdam Pounds	86
" Spanish Arrobas	86
" French Killogrammes	87
" French Litres	87
" French Feet	88
" Portuguese Arrobas	88
" Weights and Measures	92 to 100
Tariff Act	1
Tariff Alphabetically Arranged	17 to 70
Tares, List of	102
Tares, Rates of at New Orleans	258
Transfer of Goods in Bond	173
Transfer of Property in Vessels	250
Treasury Circulars	116 to 158
Time of Making Appeals, etc.	211
Time of Vessels to Discharge	222
Time of Report and Entrance of Vessels	251
Tons Reduced to Pounds, Table of	83
Tonnage of Vessels, How Ascertained	229
Towage, Rates of at New Orleans	261 to 265

U

Unlading Cargoes	222
United States Laws Continued—See Acts	105

V

Vessels in the Coasting Trade	249

W

	PAGE
Warehouse System	159
Warehouse Entry	175
Warehouse and Transportation Entry	192
Warehouse and Exportation Entry	197
Weights and Measures, Tables of	92 to 100
Weights of Grain, Rates of at New Orleans	258
Wrecked Goods	251
Withdrawal Entry for Consumption	179
Withdrawal Entry for Transportation	180
Withdrawal Entry for Exportation	195
Withdrawal Entry for Transportation and Exportation to Mexico	201
Withdrawal of Silks for Dyeing	201

ACT

TO PROVIDE REVENUE FROM COMMODITIES IMPORTED FROM FOREIGN COUNTRIES.

SECTION 1. *The Congress of the Confederate States of America do enact,* That from and after the 31st day of August next, a duty shall be imposed on all goods, products, wares and merchandise imported from abroad into the Confederate States of America, as follows :

On all articles enumerated in Schedule A, an ad valorem duty of twenty-five per centum. On all articles enumerated in Schedule B, an ad valorem duty of twenty per centum. On all articles enumerated in Schedule C, an ad valorem duty of fifteen per centum. On all articles enumerated in Schedule D, an ad valorem duty of ten per centum. On all articles enumerated in Schedule E, an ad valorem duty of five per centum. And that all articles enumerated in Schedule F, a Specific Duty as therein named. And that all articles enumerated in Schedule G, shall be exempt from duty : to wit :

SCHEDULE A.

TWENTY-FIVE *per centum ad valorem.*

Alabaster and spar ornaments; anchovies, sardines, and all other fish preserved in oil.

Brandy and other spirits distilled from grain or other materials, not otherwise provided for; billiard and bagatelle tables, and all other tables or boards on which games are played.

Composition tops for tables, or other articles of furniture; confectionary, comfits, sweetmeats, or fruits preserved in sugar, molasses, brandy or other liquors, cordials, absynthe, arrack, curacoa, kirschenwesser, liquors, maraschino, ratafia, and all other spirituous beverages of a similar character.

Glass, cut.

Manufactures of cedarwood, granadilla, ebony, mahogany, rosewood and satinwood.

Scagliola tops for tables or other articles of furniture; segars, snuff, paper segars, and all other manufactures of tobacco.

Wines—Burgundy, champagne, clarets, madeira, port, sherry, and all other wines or imitations of wines.

SCHEDULE B.

Twenty *per centum ad valorem.*

Almonds, raisins, currants, dates, figs and all other dried or preserved fruits, not otherwise provided for; argentine, alabata, or German silver, manufactured or unmanufactured; articles embroidered with gold, silver, or other metal, not otherwise provided for.

Balsams, cosmetics, essences, extracts, pastes, perfumes and tinctures used for the toilet or for medicinal purposes; bay rum, beads or amber, composition of wax, and all other beads; benzoates; bracelets, braids, chains, curls, or ringlets, composed of hair, or of which hair is a component part, not otherwise provided for; brooms and brushes of all kinds.

Camphor, refined; canes and sticks, for walking, finished or unfinished; capers, pickles and sauces of all kinds, not otherwise provided for; card vases, pocket books, shell boxes, souvenirs, and all similar articles, of whatever material composed, not otherwise provided for; compositions of glass, set or unset; coral, cut or manufactured.

Feathers and flowers, artificial or ornamental, and parts thereof, of whatever material composed; fans and fire screens of every description, of whatever material composed.

Grapes, plums, and prunes, and other such fruit, when put up in bottles, cases or cans, not otherwise provided for.

Hair, human, cleansed or prepared for use.

Manufactures of gold, platina, or silver, not otherwise provided for; manufactures of papier maché; molasses.

Paintings on glass; pepper, pimento, cloves, nutmegs, cinnamon and all other spices; perfumes and perfumery, of all sorts, not otherwise provided for; plated and gilt ware of all kinds, not otherwise provided for; playing cards; prepared vegetables, fruits, meats, poultry and game, sealed or enclosed in cans or otherwise.

Silver-plated metals, in sheets or other form; soap, castile, perfumed, windsor, and other toilet soaps; sugar of all kinds; syrup of sugar.

Epaulettes, galloons, laces, knots, stars, tassels, tresses, and wings of gold or silver, or imitations thereof.

SCHEDULE C.

Fifteen *per centum ad valorem.*

Alum; arrow-root; articles of clothing or apparel, including hats, caps, gloves, shoes and boots of all kinds, worn by men, women, or children, of whatever material composed, not otherwise provided for.

Baizes, blankets, bockings, flannels and floor-cloths, of whatever material composed, not otherwise provided for; baskets and all articles composed of grass, osier, palm leaf, straw, whale-bone or willow, not otherwise provided for; beer, ale, and porter, in casks or bottles; beeswax; berries and vegetables of all sorts used for food, not otherwise provided for; blue or roman vitriol, or sulphate of copper; Bologna sausages; braces, suspenders, webbing, or other fabrics, composed wholly or in part of India rubber, not otherwise provided for; breccia; burgundy pitch; buttons and button moulds of all kinds.

Cables and cordage, of whatever material made; cadmium; calamine; calomel and all other mercurial preparations; carbonate of soda; castor beans; castor oil; candles and tapers of spermaceti, stearine, parafine, tallow or wax and all other candles; caps, hats, muffs and tippets, and all other manufactures of fur, or of which fur shall be a component part; caps, gloves, leggins, mits, socks, stockings, wove shirts and drawers, and all similar articles worn by men, women and children, and not otherwise provided for; carpets, carpeting, hearth-rugs, bed-sides, and other portions of carpeting, being either Aubusson, Brussels, ingrain, Saxony, Turkey, Venetian, Wilton, or any other similar fabric, not otherwise provided for; carriages and parts of carriages; castorum; chains, of all sorts; cider and other beverages not containing alcohol, and not otherwise provided for; chocolate; chromate of lead; chromate, bi-chromate, hydriodate, and prussiate of potash; clocks and parts of clocks; coach and harness furniture of all kinds; cobalt; combs of all kinds; copper bottoms; copper rods, bolts, nails, and spikes; copper in sheets or plates, called braziers' copper, and other sheets of copper, not otherwise provided for; copperas, or green vitriol, or sulphate of iron; corks; cotton cords, gimps, and galloons; cotton laces, cotton insertings, cotton trimming laces, cotton laces and braids; court plaster; coral unmanufactured; crayons of all kinds; cubebs; cutlery of all kinds.

Delaines; dolls and toys of all kinds; dried pulp; drugs, medicinal.

Earthen, china, and stone ware, and all other wares composed of earthy and mineral substances, not otherwise provided for; encaustic tiles; ether; felspar; fig blue; fire crackers, sky-rockets, Roman candles, and all similar articles used in pyrotechnics; fish, whether fresh, smoked, salted, dried or pickled, not otherwise provided for; fruits, preserved in their own juice, or pie fruits; fish-glue, or isin-glass; fish skins; flats, braids, plaits, sparterre and willow squares, used for making hats or bonnets; floss silks, feather beds, feathers for beds, and downs of all kinds; frames and sticks for umbrellas, parasols, and sunshades, finished or unfinished; Frankford black; fulminates or fulminating powders; furniture, cabinet and household, not otherwise provided for; furs, dressed on the skin.

Ginger, dried, green, ripe, ground, preserved, or pickled; glass, colored, stained, or painted; glass, window; glass crystals for watches; glasses or pebbles for spectacles; glass tumblers, plain, moulded and pressed; bottles, flasks, and all other vessels of glass, not otherwise provided for; glue; grass cloth; green turtle; gum, benzoin or benjamin; guns, except muskets and rifles, fire arms and all parts thereof not intended for military purposes; gunny cloth and India baggings and India mattings of all sorts, not otherwise provided for.

Hair, curled, moss, seaweed, and all other vegetable substances, used for beds or mattresses; hair pencils; hat bodies of cotton or wool; hats and bonnets for men, women and children, composed of straw, satin straw, chip, grass, palm leaf, willow or any other vegetable substance, or of hair, whalebone, or other materials, not otherwise provided for; hatter's plush of whatever material composed; honey.

Ink and ink powder; ipecacuanha; iridium; iris, or orris root; iron castings; iron liquor; iron in bars, bolts, rods, slabs, and railroad rails, spikes, fishing plates and chairs used in constructing railroads; ivory black.

Jalap; japanned ware of all kinds, not otherwise provided for; jet, and manufactures of jet, or imitations thereof; jewelry or imitations thereof; juniper berries.

Laces of cotton, of thread or other materials, not otherwise provided for; lampblack; lastings, cut in strips, or patterns of the size or shape for shoes, boots, bootees, slippers, gaiters or buttons, of whatever material composed; lead pencils; leaden pipes; leather, japanned; leeches; linens, of all kinds; liquorice paste, juice or root; litharge.

Maccaroni, vermicelli, gelatine, jellies, and all other similar preparations, not otherwise provided for; machinery of every description, not otherwise provided for; malt; magnesia; manganese; manna; manufactures of the bark of the cork tree; manufactures of silk; manufactures of wool of all kinds, or worsted, not otherwise provided for; manufactures of hair of all kinds, not otherwise provided for; manufactures of cotton of all kinds, not otherwise provided for; manufactures of flax of all kinds, not otherwise provided for; manufactures of hemp of all kinds, not otherwise provided for; manufactures of bone, shell, horn, pearl, ivory, or vegetable ivory, not otherwise provided for; manufactures, articles, vessels and wares, not otherwise provided for, of brass, copper, iron, steel, lead, pewter, tin, or of which either of these metals shall be a component part; manufactures, articles, vessels, and wares, of glass, or of which glass shall be a component material, not otherwise provided for; manufactures and articles of leather, or of which leather shall be a component part, not otherwise provided for; manufactures and articles of marble, marble paving tiles, and all other marble more advanced in manufacture than in slabs or blocks in the rough, not otherwise provided for; manufactures of paper, or of which paper is a component material, not otherwise provided for; manufactures of wood or of which wood is a component part, not otherwise provided for; matting, china or other floor matting, and mats made of flags, jute, or grass; medicinal preparations, drugs, roots, and leaves in a crude state, not otherwise provided for; morphine; metallic pens; mineral waters; musical instruments of all kinds, and strings for musical instruments, of whipgut, catgut, and all other strings of the same material; mustard, in bulk or in bottles; mustard seed.

Needles of all kinds for sewing, darning and knitting; nitrate of lead.

Ochres and ochrey earths; oil-cloths of every description, of whatever material composed; oils of every description, animal, vegetable and mineral, not otherwise provided for; olives; opium; orange and lemon peal; osier or willow, prepared for basket-makers' use.

Paints, dry or ground in oil, not otherwise provided for; paper, antiquarian, demy, drawing, elephant, foolscap, imperial, letter, and for printing newspapers, hand-bills, and other printing, and all other paper, not otherwise provided for; paper boxes, and all other fancy boxes; paper envelopes; paper hangings; paper for walls, and paper for screens or fire-boards; parchment; parasols and sun-shades and umbrellas; patent mordant; paving and roofing tiles and bricks, and roofing slates, and fire-bricks; periodicals and other works, in course of printing and republication in the Confederate States; pitch; plaster of Paris, calcined; plumbago; potassium; putty.

Quicksilver; quills; quasia, manufactured or unmanufactured.

Red chalk pencils; rhubarb; roman cement.

Saddlery of all kinds, not otherwise provided for; saffron, and saffron cake; sago; salts, epsom, glauber, rochelle, and all other salts and preparations of salts, not otherwise provided for; sarsaparilla; screws of all kinds; sealing wax; seines; seppia; sewing silk, in the gum and purified; shaddocks; skins of all kinds, tanned, dressed, or japanned; slate pencils; smaltz; soda of every description, not otherwise provided for; spirits of turpentine; spunk; squills; starch; stereotype plates; still bottoms;

sulphate of barytes, crude or refined; sulphate of quinine, and quinine in all its various preparations.

Tapioca; tar; textile fabrics of every description, not otherwise provided for; twine and packed thread, of whatever material composed; thread, lacings and insertings; types, old or new, and type metals.

Umbrellas; vandyke brown; vanilla beans; varnish of all kinds, vellum; venetian red; velvet in piece, composed wholly of cotton, or of cotton and silk, but of which cotton is the component material of chief value; verdigris; vermillion; vinegar.

Wafers; water colors; whalebone; white and red lead; white vitrol or sulphate of zinc; whiting or Paris white; window glass, broad, crown or cylinder; woollen and worsted yarns and woollen listings; shot of lead, not otherwise provided for; wheelbarrows and hand-barrows; wagons and vehicles of every description, or parts thereof.

SCHEDULE D.

Ten per centum ad valorem.

Acids of every description, not otherwise provided for; alcornoque; aloes; ambergris; amber; ammonia, and sal ammonia; anatto, roucon or orleans; angora, thibet, and other goats' hair, or mohair, unmanufactured, not otherwise provided for; anniseed; antimony, crude or regulus of; argol, or crude tartar; arsenic; ashes, pot, pearl and soda; asphaltum; assafœtida.

Bananas, cocoa nuts, pine apples, plantains, oranges and all West India fruits in their natural state; barilla; bark of all kinds, not otherwise provided for; bark, Peruvian; bark, guilla; bismuth; bitter apples; bleaching powder of chloride of lime; bones, burnt; boards, planks, staves, shingles, laths, scantling, and all other sawed lumber; also spars and hewn timber, of all sorts, not otherwise provided for; bone black, or animal carbon, and bone dust; bolting cloths; books, printed magazines, pamphlets, periodicals, and illustrated newspapers, bound or unbound, not otherwise provided for; books, blank, bound or unbound; borate of lime; borax, crude or tincal; borax, refined; bouchu leaves; box-wood, unmanufactured; Brazil paste, Brazil wood, braziletto, and all dye-woods in sticks; bristles; bronze and Dutch metal in leaf; bronze liquor and bronze powder; building stones; butter; burr stones, wrought or unwrought.

Cabinets of coins, medals, and all collections of antiquities; camphor; crude; cantharides; cassia and cassia buds; chalk; cheese; chickory root, chronometers, box or ship, and parts thereof; clay, burnt or unburnt bricks, paving and roofing tiles, gas retorts, and roofing slates; coal, coke, and culm of coal; cochineal; cocoa nuts, cocoa, and cocoa shells; coculus indicus; coir yarn; codilla, or tow of hemp or flax; cowhage down; cream of tartar; cudbear.

Diamonds, cameos, mosaics, gems, pearls, rubies and other precious stones, and imitations thereof, when set in gold or silver, or other metal; diamonds, glaziers', set or not set; dragon's blood.

Engravings, bound or unbound; extract of indigo, extracts and decoctions of log-wood and other dye-woods, not otherwise provided for; extract of madder; ergot.

Flax, unmanufactured; flaxseed and linseed; flints and flint ground; flocks, waste or shoddy; French chalk; furs, hatters', dressed or undressed, not on the skin; furs, undressed, when on the skin.

Glass, when old and fit only to be remanufactured; gamboge; gold and silver leaf; gold beaters' skin; grindstones; gums— Arabic, Barbary, copal, East Indies, Senegal, substitute, tragacanth, and all other gums and resins, in a crude state, not otherwise provided for.

Hair, of all kinds, uncleansed and unmanufactued; hemp, unmanufactured; hemp seed and rape seed; hops, horns, horn-tips, bone, bone-tips, and teeth, unmanufactured.

Ivory, unmanufactured; ivory nuts, or vegetable ivory.

Jute, sisal grass, coir, and other vegetable substances, unmanufactured, not otherwise provided for.

Kelp; kermes.

Lac spirits, lac sulphur, and lac dye; leather, tanned, bend, sole, and upper of all kinds, not otherwise provided for; lemons and limes, and lemon and lime juice, and juices of all other fruits without sugar; lime.

Madder, ground or prepared; madder root; marble, in the rough, slab or block, unmanufactured; metals, unmanufactured, not otherwise provided for; mineral kermes; mineral and bituminous substances in a crude state, not otherwise provided for; moss, iceland; music, printed with lines, bound or unbound.

Natron; nickel; nuts, not otherwise provided for; nut galls; nux vomica.

Oakum; oranges, lemons, and limes; orpiment.

Palm leaf, unmanufactured; pearl, mother of; pine apples; plantains; platina, unmanufactured; polishing stones; potatoes; Prussian blue; pumice and pumice stone.

Ratans, and reeds, unmanufactured; red chalk; rotten stone.

Safflower; sal soda; and all carbonates and sulphates of soda, by whatever names designated, not otherwise provided for; seedlac; shellac; silk, raw, not more advanced in manufacture than singles, tram and thrown, or organzine; sponges; steel in bars, sheets and plates, not further advanced in manufacture than by rolling, and cast steel in bars; sumac; sulphur, flour of.

Tallow, marrow, and all other grease or soap stocks and soap stuffs, not otherwise provided for; tea, terne tin, in plates or sheets; teazle, terra, japonica, catechu, tin in plates or sheets and tin foil; tortoise and other shells, unmanufactured; trees, shrubs, bulbs, plants and roots, not otherwise provided for; turmeric.

Watches and parts of watches; woad or pastel; woods; viz: cedar, box, ebony, lignumvitæ, granadilla, mahogany, rose-wood, satin-wood, and all other woods, unmanufactured.

Iron ore, and iron in blooms, loops and pigs.

Maps and charts.

Paintings and statuary not otherwise provided for.

Wool, unmanufactured, of every description, and hair of the Alapaca goat and other like animals.

Specimens of natural history, mineralogy or botany, not otherwise provided for.

Yams.

Leaf and unmanufactured tobacco.

SCHEDULE E.

Five per centum ad valorem.

Articles used in dyeing and tanning, not otherwise provided for.

Brass, in bars or pigs, old and fit only to be remanufactured; bells, old; bell metal.

Copper in pigs or bars; copper ore; copper, when old and fit only to be remanufactured; cutch.

Diamonds, cameos, mosaics, pearls, gems, rubies, and other precious stones, and imitations thereof, when not set.

Emery in lump or pulverized.

Felt, adhesive for sheathing vessels; fuller's earth.

Gums of all sorts, not otherwise provided for; gutta percha, unmanufactured

Indigo; india rubber, in bottles, slabs or sheets, unmanufactured; india rubber, milk of.

Junk, old.

Plaster of Paris or sulphate of lime, ground or unground; raw hides and skins of all kinds, undressed.

Sheathing copper, but no copper to be considered as such except in sheets forty-eight inches long and fourteen inches wide, and weighing from eleven to thirty-four ounces; sheathing or yellow metal not wholly or part of iron; sheathing or yellow metal nails, expressly for sheathing vessels; sheathing paper, stave bolts and shingle bolts.

Tin ore and tin in pigs or bars; type, old and fit only to be remanufactured.

Wold.

Zinc, spelter, or tentenegue, unmanufactured.

SCHEDULE F.

Specific Duties.

Ice—one dollar and fifty cents per ton.

Salt, ground, blown, or rock—two cents per bushel, of fifty-six pounds per bushel.

SCHEDULE G.

Exempt from Duty.

Books, maps, charts, mathematical and nautical instruments, philosophical apparatus, and all other articles whatever, imported for the use of the Confederate States; books, pamphlets, periodicals and tracts, published by religious associations.

All philosophical apparatus, instruments, books, maps and charts, statues, statuary, busts and casts of marble, bronze, alabaster or plaster of Paris, paintings and drawings, etchings, specimens of sculpture, cabinet of coins, medals, gems, and all collections of antiquities. *Provided* the same be specially imported in good faith for the use of any society, incorporated or established for philosophical and literary purposes, or for the encouragement of the fine arts, or for the use or by the order of any church, college, academy, school, or seminary of learning in the Confederate States.

Bullion, gold, and silver.

Coins, gold, silver and copper; coffee; cotton; copper, when imported for the mint of the Confederate States.

Garden seeds, and all other seeds for agricultural and horticultural purposes; goods, wares and merchandize, the growth, produce or manufacture of the Confederate States, exported to a foreign country, and brought back to the Confederate States in the same condition as when exported, upon which no drawback has been allowed. *Provided* that all regulations to ascertain the identity thereof, prescribed by existing laws, or which may be prescribed by the Secretary of the Treasury, shall be complied with; guano, manures and fertilizers of all sorts.

Household effects, old and in use, of persons or families from foreign countries, if used abroad by them, and not intended for any other purpose or purposes, or for sale.

Models or inventions or other improvements in the arts. *Provided* that no article or articles shall be deemed a model which can be fitted for use.

Paving stones; personal and household effects, not merchandise, of citizens of the Confederate States dying abroad.

Specimens of natural history, mineralogy or botany. *Provided* the same be imported in good faith for the use of any society incorporated or established for philosophical, agricultural or horticultural purposes, or for the use or by the order of any college, academy, school, or seminary of learning in the Confederate States.

Wearing apparel, and other personal effects not merchandize; professional books, implements, instruments and tools of trades, occupation or employment, of persons arriving in the Confederate States. *Provided* that this exemption shall not be construed to include machinery, or other articles imported for use in any manufacturing establishment, or for sale.

Bacon, pork, hams, lard, beef, wheat, flour and bran of wheat, flour and bran of all other grains, Indian corn and meal, barley, rye, oats, and oatmeal, and living animals of all kinds, not otherwise provided for; also, all agricultural productions, including those of the orchard and garden, in their natural state, not otherwise provided for.

Gunpowder, and all the materials of which it is made.

Lead, in pigs or bars, in shot or balls, for cannon, muskets, rifles, or pistols.

Rags, of whatever material composed.

Arms of every description, for military purposes and parts thereof, munitions of war, military accoutrements and percussion caps.

Ships, steamers, barges, dredging vessels, machinery, screw pile jetties, and articles to be used in the construction of harbors, and for dredging and improving the same.

SEC. 2. *And be it further enacted*, That there shall be levied, collected and paid, on each and every non-enumerated article which bears a similitude, either in material, quality, texture, or the uses to which it may be applied, to any enumerated article chargeable with duty, the same rate of duty which is levied and charged on the enumerated article by the foregoing schedules, which it most resembles in any of the particulars before mentioned; and if any non-enumerated article equally resembles two or more enumerated articles on which different rates of duty are chargeable, there shall be levied, collected and paid, on such non-enumerated article, the same rate of duty as is chargeable on the article which it resembles, paying the highest duty. *Provided*, That on all articles manufactured from two or more materials, the duty shall be assessed at the highest rates at which any of its component parts may be chargeable. *Provided further*, That on all articles which are not enumerated in the foregoing schedules, and cannot be classified under this section, a duty of ten per cent. ad valorem shall be charged.

SEC. 3. *And be it further enacted*, That all goods, wares and merchandize, which may be in the public stores as unclaimed, or in warehouse under warehousing bonds, on the 31st day of August next, shall be subject, on entry thereof for consumption, to such duty as if the same had been imported, respectively after that day.

SEC. 4. *And be it further enacted*, That on the entry of any goods, wares or merchandize, imported on or after the 31st day of August aforesaid, the decision of the collector of customs at the port of importation and entry, as to their liability to duty or exemption therefrom, shall be final and conclusive against the owner, importer, consignee, or agent of any such goods, wares and merchandize, unless the owner, importer, consignee or agent shall, within ten days after such entry, give notice to the collector, in writing, of his dissatisfaction with such decision, setting forth therein distinctly and specifically his ground of objection thereto, and shall, within thirty days after the date of such decision, appeal therefrom to the Secretary of the Treasury, whose decision on such appeal shall be final and conclusive; and the said goods, wares and merchandze shall be liable to duty or exemption therefrom accordingly, any Act of Congress to the contrary notwithstanding, unless suit shall be brought within thirty days after such decision, for any duties that may have been paid, or may hereafter be paid on said goods, or within thirty days after the duties shall have been paid in cases where such goods shall be in bond.

SEC. 5. *And be it further enacted*, That it shall be lawful for the owner, consignee, or agent of imports which have been actually purchased or procured otherwise than by purchase, on entry of the same, to make such addition in the entry to the cost or value given in the invoice as, in his opinion, may raise the same to the true market value of such imports in the principal markets of the country whence the importation shall have been made, and to add thereto all costs and charges which, under existing laws, would form part of the true value at the port where the same may be entered, upon which the duty should be assessed And it shall be the duty of the collector within whose district the same may be imported or entered, to cause the dutiable value of such imports to be appraised, estimated and ascertained, in accordance with the provisions of existing laws; and if the appraised value thereof shall exceed by ten per centum, or more, the value so declared on entry, then in addition to the duties imposed by law on the same, there shall be levied, collected and paid a duty of twenty per centum ad valorem, on such appraised value. *Provided nevertheless,* That under no circumstances shall the duty be assessed upon an amount less than the invoice or entered value, any law of Congress to the contrary notwithstanding.

SEC. 6. *And be it further enacted,* That so much of all Acts or parts of Acts as may be inconsistent with the provisions of this Act shall be, and the same are hereby repealed.

Approved May 21, 1861.

AN ACT

TO AMEND "AN ACT TO PROVIDE REVENUE FROM COMMODITIES IMPORTED FROM FOREIGN COUNTRIES," APPROVED MAY 21, 1861.

The Congress of the Confederate States of America do enact, That the following alterations and amendments be, and the same are hereby, made to the "Act to provide revenue from commodities imported from foreign countries," approved May 21, 1861, to-wit: That the words "carbonate of soda," and the words, "paving and roofing tiles, and bricks and roofing slates and fire bricks," in schedule C of said Act be, and the same are hereby, strickn out and repealed in said schedule, and that in the same schedule C, in the enumeration of the various kinds of iron, after the word "slabs," the words "sheet or other form," are hereby inserted and made part of said schedule; and in schedule D of said Act, the terms "lac sulphur," and "sulphur, flour of," be, and the same are hereby, stricken out of and repealed in said schedule. And the terms "terra japonica and catechu," are hereby transferred from schedule D to schedule C, they being considered in commerce as the same articles of merchandise as cutch, which is enumerated in schedule C of said Act.

APPROVED August 3, 1861.

TARIFF

OF

DUTIES PAYABLE ON IMPORTATIONS OF MERCHANDISE UNDER THE TARIFF ACT OF 21st MAY, 1861, ALPHABETICALLY ARRANGED.

	SCHED.	PER CENT.
Absynthe—see Cordials........................	A	25
Acids of every description, not otherwise provided for...	D	10
Acetic acid—see Acids, acetic, &c..............	D	10
Acetous acid— see Acid, acetous, &c...........	D	10
Acids, acetic, benzoic, boracic, citric, muriatic, white and yellow, oxalic, pyroligneous, and tartaric, and all other acids of every description, used for chemical or for manufacturing purposes, not otherwise provided for.....................	D	10
Acids, acetous, chromic, nitric, and all other acids of every description, used for medicinal purposes, or in the fine arts, not otherwise provided for..	D	10
Acid, sulphuric—see Sulphuric acid.............	D	10
Adhesive felt, &c.—see Felt, adhesive...........	E	5
Alabaster statuary, &c., for use of colleges, &c.— see All Philosophical apparatus, &c...........	G	Free
Alabaster and spar ornaments.................	A	25

	SCHED.	PER CENT.
Alabata—see Argentine....................	B	20
Alcornoque................................	D	10
Ale, beer, and porter, in casks or bottles........	C	15
All agricultural productions, including those of the orchard and garden, in their natural state, not otherwise provided for......................	G	Free
Almonds, raisins, currants, dates, figs, and all other dried or preserved fruits, not otherwise provided for....................................	B	20
Aloes...................................	D	10
Alum....................................	C	15
All philosophical apparatus, instruments, books, maps and charts, statues, statuary, busts and casts of marble, bronze, alabaster, or plaster of Paris, paintings and drawings, Etchings, specimens of sculpture, Cabinet of Coins, medals, gems, and all collections of antiquities, *provided* the same be specially imported in good faith, for the use of any Society, incorporated or established for philosophical or literary purposes, or for the encouragement of the fine arts, or for the use, or by the order of any church, college, academy, school, or seminary of learning, in the Confederate States......................................	G	Free
Amber beads—see Beads.....................	B	20
Amber..................................	D	10
Ambergris	D	10
Ammonia................................	D	10
Ammonia, sal—see Sal ammonia..............	D	10
Anatto, roucou, or orleans...................	D	10
Anchovies, sardines, and all other fish preserved in oil....................................	A	25
Angora, Thibet, and other goats' hair or mohair,		

	SCHED.	PER CENT.
unmanufactured, not otherwise provided for....	D	10
Animal carbon—see Bone black................	D	10
Animal oils—see Oils of every description, &c...	C	15
Animals, living, of all kinds, not otherwise provided for...	G	Free
Anniseed...	D	10
Antimony, crude or regulus of.................	D	10
Antiquarian paper—see Paper..................	C	15
Antiquities, collections of—see All Philosophical apparatus, &c.................................	G	Free
Antiquities, collections of—see Cabinets of coins, &c..	D	10
Apparatus for use of Confederate States—see Books, maps, &c...............................	G	Free
Apparatus for use of colleges, &c.—see All Philosophical apparatus, &c.......................	G	Free
Apparel—see Articles of clothing, &c..........	C	15
Apples, bitter—see Bitter apples...............	D	10
Arabic, gum—see Gum Arabic..................	D	10
Argentine, alabata, or German silver, manufactured or unmanufactured.........................	B	20
Argol, or crude tartar.........................	D	10
Arms, of every description for military purposes, and parts thereof.............................	G	Free
Arrack—see Cordials...........................	A	25
Arrow-root......................................	C	15
Arsenic..	D	10
Articles embroidered with gold, silver, or other metal, not otherwise provided for.............	B	20
Articles of clothing or apparel, including hats, caps, gloves, shoes and boots of all kinds, worn by men, women, or children, of whatever material composed, not otherwise provided for.......	C	15

	SCHED.	PER CENT.
Articles of metal—see Manufactures	C	15
Articles of leather—see Manufactures	C	15
Articles of marble—see Manufactures	C	15
Articles of glass—see Manufactures	C	15
Articles of papier-maché—see Manufactures	B	20
Articles, all, imported for the use of the Confederate States—see Books, maps, &c	G	Free
Articles used in dyeing or tanning, not otherwise provided for	E	5
Artificial flowers or feathers—see Feathers and flowers	B	20
Ash, Pot, Pearl, and Soda	D	10
Asphaltum	D	10
Assafœtida	D	10
Asses' skins (or parchment)	C	15
Aubusson carpeting—see Carpets	C	15
Bacon	G	Free
Baizes, blankets, bockings, flannels, and floorcloths, of whatever material composed, not otherwise provided for	C	15
Balsams, cosmetics, essences, extracts, pastes, perfumes, and tinctures, used for the toilet or for medicinal purposes	B	20
Bananas, cocoa nuts, pine apples, plaintains, oranges, and all other West India fruits, in their natural state	D	10
Barbary gum—see Gum Arabic	D	10
Barilla	D	10
Bark of the cork tree, manufactures of—see Manufactures	C	15
Bark of the cork tree unmanufactured—see Cork tree bark	D	10
Barks of all kinds, not otherwise provided for	D	10

	SCHED.	PER CENT.
Bark, Peruvian	D	10
Bark, quilla	D	10
Barley	G	Free
Barley, pearl or hulled—see Pearl or hulled barley.	G	Free
Bars, iron—see Iron in bars	C	15
Bars, steel, in—see Steel in bars	D	10
Bars, brass—see Brass in bars, &c	E	5
Bars, copper—see Copper in pigs, &c	E	5
Bar, tin—see Tin in pigs, &c	E	5
Barytes, sulphate of—see Sulphate of barytes	C	15
Baskets, and all other articles composed of grass, osier, palm-leaf, straw, whalebone, or willow, not otherwise provided for	C	15
Bay rum	B	20
Beads, of amber, composition, or wax, and all other beads	B	20
Beans, Vanilla—see Vanilla beans	C	15
Bed-sides—see Carpets	C	15
Beds, feather—see Floss silks, &c	C	15
Beef	G	Free
Beer, in casks or bottles—see Ale beer, &c	C	15
Beeswax	C	15
Bells, old, bell metal	E	5
Bend leather—see Leather, tanned, &c	D	10
Benzoates	B	20
Benzoin, or Benjamin gum—see Gum benzoin, &c.	C	15
Benzoic acid—see Acids, acetic, &c	D	10
Berries and vegetables, of all sorts used for food, not otherwise provided for	C	15
Berries, juniper—see Juniper berries	C	15
Berries, nuts, flowers, plants, and vegetables, used exclusively in dyeing, or in composing dyes—see Articles used in dyeing, &c	E	5
Bichromate of potash—see Chromate	C	15

	SCHED.	PER CENT.
Billiard, and bagatelle tables, and all other tables or boards on which games are played	A	25
Bismuth	D	10
Bitter apples	D	10
Bituminous substances in a crude state—see Mineral and bituminous substances	D	10
Black, Frankfort—see Frankfort black	C	15
Black, ivory—see Ivory black	C	15
Blank books, bound or unbound	D	10
Blankets, of whatever material composed, not otherwise provided for—see Baizes, &c.	C	15
Bleaching powder, or chloride of lime	D	10
Blocks, tin—see Tin in pigs, &c.	E	5
Blooms—see Iron ore, &c.	D	10
Blue or Roman vitriol, or sulphate of copper	C	15
Blue, fig—see Fig blue	C	15
Blue, Prussian—see Prussian blue	D	10
Bone black—see Animal carbon	D	10
Boards, planks, staves, shingles, laths, scantlings, and all other sawed lumber; also spars and hewn timber of all sorts, not otherwise provided for,	D	10
Bockings—see Baizes	C	15
Bodies, hat, of cotton or wool—see Hat bodies	C	15
Bologna sausages	C	15
Bolts—see Iron in bars	C	15
Bolts, shingle and stave	E	5
Bolts, copper—see Copper rods, &c.	C	15
Bolting cloths	D	10
Bone, manufactures of—see manufactures of bone,	C	15
Bone Black or animal carbon	D	10
Bone dust	D	10
Bones and bone-tips, unmanufactured—see Horn and horn-tips	D	10

	SCHED.	PER CENT.
Bones, burnt...............................	D	10
Bonnets, flats, braids, &c., used for making—see Flats, &c.................................	C	15
Bonnets composed of certain materials—see Hats and bonnets................................	C	15
Books, pamphlets, periodicals and tracts published by religious associations.....................	G	Free
Books, maps, charts, mathematical and nautical instruments, philosophical apparatus, and all other articles whatever, imported for the use of the Confederate States.......................	G	Free
Books as personal effects of persons arriving in the Confederate States—see Wearing apparel......	G	Free
Books specially imported for societies—see All Philosophical apparatus........................	G	Free
Botany, specimens of—see Specimens of natural history	D	10
Books, blank—see blank books.................	D	10
Books, printed, magazines, pamphlets, periodicals, and illustrated newspapers, bound or unbound, not otherwise provided for....................	D	10
Books in course of printing and republication—see Periodicals.................................	C	15
Boracic acid—see Acids, acetic, &c..............	D	10
Borate of lime................................	D	10
Borax, crude or tincal........................	D	10
Borax, refined...............................	D	10
Bottles, India rubber—see India rubber in bottles,	E	5
Bottles of glass, not cut......................	C	15
Bottoms, copper—see Copper bottoms............	C	15
Bottoms, still—see Still bottoms................	C	15
Boucho leaves................................	D	10
Boxes, paper—see Paper boxes.................	C	15

	SCHED.	PER CENT.
Boxes, fancy—see Paper boxes	C	15
Box-wood, unmanufactured	D	10
Bracelets, braids, chains, curls or ringlets, composed of hair, or of which hair is a component part, not otherwise provided for	B	20
Braces, suspenders, webbing or other fabrics, composed wholly or in part, of India rubber, not otherwise provided for	C	15
Braids, of hair—see Bracelets	B	20
Braids, for making hats or bonnets—see Flats, braids, &c	C	15
Braids, cotton—see Cotton laces, &c	C	15
Bran, of wheat, and all other grains	G	Free
Brandy, and other spirits distilled from grain or other materials, not otherwise provided for	A	25
Brass, manufactures of—see Manufactures of brass,	C	15
Brass, in bars or pigs	E	5
" old, and fit only to be remanufactured	E	5
Braziers' copper—see Copper in sheets, &c	C	15
Brazil paste	D	10
Brazil-wood, brazilletto, and all dye-woods in sticks,	D	10
Breccia	C	15
Bricks, burnt or unburnt—see Paving and roofing tiles, &c	D	10
Brimstone, roll—see Roll brimstone as a material of gunpowder	G	Free
Brimstone, Crude, in bulk, as a material of gunpowder—see Gunpowder	G	Free
Bristles	D	10
Broad window-glass—see Window-glass	C	15
Bronze liquor and bronze powder	D	10
" casts of—see All Philosophical apparatus	G	Free
" casts of—not exempted	D	10

	SCHED.	PER CENT.
Bronze and Dutch metal, in leaf—see Metals, Dutch, &c.	D	10
Brooms and brushes of all kinds	B	20
Brushes	B	20
Brussels carpeting—see Carpets	C	15
Buds, cassia—see Cassia buds	D	10
Building stones	D	10
Bulbs—see Trees, shrubs, &c.	D	10
Bullion, gold and silver	G	Free
Burgundy—see Wines	A	25
Burgundy pitch	C	15
Burnt starch—see Gum substitute	D	10
Burr stones, wrought or unwrought	D	10
Busts—see All Philosophical apparatus, &c.	G	Free
Butter	D	10
Buttons and button-moulds of all kinds	C	15
Cabinet and household furniture, not otherwise provided for	C	15
Cabinets of coins, medals, gems, and all collections of antiquities	D	10
Cables and cordage of whatever material made	C	15
Cadmium	C	15
Cake, saffron—see Saffron and saffron cake	C	15
Calamine	C	15
Calomel and all other mercurial preparations	C	15
Cameos, real and imitation, and mosaics, real and imitation, when set in gold, silver, or other metal	D	10
Cameos and mosaics, imitations thereof, not set	E	5
Cameos and mosaics not set	E	5
Camphor, refined	B	20
Camphor, crude	D	10
Candles, spermaceti—see candles	C	15
Candles and tapers of spermaceti, stearine, paraf-		

	SCHED.	PER CENT.
fine, tallow or wax, and all other candles	C	15
Castor oil	C	15
Candles, stearine—see Stearine candles	C	15
Candles, tallow—see Tallow candles	C	15
Candles, wax—see Wax candles	C	15
Candles, paraffine—see candles	C	15
Canes and sticks for walking, finished or unfinished	B	20
Cantharides	D	10
Capers, pickles, and sauces of all kinds, not otherwise provided for	B	20
Caps, hats, muffs, and tippets of fur, and all other manufactures of fur, or of which fur shall be a component part	C	15
Caps, gloves, leggins, mits, socks, stockings, wove shirts and drawers, and all similar articles worn by men, women and children, and not otherwise provided for—see articles of clothing	C	15
Caps, gloves, leggins, mits, socks, stockings, wove shirts and drawers, composed wholly of cotton, worn by men, women, and children	C	15
Carbonate of soda	D	10
Carbon, animal—see Animal carbon	D	10
Card cases, pocket books, shell boxes, souvenirs, and all similar articles of whatever material composed, not otherwise provided for	B	20
Cards, playing—see playing cards	B	20
Carpets, carpeting, hearth rugs, bed-sides, and other portions of carpeting, being either Aubusson, Brussels, ingrain, Saxony, Turkey, Venetian, Wilton, or any other similar fabric, not otherwise provided for	C	15
Carriages, and parts of carriages	C	15
Cassia, and cassia buds	D	10
Castings of iron	C	15

	SCHED.	PER CENT.
Cast iron vessels—see manufactures of iron	C	15
Cast steel—see steel in bars	D	10
Casts of marble, bronze, alabaster, or plaster of Paris—see All philosophical apparatus, &c	G	Free
Castile soap—see soap, Castile, &c	B	20
Castor beans	C	15
Castorum	C	15
Cayenne pepper	B	20
Cedar-wood, manufactures of—see Manufactures of cedar-wood	A	25
Cedar-wood, box-wood, ebony, granadilla, lignum-vitæ, mahogany, rose-wood and satin-wood, and all other woods, unmanufactured—see Woods,	D	10
Cement, Roman—see Roman cement	C	15
Chains of all sorts	C	15
Chains of hair—see Bracelets, braids, &c	B	20
Chalk, red, pencils—see Red chalk pencils	C	15
Chalk	D	10
Chalk, French—see French chalk	D	10
Chalk, red—see Red chalk	D	10
Charts—see Maps and charts	D	10
Cheese	D	10
Chickory root	D	10
China ware—see Earthen, China and stone ware	C	15
China matting—see Matting, China, &c	C	15
Chip hats and bonnets—see Hats and bonnets	C	15
Chocolate	C	15
Chloride of lime—see Bleaching powder	D	10
Chromate of Lead	C	15
Chromate, bichromate, hydromate and prussiate of potash	C	15
Chromic acid—see Acids, acetous, &c	D	10
Chronometers, box or ship, and parts thereof	D	10

	SCHED.	PER CENT
Cider and other beverage not containing alcohol, and not otherwise provided for	C	15
Cinnamon	B	20
Citric acid—see Acids, acetic, &c	D	10
Claret—see Wines	A	25
Clay	D	10
Clay, unwrought	D	10
Clocks, and parts of clocks	C	15
Clothing, ready-made, and wearing apparel of every description, of whatever material composed—see articles of clothing	C	15
Cloth, suitable for the manufacture of shoes, buttons, &c., exclusively—see Lastings, &c	C	15
Cloths, bolting—see Bolting cloths	D	10
Cloves	B	20
Coach and harness furniture of all kinds	C	15
Coal	D	10
Cobalt	C	15
Cochineal	D	10
Cocoa nuts	D	10
Cocoa	D	10
Cocoa shells	D	10
Cocoa nut oil—see Oils, &c	C	15
Coculus indicus	D	10
Codilla, or tow of hemp or flax	D	10
Coffee	G	Free
Coins, gold, silver and copper	G	Free
Coins—see Cabinets of coins	D	10
Coir, and coir yarn—see Jute, &c	D	10
Coke and culm of coal	D	10
Collections of antiquities—see All Philosophical apparatus, &c	G	Free
Collections of antiquities—see cabinets of coins, &c	D	10

	SCHED.	PER CENT.
Colored glass—see Glass, colored	C	15
Colors, water—see Water colors	C	15
Combs of all kinds	C	15
Comfits, confectionary, sweetmeats or fruit, preserved in sugar, molasses, brandy or other liquors,	A	25
Common saddlery—see Saddlery	C	15
Composition tops for tables, or other articles of furniture	A	25
Composition beads—see Beads	B	20
Compositions of glass, when set	B	20
Compositions of glass, not set	B	20
Confectionary—see Comfits	A	25
Copal, gum—see Gums	D	10
Copper articles, vessels and wares—see Manufactures	C	15
Copper bottoms	C	15
Copper rods, bolts, nails and spikes	C	15
Copper in sheets or plates called brazier's copper, and other sheets of copper, not otherwise provided for	C	15
Copperas, or green vitriol, or sulphate of iron	C	15
Copper, in pigs or bars	E	5
Copper, when old, and fit only to be remanufactured,	E	5
Copper, when imported for the mint of the Confederate States	G	Free
Copper ore	E	5
Copper sheathing—see Sheathing copper	E	5
Copper coins—see Coins	G	Free
Coral, cut or manufactured	B	20
Coral, marine—see Marine coral, unmanufactured,	C	15
Cordage—see Cables and cordage	C	15
Cordials, absynthe, arrack, curraçoa, kirschenwasser, liqueurs, maraschino, ratafia, and all		

	SCHED.	PER CENT.
other spirituous beverages of a similar character,	A	,25
Cords, cotton—see Cotton cords	C	15
Corks	C	15
Cork tree bark—see Manufactures of the bark of the cork tree	C	15
Cork tree bark	D	10
Corn, Indian—see Indian corn	G	Free
Corn meal, Indian—see Indian corn and meal	G	Free
Cosmetics—see Balsams, cosmetics, &c	B	20
Cotton	G	Free
Cotton cords, gimps and gallons	C	15
Cotton, hat bodies of—see Hat bodies of cotton	C	15
Cotton, embroidered—see Manufactures of cotton, &c., embroidered	C	15
Cotton, all manufactures of—see Manufactures of cotton	C	15
Cotton laces, cotton insertings, cotton trimming laces, cotton laces and braids	C	15
Cotton, manufactures of, not otherwise provided for—see Manufactures of cotton not otherwise provided for	C	15
Cotton, articles of—see Caps, gloves, &c	C	15
Cotton and silk, hatters' plush—see Hatters' plush,	C	15
Cotton velvet in the piece, composed wholly of cotton—see Velvet in the piece, &c	C	15
Cotton and silk velvet in the piece, cotton of chief value—see Velvet in the piece, composed of cotton and silk, &c	C	15
Court plaster	C	15
Cowhage, down	D	10
Crackers, fire—see Fire-crackers	C	15
Crayons of all kinds	C	15
Cream of tartar	D	10

	SCHED.	PER CENT.
Crown window-glass—see Window-glass	C	15
Crude tartar—see Argol	D	10
Crude articles for dyeing—see Articles used in dyeing, &c.	E	5
Crystals for watches—see Glass crystals	C	15
Cubebs	C	15
Cudbear	D	10
Culm of coal—see Coke	D	10
Curacoa—see Cordials	A	25
Curls of hair—see Bracelets	B	20
Curled hair for beds—see Hair curled, &c.	C	15
Currants—see Almonds, &c.	B	20
Cutlery of all kinds	C	15
Cutch, catechu and terra japonica	E	5
Cylinder window-glass—see Window-glass	C	15
Darning needles—see Needles of all kinds	C	15
Dates—see Almonds, &c.	B	20
Demy paper—Paper, demy, &c.	C	15
Decoctions of log-wood, &c.—see Extracts and decoctions	D	10
De laines	C	15
Diamonds, cameos, mosaics, gems, pearls, rubies, and other precious stones, and imitations thereof, when set in gold, silver, or other metal	D	10
Diamonds, cameos, mosaics, gems, pearls, rubies, and other precious stones, and imitations thereof, when not set	E	5
Diamonds, glaziers', set or not set	D	10
Dolls, and toys of all kinds	C	15
Downs of all kinds—see Floss silk &c.	C	15
Dragon's blood	D	10
Drawers, wove—see Caps, gloves, &c.	C	15
Drawers, wove on frames, wholly of cotton—see		

	SCHED.	PER CENT.
Caps, gloves, &c............................	C	15
Drawing paper—see Paper, demy, &c.............	C	15
Drawings—see All Philosophical apparatus, &c...	G	Free
Dressed and tanned skins—see Skins, tanned, &c..	C	15
Dried pulp...............................	C	15
Dried fish—see Fish, &c......................	C	15
Drugs, medicinal, in a crude state—see Medicinal drugs......................................	C	15
Dutch metal in leaf—see Metal, Dutch, &c........	D	10
Dye-woods, extracts and decoctions of—see Extracts and decoctions............................	D	10
Dye-woods, in sticks—see Brazil-wood, &c.......	D	10
Dye, lac—see Lac dye........................	D	10
Dyeing, articles used for—see Articles used in dyeing &c.................................	E	5
Dyeing—see Berries, nuts, &c..................	E	5
Earthen, China, and stone ware, and all other wares composed of earthy and mineral substances, not otherwise provided for......................	C	15
Earths, ochrey, crude or ground—see Ochres and ochrey earths..............................	C	15
Earth, ochrey—see Ochres and ochrey earths....	C	15
Earth, fullers'—see Fullers' earth...............	E	5
East India gum—see Gum Arabic, &c...........	D	10
Ebony-wood, manufactures of—see Manufactures of cedar-wood, &c	A	25
Ebony-wood, unmanufactured—see Cedar-wood...	D	10
Effects, household—see Household effects........	G	Free
Effects, personal and household—see Personal and household effects...........................	G	Free
Effects, not merchandize, of persons arriving in the Confederate States—see Wearing apparel in actual use..................................	G	Free
Elephant paper—see Paper, demy, &c........	C	15

SCHED. PER CENT.

Embroideries of gold, silver, &c.—see Articles embroidered, &c.	B	20
Embroidered manufactures, of cotton, silk, wool, worsted—see Manufactures of cotton, &c., embroidered	C	15
Emery in lump or pulverized	E	5
Encaustic tiles	C	15
Engravings or plates, bound or unbound	D	10
Envelopes, paper—see Paper envelopes	C	15
Epaulets, galloons, laces, knots, stars, tassels, tresses and wings of gold, silver, or imitations thereof,	B	20
Epsom salts—see Salts, epsom, &c.	C	15
Ergot	D	10
Essential oils—see Oils, &c.	C	15
Etchings—see All Philosophical apparatus, &c.	G	Free
Ether	C	15
Expressed oils—see Oils, &c.	C	15
Extracts—see Balsams	B	20
Extract of Indigo	D	10
Extracts and decoctions of log-wood and other dye-woods, not otherwise provided for	D	10
Extract of madder	D	10
Fabrics, wholly or in part of India rubber—see Braces, &c.	C	15
Fancy boxes—see Paper boxes	C	15
Fans and fire screens of every description, of whatever material composed	B	20
Feathers and flowers, artificial or ornamental, and parts thereof, of whatever material composed	B	20
Feather beds—see Floss silk, &c.	C	15
Feathers for beds—see Floss silk, &c.	C	15
Felspar	C	15
Felt, adhesive, for sheathing vessels	E	5

	SCHED.	PER CENT.
Figs..	B	20
Fig-blue..	C	15
Fire-arms for military purposes.................	G	Free
Fire-arms—see Guns, &c........................	C	15
Fire-crackers, Sky rockets, Roman candles, and all similar articles used in pyrotechnics............	C	15
Fire-screens—see Fans and fire-sceens...........	B	20
Fire-wood—see Wood, unmanufactured..........	D	10
Fish, preserved in oil—see Anchovies...........	A	25
Fish, whether fresh, smoked, salted, dried or pickled, not otherwise provided for.................	C	15
Fish glue, or isinglass...........................	C	15
Fish skins..	C	15
Fish oils—see Oils, &c............................	C	15
Flags, mattings, or mats of—see Matting, China, &c.	C	15
Flannels—see Baizes, &c.........................	C	15
Flasks of glass, not cut—see Glass, &c...........	C	15
Flats, braids, plaits, sparterre and willow squares, used for making hats or bonnets...............	C	15
Flax, manufactures of—see Manufactures of flax, &c,...	C	15
Flax, unmanufactured............................	D	10
Flax, tow of—see Codilla........................	D	10
Flaxseed and linseed.............................	D	10
Flints, and flint ground.........................	D	10
Flocks waste, or shoddy.........................	D	10
Floor cloths—see Baizes, &c.....................	C	15
Floor matting—see Matting, China, &c...........	C	15
Floss silks, feather beds, feathers for beds, and downs of all kinds..............................	C	15
Flour, of wheat, and of all other grains—see Wheat and wheat flour..............................	G	Free
Flour, rye—see Rye and rye flour................	G	Free

	SCHED.	PER CENT.
Flour of sulphur, as a material of gunpowder....	G	Free
Flowers, artificial or ornamental—see Feathers...	B	20
Flowers, used exclusively in dyeing, &c—see Berries, nuts, &c..............................	E	5
Flowers, not otherwise provided for.............	D	10
Foolscap paper—see Paper, demy, &c...........	C	15
Frames and sticks for umbrellas, parasols, and sunshades, finished or unfinished..............	C	15
Frankfort black................................	C	15
French chalk...................................	D	10
Fresh fish—see Fish............................	C	15
Fruit preserved in sugar, molasses, brandy, or other liquors—see Comfits.........................	A	25
Fruits, prepared, dried or preserved, not otherwise provided for.................................	B	20
Fruits preserved in their own juice, or pie fruits..	C	15
Fullers' earth..................................	E	5
Fulminates, or fulminating powders..............	C	15
Furniture, cabinet and household, not otherwise provided for.................................	C	15
Furniture—see Composition table-tops...........	A	25
Fur manufactures—see Caps, hats, muffs, and tippets of fur....................................	C	15
Fur caps—see Caps, &c., of fur.................	C	15
Furs, dressed on the skin......................	C	15
Furs, hatters', dressed or undressed, not on the skin..	D	10
Furs, undressed, when on the skin..............	D	10
Galloons, gold, silver, &c.—see Epaulets........	B	20
Galloons, cotton—see Cotton cords, &c..........	C	15
Galvanized tin plates—see Tin in plates, &c.....	D	10
Gamboge......................................	D	10
Game, prepared—see Prepared vegetables, meats,	B	20

	SCHED.	PER CENT.
Garden seeds, and all other seeds for agricultural, and horticultural purposes	G	Free
Gas Retorts—see Clay	D	10
Gelatine—see Maccaroni, &c	C	15
Gems, set—see Diamonds, &c., set	D	10
Gems—see All Philosophical apparatus, &c	G	Free
Gems, not set—see Cameos, &c., not set	E	5
Gems, imitations of, not set—see Diamonds, &c	E	5
German silver—see Argentine	B	20
German steel—see Steel in bars, &c	D	10
Gilt ware—see Plated and gilt ware	B	20
Gimps, cotton—see Cotton cords, &c	C	15
Ginger, ground	C	15
Ginger, dried, green, ripe, ground, preserved or pickled	C	15
Glass, cut	A	25
Glass, colored, stained, or painted	C	15
Glass crystals for watches	C	15
Glasses or pebbles for spectacles	C	15
Glass tumblers, plain, moulded, and pressed, bottles, flasks, and all other vessels of glass not cut	C	15
Glass, not otherwise provided for	C	15
Glass, paintings on—see Paintings on glass	B	20
Glass, porcelain—see Porcelain glass	C	15
Glass, compositions of, set—see Compositions of glass or paste, when set	B	20
Glass, compositions of, not set—see Compositions of glass or paste not set	B	20
Glass, window—see Window glass	C	15
Glass, when old, and fit only to be re-manufactured	D	10
Glaziers' diamonds, set or not set—see Diamonds, glaziers'	D	10
Glauber salts—see Salts epsom, &c	C	15

	SCHED.	PER CENT.
Gloves, made on frames—see Caps, gloves, &c.	C	15
Gloves, wholly of cotton, made on frames—see Caps, gloves, &c.	C	15
Glue	C	15
Glue, fish	C	15
Goats' hair, manufactures of—see Manufactures of goats' hair, &c.	C	15
Goats' hair, unmanufactured—see Angora, Thibet, and other goats' hair	D	10
Gold embroideries—see Articles embroidered with gold	B	20
Gold, manufactures of, not otherwise provided for—see Manufactures of, &c.	B	20
Gold coin—see Coin	G	Free
Gold and silver leaf	D	10
Gold-beaters' skin	D	10
Goods, wares, and merchandise, the growth, produce, or manufacture of the Confederate States, exported to a foreign country, and brought back to the Confederate States in the same condition as when exported, upon which no drawback has been allowed: *provided*, that all regulations to ascertain the identity thereof prescribed by existing laws, or which may be prescribed by the Secretary of the Treasury, shall be complied with	G	Free
Granadilla-wood, manufactures of—see Manufactures of cedar-wood, &c.	A	25
Granadilla-wood, unmanufactured—see Woods, &c.	D	10
Grapes—see Almonds, &c.	B	20
Grapes, when in bottles, cases, or cans	B	20
Grass bonnets,—see Hats and bonnets composed of straw, &c.	C	15

	SCHED.	PER CENT.
Grass baskets—see Baskets, &c., composed of grass, &c.	C	15
Grass cloth	C	15
Grass, Sisal—see Jute, &c., unmanufactured	D	10
Grass mats and matting—see Matting, China, &c.	C	15
Grease—see Tallow, &c.	D	10
Green vitriol—see Copperas	C	15
Green turtle	C	15
Grindstones	D	10
Ground plaster of Paris—see Plaster of Paris	E	5
Gum benzoin, or Benjamin	C	15
Gums—Arabic, Barbary, copal, East India, Senegal, substitute, tragacanth, and all other gums and resins in a crude state, not otherwise provided for	D	10
Gums of all sorts, not otherwise provided for	E	5
Guano, manure, and fertilizers of all sorts	G	Free
Gunny cloth	C	15
Gunpowder, and all materials of which it is made	G	Free
Gutta percha, unmanufactured	E	5
Guns' except muskets and rifles, fire-arms, and all parts thereof, not intended for military purposes,	C	15
Hair, human, cleansed or prepared for use	B	20
Hair of all kinds, uncleansed and unmanufactured,	D	10
Hair, goats', unmanufactured—see Angora, Thibet, and other goats' hair	D	10
Hair, curled, moss, sea-weed, and all other vegetable substances used for beds or mattresses	C	15
Hair cloth, hair seating, and all other manufactures of hair not otherwise provided for	C	15
Hair, hats, &c., of—see hats and bonnets of straw, hair, &c.	C	15
Hair pencils	C	15

	SCHED.	PER CENT.
Hair seating—see Hair cloth, &c	C	15
Hams	G	Free
Harness furniture—see Coach furniture	C	15
Hats—see Hats and bonnets, &c	C	15
Hats, flats, braids for making—see Flats, &c	C	15
Hat bodies of cotton or wool	C	15
Hats and bonnets, for men, women and children, composed of straw, satin-straw, chip, grass, palm-leaf, willow, or any other vegetable substance, or of hair, whale-bone, or other materials, not otherwise provided for	C	15
Hats, of wool	C	15
Hat bodies, made of wool, or of which wool shall be a component material of chief value	C	15
Hatters' plush, of whatever material composed	C	15
Hearth rugs—see Carpets	C	15
Hemp, unmanufactured	D	10
Hemp, manufactured—see Manufactures of hemp,	C	15
Hemp, tow of—see Codilla	D	10
Hemp seed, and rape seed	D	10
Hemp seed or linseed, and rape seed oil, and all other oils used in painting—see Oils	C	15
Hides, raw, of all kinds—see Raw hides and skins,	E	5
Honey	C	15
Hops	D	10
Horn, manufactures of—see Manufactures of bone, &c	C	15
Horns, horn-tips, bone, bone-tips and teeth, unmanufactured	D	10
Household furniture—see Furniture	C	15
Household effects, old and in use, of persons or families from foreign countries, if used abroad by		

	SCHED.	PER CENT.
them, and not intended for any other purpose or purposes, or for sale	G	Free
Hulled barley—see Pearl or hulled barley	G	Free
Human hair, cleansed or prepared for use	B	20
Hydriodate of potash—see Chromate, bichromate, &c	C	15
Ice	F	$1 50 per ton
Illustrated newspapers—see Books, &c	D	10
Imitations of wines—see Wines	A	25
Imitations of cameos or mosaics, set—see Cameos, &c., set	D	10
Imitations of precious stones, set—see Diamonds, &c., set	D	10
Imitations of jewelry—see Jewelry	C	15
Imitations of cameos and mosaics, not set—see Cameos and mosaics, imitations of, not set	E	5
Imitations of diamonds, gems, &c., not set—see Diamonds, imitations of, &c., not set	E	5
Imitations of jet—see Jet and manufactures of	C	15
Imperial paper—see Paper, antiquarian, &c	C	15
India rubber, fabrics of—see Braces, &c	C	15
India rubber shoes—see Articles of clothing	C	15
India rubber in bottles, slabs or sheets, unmanufactured	E	5
India rubber, milk of	E	5
Indian corn and meal	G	Free
Indigo, extract of—see Extract of indigo	D	10
Indigo	E	5
Ingrain carpeting—see Carpets	C	15
Ink and ink-powder	C	15
Insertings, cotton—see Cotton insertings	C	15
Insertings, thread—see Thread laces, &c	C	15
Instruments, musical—see Musical instruments	C	15

	SCHED.	PER CENT.
Ipecacuanha	C	15
Iridium	C	15
Iris, or orris-root	C	15
Iron in bars, bolts, rods, slabs, sheet or other form, and rail road rails, spikes, fishing plates, and chairs used in constructing rail roads	C	15
Iron castings—see Castings of iron	C	15
Iron ore, and iron in bloom, loops and pigs	D	10
Iron, old or scrap—see Old or scrap iron	C	15
Iron, vessels of—see Vessels of iron	C	15
Iron, manufactures of—see Manufactures of brass,	C	15
Iron, sulphate of—see Copperas, &c	C	15
Iron, liquor	C	15
Isinglass—see Fish glue	C	15
Ivory, manufactures of—see Manufactures of bone,	C	15
Ivory, vegetable, manufactures of—see Manufactures of bone, &c	C	15
Ivory black	C	15
Ivory, unmanufactured	D	10
Ivory nuts, or vegetable ivory	D	10
Jalap	C	15
Japanned ware of all kinds, not otherwise provided for	C	15
Japanned saddlery—see Saddlery, &c	C	15
Jeddo gum—see Gum Arabic	D	10
Jellies—see Maccaroni	C	15
Jet, and manufactures of jet, and imitations thereof,	C	15
Jewelry, or imitations thereof	C	15
Juice, liquorice—see Liquorice paste, &c	C	15
Juice, lemon or lime—see Lemon and lime juice	D	10
Juniper berries	C	15
Junk, old	E	5
Jute, sisal grass, coir, and other vegetable substan-		

	SCHED.	PER CENT.
ces, unmanufactured, not otherwise provided for,	D	10
Jute, mats or matting—see Matting, china, &c....	C	15
Kelp	D	10
Kirschenwasser—see Cordials	A	25
Kermes, mineral—see Mineral kermes	D	10
Kermes	D	10
Knitting needles—see Needles of all kinds for sewing, darning, or knitting	C	15
Knots, of gold or silver, or imitations thereof—see Epaulets, &c	B	20
Lac spirits	D	10
Lac sulphur*—see Medicinal preparations, &c....	C	15
Lac dye	D	10
Laces of gold or silver, or imitations thereof—see Epaulets	B	20
Laces, cotton—see Cotton laces, &c	C	15
Laces, thread—see Thread laces	C	15
Lampblack	C	15
Lard	G	Free
Lastings, cut in strips or patterns of the size or shape for shoes, boots, bootees, slippers, gaiters or buttons, of whatever material composed	C	15
Laths—see Boards, plank, &c	D	10
Lead pencils	C	15
Lead, manufactures of, not otherwise provided for—see Manufactures of brass, &c	C	15
Lead, chromate of—see Chromate	C	15
Lead in pigs or bars, in shot or balls, for cannon, musket, rifle or pistols	G	Free
Lead in sheets	D	10
Lead, nitrate of—see Nitrate of lead	C	15

*Lac sulphur is not enumerated in the Tariff Act, but as it is prepared for and used exclusively in medicine, I have classed it by virtue of the second section of the Act, in schedule C, as a "medicinal preparation," rather than as a "material of gunpowder," it not being used in the manufacture of that article.

	SCHED.	PER CENT.
Lead, white and red—see White and red lead	C	15
Leaden pipes	C	15
Leaden shot, not otherwise provided for	C	15
Leaf, gold and silver—see Gold and silver leaf	D	10
Leaf and unmanufactured tobacco	D	10
Leather, manufactures of—see Manufactures of leather	C	15
Leather, tanned, band, sole and upper, of all kinds, not otherwise provided for	D	10
Leather, Japanned	C	15
Leaves, medicinal—see Medicinal drugs, &c	C	15
Leeches	C	15
Leggins—see Caps, &c	C	15
Leggins, wholly of cotton—see Caps, &c	C	15
Lemons and limes	D	10
Lemon peel—see Orange and lemon peel	C	15
Lemon and lime juice, and juices of all other fruits without sugar	D	10
Letter paper—see Paper, antiquarian, &c	C	15
Limes—see Lemons and limes	D	10
Lime juice—see Lemon and lime juice	D	10
Lime	D	10
Lime, sulphate of, unground—see Plaster of Paris	E	5
Lime, chloride of—see Bleaching powder	D	10
Linen, manufactures of, embroidered—see Manufactures of cotton, linen, &c	C	15
Linens of all kinds	C	15
Linseed and flaxseed	D	10
Linseed oils—see oil, &c	C	15
Liquors—see Cordials	A	25
Liquor, iron—see Iron liquor	C	15
Liquorice, paste, juice or root	C	15
Listings, woolen—see Woolen listings	C	15
Litharge	C	15

	SCHED.	PER CENT.
Living animals of all kinds, not otherwise provided for	G	Free
Logwood, extract or decoction of—see Extracts and decoctions	D	10
Loops, iron—see Iron ore, &c.	D	10
Maccaroni, vermicelli, gelatine, jellies, and all other similar preparations, not otherwise provided for,	C	15
Mace—see Spcies, &c.	B	20
Machinery, screw, pile, jetties, and articles to be used in the construction of harbors, and for dredging and improving the same	G	Free
Machinery of every description, not otherwise provided for	C	15
Madder, extract of—See Extract of madder	D	10
Madder, ground or prepared	D	10
Madder root	D	10
Madeira—see Wines	A	25
Magazines—see Books	D	10
Magnesia	C	15
Mahogany-wood, manufactures of—see Manufactures of cedar-wood, &c.	A	25
Mahogany-wood, unmanufactured—see Woods, &c.	D	10
Malt	C	15
Manganese	C	15
Manna	C	15
Manufactures of cedar-wood, granadilla, ebony, mahogany, rose-wood, and satin-wood	A	25
Manufactures of jet—see Jet	C	15
Manufactures of the bark of the cork tree	C	15
Manufactures of bone, shell, horn, pearl, ivory, or vegetable ivory, not otherwise provided for	C	15
Manufactures, articles, vessels, and wares, not otherwise provided for, of brass, copper, iron,		

	SCHED.	PER CENT.
steel, lead, pewter, tin, or of which either of those metals, shall be a component part......	C	15
Manufactures of cotton of all kinds, not otherwise provided for................................	C	15
Manufactures of silk.............................	C	15
Manufactures, articles, vessels, and wares, of glass, or of which glass shall be a component material, not otherwise provided for....................	C	15
Manufactures, and articles of leather, or of which leather shall be a component part, not otherwise provided for.................................	C	15
Manufactures and articles of marble, marble paving tiles, and all other marble more advanced in manufacture than in slabs or blocks in the rough, not otherwise provided for....................	C	15
Manufactures of paper or of which paper is a component material, not otherwise provided for....	C	15
Manufactures of papier maché....................	B	20
Manufactures of wood, or of which wood is a component part, not otherwise provided for.........	C	15
Manufactures of wool of all kinds, or worsted, not otherwise provided for........................	C	15
Manufactures of hair of all kinds, not otherwise provided for.................................	C	15
Manufactures of fur—see Caps, hats, muffs, and tippets of fur, &c.............................	C	15
Manufactures composed wholly of cotton, not otherwise provided for.............................	C	15
Manufactures of goats' hair or mohair, or of which goats' hair or mohair shall be a component material, not otherwise provided for..............	C	15
Manufactures of silk, or of which silk shall be a component material, not otherwise provided for.	C	15

	SCHED.	PER CENT.
Manufactures of worsted, not otherwise provided for	C	15
Manufactures of flax, of all kinds, not otherwise provided for	C	15
Manufactures of hemp of all kinds, not otherwise provided for	C	15
Manufactures of mohair cloth, silk twist, or other manufacture of cloth suitable for the manufacture of shoes, cut in slips or patterns of the size and shape for shoes, slippers, boots, bootees, gaiters, or buttons—see Lastings	C	15
Manures, and fertilizers of all sorts—see Guano	G	Free
Maps and charts	D	10
Maraschino—see Cordials	A	25
Marble, manufactures of—see Manufactures of marble	C	15
Marble paving tile—see Manufactures of marble	C	15
Marble in the rough slab or block, unmanufactured	D	10
Marine coral, unmanufactured	C	15
Marrow—see Tallow, marrow, &c	D	10
Matting, China, and other floor matting and mats, made of flags, jute, or grass	C	15
Meal, Indian corn—see Indian corn	G	Free
Meats, prepared—see Prepared vegetables, meats, &c	B	20
Medals—see Cabinets of coins, &c	D	10
Medicinal preparations, drugs, roots, and leaves in a crude state, not otherwise provided for	C	15
Mercurial preparations—see Calomel	C	15
Metal embroideries—see Articles embroidered	B	20
Metals, manufactures of—see Manufactures of brass &c	C	15
Metals, silver plated—see Silver plated metals	B	20

	SCHED.	PER CENT.
Metal, Dutch and bronze, in leaf	D	10
Metals, unmanufactured, not otherwise provided for	D	10
Metal, type—see Type metal	C	15
Metallic pens	C	15
Military accoutrements	G	Free
Mineral waters	C	15
Mineral and bituminous substances in a crude state, not otherwise provided for	D	10
Mineral kermes	D	10
Minerals—see Specimens of natural history	D	10
Mits, made on frames—see Caps, gloves, &c	C	15
Mits, made on frames, when wholly of cotton—see Caps, gloves, &c	C	15
Models of inventions or other improvements in the arts: provided, that no article or articles shall be deemed a model, which can be fitted for use	G	Free
Mohair and silk twist—see Silk twist, &c	C	15
Mohair, manufactures of—see Manufactures of hair, &c	C	15
Molasses	B	20
Mordant, patent—see Patent mordant	C	15
Morphine	C	15
Mosaics, real, and imitations, when set—see Cameos, &c	D	10
Mosaics, not set—see Cameos, &c., not set	E	5
Mosaics, imitations of, not set—see Diamonds, &c., not set	E	5
Moss, Iceland	D	10
Moss, for beds or mattresses—see Hair, curled, &c	C	15
Moulds, button—see Button and button moulds	C	15
Muffs—see Caps, hats, muffs, &c	C	15

	SCHED.	PER CENT
Muriatic acid—see Acids, acetic, &c.	D	10
Munitions of war	G	Free
Musical instruments of all kinds, and strings for musical instruments, of whipgut, catgut, and all other strings of the same material	C	15
Music printed with lines, bound or unbound	D	10
Muskets and rifles—see Arms for military purposes,	G	Free
Mustard, in bulk or in bottles	C	15
Mustard seed	C	15
Nails, copper—see Copper rods, &c.	C	15
Natron	D	10
Natural history, specimens of—see Specimens, &c.,	D	10
Neatsfoot oil—see Oils, neatsfoot, &c.	C	15
Needles of all kinds, for sewing, darning and knitting	C	15
Newspapers, illustrated—see Books, &c.	D	10
Nickel	D	10
Nitrate of lead	C	15
Nitrate of soda, refined, &c—see Salpetre, refined, &c.	G	Free
Nitrate of soda, when crude—see Saltpetre, when crude	G	Free
Nitric acid—see Acids, acetous, &c.	D	10
Nutmegs	B	20
Nuts, not otherwise provided for	D	10
Nuts, cocoa—see Cocoa nuts	D	10
Nuts, used exclusively in dyeing, &c.—see Berries, nuts, &c.	E	5
Nuts, ivory—see Ivory nuts	D	10
Nut galls	D	10
Nux vomica	D	10
Oakum	D	10
Oats and oat meal	G	Free

	SCHED.	PER CENT.
Ochres and ochrey earths	C	15
Oil cloth of every description, of whatever material composed	C	15
Oils of every description, animal, vegetable and mineral, not otherwise provided for	C	15
Oil, castor—see Castor oil	C	15
Oil, spermaceti, whale, and other fish	C	15
Oils, hempseed, linseed, rapeseed, and all other oils used in painting—see Oils, &c.	C	15
Oils, neatsfoot, and other animal oil, spermaceti, whale, and other fish oil, the produce of foreign fisheries	C	15
Oils, palm, seal and cocoa nut	C	15
Oil of vitriol—see Sulphuric acid	D	10
Old or scrap iron—see Iron, old, &c	D	10
Old pewter—see Pewter, when old, &c	D	10
Olive oil in casks, other than salad oil	C	15
Olive salad oil, and all other olive oil, not otherwise provided for	C	15
Olives	C	15
Opium	C	15
Oranges, lemons and limes	D	10
Orange and lemon peel	C	15
Orleans—see Anatto	D	10
Ornamental feathers or flowers—see Feathers	B	20
Orpiment	D	10
Orris or iris root—see Iris or orris root	C	15
Osier baskets—see Baskets composed of grass, osier, &c	C	15
Osier or willow, prepared for basket makers' use,	C	15
Oxalic acid—see Acids, acetic, &c	D	10
Packthread—see Twines and packthread	C	15
Paddy—see Rice or paddy—see agricultural pro-		

	SCHED.	PER CENT
ductions	G	Free
Paintings and statuary, not otherwise provided for,	D	10
Paintings on glass	B	20
Painted glass—see Glass painted	C	15
Paints, dry, or ground in oil, not otherwise provided for	C	15
Palm-leaf, unmanufactured	D	10
Palm-leaf baskets—see Baskets	C	15
Palm-leaf hats—see Hats and bonnets	C	15
Palm oils—see Oils, palm, &c.	C	15
Pamphlets—see Books, printed, &c.	D	10
Paper segars—see segars, snuff, &c.	A	25
Paper, manufactures of—see Manufactures of paper, &c.	C	15
Paper, antiquarian, demy, drawing, elephant, foolscap, imperial, letter, and for printing newspapers, handbills, and other printing, and all other paper not otherwise provided for	C	15
Paper boxes, and all other fancy boxes	C	15
Paper envelopes	C	15
Paper hangings	C	15
Paper for walls	C	15
Paper for screens or fire boards	C	15
Paper, sheathing—see Sheathing paper	E	5
Paper, music, bound or unbound—see Music paper,	D	10
Papier-maché—see Manufactures of papier-maché,	B	20
Paraffine candles—see Candles	C	15
Parchment	C	15
Parasols, frames or sticks for—see frames or sticks,		
Parasols, sunshades and umbrellas	C	15
Paris white—see whiting or Paris white	C	15
Pastes—see Balsams	B	20
Paste composition—see Compositions of glass or		

	SCHED.	PER CENT.
paste, when set	B	20
Paste, liquorice—see Liquorice paste	C	15
Paste, Brazil—see Brazil paste	D	10
Paste, compositions, if not set—see Compositions of glass or paste, not set	B	20
Pastel—see Woad or Pastel	D	10
Patent mordant	C	15
Paving tiles, marble—see Manufactures of marble,	C	15
Paving stones	G	Free
Paving and roofing tiles and bricks, and roofing slates	D	10
Pearls, when set—see Diamonds, &c., set	D	10
Pearl, manufactures of—see Manufactures of bone, shell, pearl, &c	C	15
Pearl, or hulled barley—see Agricultural productions	G	Free
Pearls, not set—see Cameos, mosaics, diamonds, gems, pearls, &c., not set	E.	5
Pearls, imitations thereof, not set—see Diamonds, pearls, &c., imitations thereof, not set	E	5
Pearl, mother of	D	10
Pebbles for spectacles—see Glasses or pebbles for spectacles	C	15
Pencils, hair—see Hair pencils	C	15
Pencils, lead—see Lead pencils	C	15
Pencils, red chalk—see Red chalk pencils	C	15
Pens, metallic—see Metallic pens	C	15
Pepper, pimento, cloves, nutmegs, cinnamon, and all other spices	B	20
Percussion caps	G	Free
Perfumes, and perfumery of all sorts, not otherwise provided for—see Balsams, &c	B	20
Perfumed soap—see Soap perfumed	B	20

	SCHED.	PER CENT.
Periodicals, and all other works in course of printing and republication in the Confederate States,	C	15
Periodicals—see Books printed, &c..............	D	10
Personal and household effects (not merchandise) of citizens of the Confederate States dying abroad,	G	Free
Peruvian bark—see Bark Peruvian..............	D	10
Pewter, manufactures of—see Manufactures of brass, &c....................................	C	15
Pewter, when old, and fit only to be remanufactured,	D	10
Pickles, capers, &c.—see Capers, &c............	B	20
Pickled fish—see Fish, whether fresh, &c........	C	15
Pie fruit....................................	C	15
Pigs, iron—see Iron ore.........................	D	10
Pigs, lead—see Lead in pigs, &c................	G	Free
Pigs, brass—see Brass in bars and pigs.........	E	5
Pigs, copper—see Copper in pigs, &c............	E	5
Pigs tin—see Tin, in pigs, &c..................	E	5
Pimento—see pepper...........................	B	20
Pine apples...................................	D	10
Pipes, lead—see Leaden pipes, &c..............	C	15
Pitch...	C	15
Pitch, Burgundy—see Burgundy pitch...........	C	15
Plaits for bonnets, &c.—see Flats, braids, plaits, &c.,	C	15
Planks—see Boards, planks, &c.................	D	10
Plants not otherwise provided for—see Trees, shrubs, &c....................................	D	10
Plants used exclusively in dyeing—see Berries, nuts, &c......................................	E	5
Plantains......................................	D	10
Plaster of Paris, calcined......................	C	15
Plaster of Paris, or sulphate of lime, ground or unground.....................................	E	5
Plated metal, silver—see Silver plated metal, &c.,	B	20

	SCHED.	PER CENT.
Plates, copper—see Copper in sheets, &c.	C	15
Plates, stereotype—see Stereotype plates	C	15
Plates, Terne tin—see Terne tin plates	D	10
Plates, tin, galvanized or ungalvanized—see Tin plates	D	10
Plates, bound or unbound—see Engravings or plates,	D	10
Plated and gilt ware of all kinds, not otherwise provided for	B	20
Platina, manufactures of—see Manufactures of Gold, &c.	B	20
Platina, unmanufactured	D	10
Playing cards	B	20
Plumbago	C	15
Plums, in bottles, cases or cans—see Grapes	B	20
Plush, hatters'—see Hatters' plush	C	15
Pocket-books—see Card-cases, &c.	B	20
Polishing stones	D	10
Porcelain glass—see Glass, not otherwise provided for	C	15
Pork	G	Free
Porter, in casks or bottles—see Ale, beer and Porter	C	15
Port wine—see Wines	A	25
Potash, nitrate of—see Saltpetre, refined, or partially refined, as a material of gunpowder	G	Free
Potash, nitrate of, when crude—see Saltpetre or nitrate of soda, &c., when crude	G	Free
Potassium	C	15
Potash, chromate, bichromate, hydriodate and prussiate of—see Chromate	C	15
Potatoes	D	10
Poultry, prepared—see Prepared meats, vegetables, &c.	B	20

	SCHED.	PER CENT.
Powder, gun—see Gunpowder	G	Free
Powders, fulminating—see Fulminates	C	15
Powders, bleaching—see Bleaching powder, &c	D	10
Powder, ink—see Ink and ink powder	C	15
Precious stones, and imitations thereof—see Diamonds, &c., when set	D	10
Precious stones, not set—see Cameos, &c., when not set	E	5
Precious stones, imitations of, not set—see Diamonds, &c., imitations of, not set	E	5
Prepared vegetables, meats, poultry and game, sealed or enclosed in cans, or otherwise	B	20
Preparations, medicinal—see Medicinal preparations	C	15
Preparations, mercurial—see Calomel, &c	C	15
Preparations of salts—see Salts, epsom, &c	C	15
Preserved salmon—see Salmon, preserved	C	15
Printed books, magazines, &c—see Books, printed,	D	10
Prunes—see Grapes, &c	B	20
Prussian blue	D	10
Prussiate of potash—see Chromate, &c	C	15
Pulp, dried—see Dried pulp	C	15
Pumice and Pumice stone	D	10
Pumpkins—see all agricultural productions, &c.,	G	Free
Putty	C	15
Pyroligneous acid—see Acids, &c	D	10
Quassia, manufactured or unmanufactured	C	15
Quicksilver	C	15
Quilla bark—see Bark, quilla	D	10
Quills	C	15
Quinine, sulphate, in all its various preparations—see Sulphate	C	15
Quinine, valerienate, &c	C	15

	SCHED.	PER CENT.
Rags, of whatever material composed	G	Free
Raisins—see Almonds	B	20
Rapeseed—see Hempseed	D	10
Rapeseed oil—see Oils, &c.	C	15
Ratafia—see Cordials	A	25
Ratans and reeds, unmanufactured	D	10
Raw silk—see Silks, raw, not more advanced, &c.	D	10
Raw silk—see Silk, raw, or as reeled from the cocoon, &c.	D	10
Raw hides and skins of all kinds, undressed	E	5
Red chalk pencils	C	15
Red chalk	D	10
Red lead—see White and red lead	C	15
Reeds, unmanufactured—see Ratans, &c.	D	10
Regulus of antimony—see Antimony, &c.	D	10
Rhubarb	C	15
Rice or paddy—see Agricultural productions	G	Free
Rigotine, (a kind of woolen cloth,)	C	15
Rifles for military purposes—see Arms	G	Free
Ringlets of hair—see Bracelets	B	20
Rods, iron—see Iron in bars, &c.	C	15
Rods, copper—see Copper rods, &c.	C	15
Roll brimstone, as a material of gunpowder	G	Free
Roman Vitriol—see Blue or Roman vitriol	C	15
Roman candles—see Fire crackers	C	15
Roman cement	C	15
Roofing slates, &c.	D	10
Roofing tiles—see Paving and roofing, &c.	D	10
Root, iris or orris—see Iris or orris root	C	15
Root, liquorice—see Liquorice paste, &c.	C	15
Roots, medicinal—see Medicinal drugs, &c.	C	15
Root, madder—see Madder root	D	10
Roots used exclusively in dyeing—see Articles		

	SCHED.	PER CENT.
used in dyeing, &c.	E	5
Rose-wood, manufactures of—see Manufactures of cedar wood, &c.	A	25
Rose-wood, unmanufactured—see Woods.	D	10
Rotten stone.	D	10
Roucou—see Anatto.	D	10
Rough marble—see Marble in the rough.	D	10
Rubies and imitations, when set—see Diamonds, &c.	D	10
Rubies, not set—see Cameos, &c., not set.	E	5
Rubies, imitations thereof, not set—see Diamonds, &c., imitations of, not set.	E	5
Rugs—see Carpets.	C	15
Rye and rye flour.	G	Free
Saddlery of all kinds, not otherwise provided for.	C	15
Saddlery, common tinned or japanned.	C	15
Safflower.	D	10
Saffron and saffron cake.	C	15
Sago.	C	15
Salad oil—see Olive salad oil.	C	15
Sal ammonia.	D	10
Salmon, preserved.	C	15
Sal soda, and all carbonates and sulphates of soda, by whatever names designated, not otherwise provided for.	D	10
Salted fish—see Fish, &c.	C	15
Saltpetre, or nitrate of soda, or potash, when refined or partially refined—see Gunpowder.	G	Free
Salt, ground, blown or rock (2 cents per bushel of 56 pounds)	F	2 cts. per bu.
Saltpetre, or nitrate of soda, or potash, when crude—see Gunpowder, &c.	G	Free
Salts, Epsom, glauber, Rochelle, and all other salts		

	SCHED.	PER CENT.
and preparations of salts, not otherwise provided for	C	15
Sardines—see Anchovies	A	25
Sarsaparilla	C	15
Satin-wood, manufactures of—see Manufactures of cedar-wood, &c.	A	25
Satin wood, unmanufactured—see Woods	D	10
Satin-straw hats, bonnets, &c.—see Hats, bonnets, &c.	C	15
Sauces—see Capers	B	20
Saxony carpeting—see Carpets	C	15
Scagliola tops for tables, or other articles of furniture	A	25
Scantling—see Boards, &c.	D	10
Scrap iron—see Old or scrap iron	C	15
Sculpture, specimens of—see All philosophical apparatus, &c.	G	Free
Screws of all kinds	C	15
Sealing wax	C	15
Seating, hair—see Hair cloth	C	15
Sea-weed, for beds, mattresses, &c.—see Hair, curled, &c.	C	15
Seeds—see Garden seeds, &c.	G	Free
Seeds, hempseed and rapeseed—see Hempseed	D	10
Seedlac	D	10
Segars, snuff, paper segars, and all other manufactures of tobacco	A	25
Senegal gum—see Gum Arabic, &c.	D	10
Seines	C	15
Seppia	C	15
Sewing silk, in the gum and purified	C	15
Sewing needles—see Needles of all kinds	C	15
Shaddocks	C	15

8

	SCHED.	PER CENT.
Shear steel—see Steel in bars..................	D	10
Sheathing paper.............................	E	5
Sheathing copper; but no copper to be considered such, except in sheets of forty-eight inches long, and fourteen inches wide, and weighing from eleven to thirty-four ounces, [the square foot,]	E	5
Sheathing or yellow metal, not wholly or part of iron,	E	5
Sheathing or yellow metal nails expressly for sheathing vessels...........................	E	5
Sheathing felt—see Felt, adhesive, &c...........	E	5
Sheeps' wool—see Wool.......................	D	10
Sheets, silver plated metal—see Silver plated metal,	B	20
Sheets, copper—see Copper in sheets............	C	15
Sheets, iron	C	15
Sheets, lead.................................	D	10
Sheets, tin—see Tin in plates or sheets..........	D	10
Sheets, zinc, unmanufactured—see Zinc, unmanufactured, &c.................................	E	5
Sheets, India rubber—see India rubber, &c.......	E	5
Shell, manufactures of—see Manufactures of bone, &c...	C	15
Shells of cocoa—see Cocoa shells................	D	10
Shell boxes—see Card cases, &c................	B	20
Shells, unmanufactured—see Tortoise and other shells	D	10
Shellac......................................	D	10
Sherry—see Wines............................	A	25
Ships, steamers, barges, dredging vessels, machinery, screw pile jetties, and articles to be used in the construction of harbors, and for dredging and improving the same.............	G	Free
Shingle bolts and stave bolts...................	E	5
Shirts, wove—see Caps, gloves, &c..............	C	15
Shirts, made on frames, if wholly of cotton—see		

	SCHED.	PER CENT.
Caps, gloves, &c	C	15
Shoes, composed wholly of India rubber	C	15
Shoddy—see Waste or shoddy	D	10
Shot, leaden, not otherwise provided for	C	15
Shrubs—see Trees, shrubs, &c	D	10
Side-arms of every description, for military purposes	G	Free
Singles, silk—see Silk, raw, not more advanced, &c	D	10
Silk, manufactures of, if embroidered—see Manufactures of silk, &c	C	15
Silk twist, and twist composed of mohair and silk	C	15
Silk, sewing, purified—see Sewing silk	C	15
Silk, sewing, in the gum—see Sewing silk	C	15
Silks, floss—see Floss silks	C	15
Silk, manufactures of—see Manufactures of silk	C	15
Silk and cotton hatters' plush—see Hatters' plush	C	15
Silk and cotton velvet in the piece, cotton chief value—see Velvet composed of cotton and silk	C	15
Silk, raw, not more advanced in manufacture than singles, tram and thrown, or organzine	D	10
Silk, raw, or as reeled from the cocoon, not being doubled, twisted, or advanced in manufacture in any way	D	10
Silk twist, suitable for the manufacture exclusively of shoes, cut in slips or patterns of the size and shape for shoes, boots, bootees, or buttons, slippers and gaiters, not combined with India rubber—see Manufactures of mohair cloth, &c	C	15
Silver embroideries—see Articles embroidered, &c	B	20
Silver, manufactures of—see Manufactures of gold, &c	B	20
Silver-plated metal, in sheets or other form	B	20

	SCHED.	PER CENT.
Silver leaf—see Gold and silver leaf	D	10
Silver coin—see Coins	G	Free
Sisal grass—see Jute, &c	D	10
Skins, fish—see Fish skins	C	15
Skins, furs dressed on—see Furs dressed on the skin	C	15
Skins, goldbeaters'—see Goldbeaters' skins	D	10
Skins of all kinds, tanned, dressed or japanned	C	15
Skins, raw, of all kinds—see Raw hides and skins, &c	E	5
Skins of all kinds, not otherwise provided for	D	10
Sky-rockets—see Fire-crackers	C	15
Slabs, iron—see Iron in bars, &c	C	15
Slabs, marble—see Marble in the rough	D	10
Slabs of India rubber, unmanufactured	E	5
Slates, roofing—see Roofing slates	D	10
Slates, other than roofing	D	10
Slate pencils	C	15
Smaltz	C	15
Smoked fish—see Fish, &c	C	15
Snuff—see Segars, snuff, &c	A	25
Soap, Castile, perfumed, Windsor, and other toilet soaps	B	20
Soap stocks and stuffs—see Tallow	D	10
Soap of every description, not otherwise provided for,	C	15
Socks, made on frames—see Caps, gloves, &c	C	15
Socks made on frames, wholly of cotton—see Caps, gloves, &c	C	15
Soda, sal—see Sal soda	D	10
Soda, carbonates of—see Sal soda	D	10
Soda, nitrate of, refined, &c.—see Salpetre, refined.	G	Free
Soda, nitrate of, when crude—see Saltpetre, crude,	G	Free
Soda ash—see Sal soda	D	10

	SCHED.	PER CENT.
Sole leather—see Leather, tanned, &c	D	10
Souvenirs—see Card cases	B	20
Spar ornaments—see Alabaster and spar ornaments	A	25
Spars—see Boards, plank, &c	D	10
Sparterre for hats, bonnets, &c—see Flats, braids, sparterre, &c	C	15
Spectacles, glasses for—see Glasses or pebbles for spectacles	C	15
Specimens of sculpture—see All philosophical apparatus, &c	G	Free
Specimens of natural history, mineralogy or botany, not otherwise provided for	D	10
Specimens of natural history, mineralogy or botany, *provided* the same be imported in good faith for the use of any society, incorporated or established for philosophical, agricultural or horticultural purposes, or for the use or by the order of any college, academy, school, or seminary of learning in the Confederate States	G	Free
Spelter in sheets—see Zinc, spelter, &c	E	5
Spelter, unmanufactured—see Zinc, spelter, &c., unmanufactured	E	5
Spermaceti oil—see Oils, &c	C	15
Spermaceti candles and tapers	C	15
Spices of all kinds	B	20
Spikes, copper—see Copper rods, &c	C	15
Spirits distilled from grain—see Brandy	A	25
Spirituous beverages—see Cordials	A	25
Spirits, lac—see Lac spirits	D	10
Spirits of turpentine	C	15
Sponges	D	10
Spunk	C	15

	SCHED.	PER CENT.
Squills	C	15
Stained glass—see Glass, colored stained or painted	C	15
Starch	C	15.
Stars, of gold or silver—see Epaulets	B	20
Statuary—see Paintings and statuary	D	10
Staves—see Boards, plank, &c	D	10
Stave bolts and shingle bolts	E	5
Stearine candles and tapers—see Candles	C	15
Steel, not otherwise provided for	D	10
Steel, in bars, sheets and plates, not farther advanced in manufacture than by rolling, and cast steel in bars	D	10
Steel in bars, cast	D	10
Stereotype plates	C	15
Sticks for walking—see Canes, &c	B	20
Sticks for umbrellas—see Frames and sticks for umbrellas, &c	C	15
Still bottoms	C	15
Stockings made on frames—see Caps, gloves, &c., made on frames	C	15
Stockings, wholly of cotton, made on frames—see Articles of clothing, &c	C	15
Stones, precious, and imitations thereof, when set—see Diamonds, &c., when set	D	10
Stones, precious, when not set—see Cameos, &c., not set	E	5
Stones, precious, imitations thereof, not set—see Diamonds, &c., imitations of, not set	E	5
Stones, paving—see Paving stones	G	Free
Stones, building—see Building stones	D	10
Stones, burr, wrought or unwrought—see Burr stones	D	10

	SCHED.	PER CENT.
Stone ware—see Earthen, China and stone ware..	C	15
Stones, polishing—see Polishing stones	D	10
Stone, pumice—see Pumice stone	D	10
Stone, rotten—see Rotten stone	D	10
Straw baskets—see Baskets composed of grass, straw, &c.	C	15
Straw hats and bonnets—see Hats and bonnets composed of straw, &c.	C	15
Strings of whip-gut or cat-gut, for musical instruments—see Musical instruments	C	15
Strings, all other, of the same material—see Musical instruments	C	15
Substances expressly used for manures—see Manures	G	Free
Substitute gums, or burnt starch—see Gum Arabic,	D	10
Sugar of all kinds	B	20
Sugar, syrup of—see Syrup of sugar	B	20
Sulphate of lime, ground or unground—see Plaster of Paris	E	5
Sulphate of copper—see Blue or Roman vitriol	C	15
Sulphate of iron—see Copperas	C	15
Sulphate of Barytes, crude or refined	C	15
Sulphate of quinine, and quinine in all its various preparations	C	15
Sulphate of zinc—see White vitriol	C	15
Sulphuric acid, or oil of vitriol—see Acids	D	10
Sulphur, flour of—see Flour of sulphur	G	Free
Sulphur, lac—see Lac sulphur	C	15
Sumac	D	10
Sunshades—see parasols and sunshades	C	15
Sunshades, frames and sticks for—see Frames and sticks for parasols	C	15
Suspenders, wholly or in part of India rubber—see Braces	C	15

	SCHED.	PER CENT.
Sweetmeats—see Comfits	A	25
Syrup of sugar	B	20
Tallow candles	C	15
Tallow, marrow, and all other grease or soap stocks and soap stuffs, not otherwise provided for	D	10
Tanned leather—see Leather, tanned	D	10
Tanned and dressed skins—see Skins tanned and dressed	C	15
Tanning, articles used in, not otherwise provided for—see Articles used in dyeing or tanning	E	5
Tapers, spermaceti—see Candles and tapers	C	15
Tapers, stearine—see Candles and tapers	C	15
Tapers, wax—see Candles and tapers	C	15
Tapioca	C	15
Tar	C	15
Tartaric acid—see Acids, acetic	D	10
Tartar, cream of—see Cream of tartar	D	10
Tartar, crude—see Argols	D	10
Tassels of gold, silver, or other metal—see Epaulets	B	20
Tea	D	10
Teazle	D	10
Teeth, unmanufactured—see Horns, &c	D	10
Terne tin in plates or sheets	D	10
Terra japonica, catechu or cutch	E	5
Teutenegue, in sheets—see Zinc, spelter and teutenegue, in sheets	E	5
Teutenegue, unmanufactured—see Zinc, &c., unmanufactured	E	5
Textile fabrics of every description, not otherwise provided for	C	15
Thibet, goats' hair, unmanufactured—see Angora, Thibet, &c	D	10

	SCHED.	PER CENT.
Thread lacings and insertings..................	C	15
Thrown silk—see Silk, raw, not more advanced, &c.,	D	10
Tiles, marble paving—see Manufactures of marble,	C	15
Tiles, encaustic...............................	C	15
Tiles, roofing or paving—see paving and roofing tiles	D	10
Timber, hewn, of all sorts—see Boards, planks, &c.,	D	10
Timber to be used in the construction of harbors—see Ships, steamers, barges, &c..............	G	Free
Tin, manufactures of—see Manufactures of brass, &c.,	C	15
Tin in plates or sheets, and tin foil..............	D	10
Tin in pigs or bars...........................	E	5
Tin foil......................................	D	10
Tinned saddlery—see Saddlery, common, &c......	C	15
Tin ore.......................................	E	5
Tincal—see Borax, crude.....................	D	10
Tinctures—see Balsams.......................	B	20
Tippets of fur—see Caps, &c., of fur............	C	15
Tobacco, manufactures of—see Segars...........	A	25
Tobacco, leaf and unmanufactured..............	D	10
Toilet soaps..................................	B	20
Tortoise and other shells, unmanufactured........	D	10
Tow of hemp or flax—see Codilla..............	D	10
Toys—see Dolls...............................	C	15
Tragacanth, gum—see Gum Arabic, &c..........	D	10
Tram, silk—see Silks, raw, not more advanced, &c.,	D	10
Trees, shrubs, bulbs, plants and roots, not otherwise provided for................................	D	10
Tresses, gold, silver or other metal—see Epaulets,	B	20
Trimming laces of cotton—see Cotton laces......	C	15
Tumblers, glass, not cut—see Glass tumblers.....	C	15
Turkey carpeting—see Carpets.................	C	15
Turmeric.....................................	D	10

	SCHED.	PER CENT.
Turpentine, spirits of—see Spirits of turpentine..	C	15
Turtle, green—see Green turtle................	C	15
Twines and packthread, of whatever materials composed	C	15
Twist, silk, or silk and mohair—see Silk twist....	C	15
Type metals....................................	C	15
Types, new or old..............................	C	15
Type, old, and fit only to be remanufactured......	E	5
Umbrellas	C	15
Umbrella frames and sticks—see Frames.........	C	15
Upper leather—see Leather.....................	D	10
Vandyke brown................................	C	15
Vanilla beans..................................	C	15
Varnish of all kinds............................	C	15
Vegetable ivory, manufactured—see Manufactures bone, &c....................................	C	15
Vegetable ivory, or ivory nuts—see Ivory nuts...	D	10
Vegetables, prepared—see Prepared vegetables...	B	20
Vegetable substances used in making hats and bonnets—see Jute, &c..........................	D	10
Vegetable substances, unmanufactured—see Jute,	D	10
Vegetables used for food, not otherwise provided for—see Berries, vegetables..................	C	15
Vegetable substances used for beds and mattresses—see Hair, curled..........................	C	15
Vegetables used exclusively in dyeing—see Berries, nuts, &c................................	E	5
Vellum..	C	15
Velvet in the piece, composed wholly of cotton, or of cotton and silk, but of which cotton is the component material of chief value............	C	15
Venetian red...................................	C	15
Venetian carpeting—see Carpets................	C	15

	SCHED.	PER CENT.
Verdigris	C	15
Vermicelli—see Maccaroni	C	15
Vermillion	C	15
Vessels of cast iron—see Iron, cast, &c	C	15
Vessels of metal—see Manufactures of Brass, &c.	C	15
Vessels of glass—see Manufactures of glass	C	15
Vessels of gold, platina or silver—see Manufactures of	B	20
Vinegar	C	15
Vitriol, green—see Copperas	C	15
Vitriol, white—see White vitriol, or sulphate of zinc	C	15
Vitriol, oil of—see Sulphuric acid	D	10
Volatile oil—see Oils, volatile	C	15
Wafers	C	15
Wagons and vehicles of every description, and parts thereof	C	15
Wares composed of earthy and mineral substances, not otherwise provided for—see Earthen, &c	C	15
Wares, japanned—see Japanned wares	C	15
Wares of metal—see Manufactures of brass, &c	C	15
Wares of glass—see Manufactures of glass	C	15
Wares of gold, platina or silver—see Manufactures of	B	20
Wares of papier-maché- -see Manufactures of papier-maché	B	20
Wares, plated and gilt—see Plated and gilt ware,	B	20
Waste or shoddy—see Flocks	D	10
Watches, crystals for—see Glass crystals for watches	C	15
Watches, and parts of watches	D	10
Watch materials and unfinished parts of watches,	D	10
Waters, mineral—see Mineral waters	C	15

	SCHED.	PER CENT.
Water colors	C	15
Wax beads—see Beads	B	20
Wax, sealing—see Sealing wax	C	15
Wax, bees'—see Beeswax	C	15
Wax candles and tapers—see Candles, &c	C	15
Wearing apparel—see Articles of clothing	C	15
Wearing apparel and other personal effects not merchandise; professional books, implements, instruments, and tools of trade, occupation or employment of persons arriving in the Confederate States: *provided*, that this exemption shall not be construed to include machinery, or other articles imported for use in any manufacturing establishment, or for sale	G	Free
Webbing, composed wholly or in part of India rubber—see Braces	C	15
Weld, or wold	E	5
Whalebone baskets—see Baskets	C	15
Whalebone hats and bonnets—see Hats and bonnets	C	15
Whale oil, foreign—see Oils of every description	C	15
Whalebone	C	15
Wheat, wheat flour, and flour of all other grains	G	Free
Wheelbarrows and hand-barrows	C	15
White acid—see Acids, acetic, &c	D	10
White and red lead	C	15
White, Paris—see Whiting, or Paris white	C	15
White vitriol, or sulphate of zinc	C	15
Whiting, or Paris white	C	15
Willow baskets—see Baskets	C	15
Willow hats and bonnets—see Hats and bonnets of straw, &c	C	15
Willow squares, for hats and bonnets—see Flats	C	15

SCHED. PER CENT.

Willow prepared for basket makers' use—see Osier and willow................................	C	15
Wilton carpeting—see Carpets..................	C	15
Window-glass, broad, crown or cylinder.........	C	15
Windsor soap—see Soap.......................	B	20
Wines, Burgundy, Champagne, claret, Madeira, port, sherry, and all other wines and imitations of wines.....................................	A	25
Wings of gold, silver or metal—see Epaulets.....	B	20
Woad, or pastel................................	D	10
Wold	E	5
Wood, manufactures of—see Manufactures of wood,	C	15
Wood, unmanufactured.........................	D	10
Wood, fire—see Fire-wood......................	D	10
Woods, viz: cedar, granadilla, ebony, mahogany, rose-wood and satin-wood, when manufactured..	A	25
Woods, viz: cedar, box, ebony, lignumvitæ, granadilla, mahogany, rose-wood, satin-wood, and all other woods, unmanufactured...............	D	10
Woods, dye, extracts and decoctions of—see Extracts and decoctions........................	D	10
Wood, dye—see Brazil-wood and all other dye-woods in sticks..............................	D	10
Wool, unmanufactured, of every description, and hair of the Alpaca goat, and other like animals..	D	10
Wools, manufactured, of all kinds...............	C	15
Woolen and worsted yarn, and woolen listings...	C	15
Wool hats—see Hats of wool....................	C	15
Wool hat bodies—see Hat bodies of wool........	C	15
Woolen listings	C	15
Worsted manufactures—see Manufactures of worsted	C	15

	SCHED.	PER CENT.
Works (foreign) in course of republication—see Periodicals	C	15
Yams	D	10
Yarn, woolen and worsted—see Woolen and worsted yarn	C	15
Yellow acid—see Acids, acetic, &c	D	10
Zinc, sulphate of—see white vitriol	C	15
Zinc, spelter or teutenegue, in sheets	E	5
Zinc, spelter or teutenegue, unmanufactured	E	5

CALCULATION

OF

STERLING MONEY,

REDUCED INTO DOLLARS AND CENTS, AT THE CUSTOM-HOUSE VALUE OF

$4.84 THE POUND STERLING,

AS FIXED BY LAW.

s. d.	$ cts.	£	$ cts.	£	$ cts.	£	$ cts.	£	$ cts.
2 6	61	9	43 56	52	251 68	95	459 80	138	667 92
3 0	73	10	48 40	53	256 52	96	464 64	139	672 76
3 6	85	11	53 24	54	261 36	97	469 48	140	677 60
4 0	97	12	58 08	55	266 20	98	474 32	141	682 44
4 6	1 09	13	62 92	56	271 04	99	479 16	142	687 28
5 0	1 21	14	67 76	57	275 88	100	484 00	143	692 12
5 6	1 33	15	72 60	58	280 72	101	488 84	144	696 96
6 0	1 45	16	77 44	59	285 56	102	493 68	145	701 80
6 6	1 57	17	82 28	60	290 40	103	498 52	146	706 64
7 0	1 69	18	87 12	61	295 24	104	503 36	147	711 48
7 6	1 82	19	91 96	62	300 08	105	508 20	148	716 32
8 0	1 94	20	96 80	63	304 92	106	513 04	149	721 16
8 6	2 06	21	101 64	64	309 76	107	517 88	150	726 00
9 0	2 18	22	106 48	65	314 60	108	522 72	151	730 84
9 6	2 30	23	111 32	66	319 44	109	527 56	152	735 68
10 0	2 42	24	116 16	67	324 28	110	532 40	153	740 52
10 6	2 54	25	121 00	68	329 12	111	537 24	154	745 36
11 0	2 66	26	125 84	69	333 96	112	542 08	155	750 20
11 6	2 78	27	130 68	70	338 80	113	546 92	156	755 04
12 0	2 90	28	135 52	71	343 64	114	551 76	157	759 88
12 6	3 03	29	140 36	72	348 48	115	556 60	158	764 72
13 0	3 15	30	145 20	73	353 32	116	561 44	159	769 56
13 6	3 27	31	150 04	74	358 16	117	566 28	160	774 40
14 0	3 39	32	154 88	75	363 00	118	571 12	161	779 24
14 6	3 51	33	159 72	76	367 84	119	575 96	162	784 08
15 0	3 63	34	164 56	77	372 68	120	580 80	163	788 92
15 6	3 75	35	169 40	78	377 52	121	585 64	164	793 76
16 0	3 87	36	174 24	79	382 36	122	590 48	165	798 60
16 6	3 99	37	179 08	80	387 20	123	595 32	166	803 44
17 0	4 11	38	183 92	81	392 04	124	600 16	167	808 28
17 6	4 24	39	188 76	82	396 88	125	605 00	168	813 12
18 0	4 36	40	193 60	83	401 72	126	609 84	169	817 96
18 6	4 48	41	198 44	84	406 56	127	614 68	170	822 80
19 0	4 60	42	203 28	85	411 40	128	619 52	171	827 64
19 6	4 72	43	208 12	86	416 24	129	624 36	172	832 48
£ 1	4 84	44	212 96	87	421 08	130	629 20	173	837 32
2	9 68	45	217 80	88	425 92	131	634 04	174	842 16
3	14 52	46	222 64	89	430 76	132	638 88	175	847 00
4	19 36	47	227 48	90	435 60	133	643 72	176	851 84
5	24 20	48	232 32	91	440 44	134	648 56	177	856 68
6	29 04	49	237 16	92	445 28	135	653 40	178	861 52
7	33 88	50	242 00	93	450 12	136	658 24	179	866 36
8	38 72	51	246 84	94	454 96	137	663 08	180	871 20

STERLING MONEY.

[CONTINUED.]

£	$ cts.	£	$ cts.	£	$ cts.	£	$ cts.	£	$ cts.
181	876 04	232	1122 88	283	1369 72	334	1616 56	385	1863 40
182	880 88	233	1127 72	284	1374 56	335	1621 40	386	1868 24
183	885 72	234	1132 56	285	1379 40	336	1626 24	387	1873 08
184	890 56	235	1137 40	286	1384 24	337	1631 08	388	1877 92
185	895 40	236	1142 24	287	1389 08	338	1635 92	389	1882 76
186	900 24	237	1147 08	288	1393 92	339	1640 76	390	1887 60
187	905 08	238	1151 92	289	1398 76	340	1645 60	391	1892 44
188	909 92	239	1156 76	290	1403 60	341	1650 44	392	1897 28
189	914 76	240	1161 60	291	1408 44	342	1655 28	393	1902 12
190	919 60	241	1166 44	292	1413 28	343	1660 12	394	1906 96
191	924 44	242	1171 28	293	1418 12	344	1664 96	395	1911 80
192	929 28	243	1176 12	294	1422 96	345	1669 80	396	1916 64
193	934 12	244	1180 96	295	1427 80	346	1674 64	397	1921 48
194	938 96	245	1185 80	296	1432 64	347	1679 48	398	1926 32
195	943 80	246	1190 64	297	1437 48	348	1684 32	399	1931 16
196	948 64	247	1195 48	298	1442 32	349	1689 16	400	1936 00
197	953 48	248	1200 32	299	1447 16	350	1694 00	401	1940 84
198	958 32	249	1205 16	300	1452 00	351	1698 84	402	1945 68
199	963 16	250	1210 00	301	1456 84	352	1703 68	403	1950 52
200	968 00	251	1214 84	302	1461 68	353	1708 52	404	1955 36
201	972 84	252	1219 68	303	1466 52	354	1713 36	405	1960 20
202	977 68	253	1224 52	304	1471 36	355	1718 20	406	1965 04
203	982 52	254	1229 36	305	1476 20	356	1723 04	407	1969 88
204	987 36	255	1234 20	306	1481 04	357	1727 88	408	1974 72
205	992 20	256	1239 04	307	1485 88	358	1732 72	409	1979 56
206	997 04	257	1243 88	308	1490 72	359	1737 56	410	1984 40
207	1001 88	258	1248 72	309	1495 56	360	1742 40	411	1989 24
208	1006 72	259	1253 56	310	1500 40	361	1747 24	412	1994 08
209	1011 56	260	1258 40	311	1505 24	362	1752 08	413	1998 92
210	1016 40	261	1263 24	312	1510 08	363	1756 92	414	2003 76
211	1021 24	262	1268 08	313	1514 92	364	1761 76	415	2008 60
212	1026 08	263	1272 92	314	1519 76	365	1766 60	416	2013 44
213	1030 92	264	1277 76	315	1524 60	366	1771 44	417	2018 28
214	1035 76	265	1282 60	316	1529 44	367	1776 28	418	2023 12
215	1040 60	266	1287 44	317	1534 28	368	1781 12	419	2027 96
216	1045 44	267	1292 28	318	1539 12	369	1785 96	420	2032 80
217	1050 28	268	1297 21	319	1543 96	370	1790 80	421	2037 64
218	1055 12	269	1301 96	320	1548 80	371	1795 64	422	2042 48
219	1059 96	270	1306 80	321	1553 64	372	1800 48	423	2047 32
220	1064 80	271	1311 64	322	1558 48	373	1805 32	424	2052 16
221	1069 64	272	1316 48	323	1563 32	374	1810 16	425	2057 00
222	1074 48	273	1321 32	324	1568 16	375	1815 00	426	2061 84
223	1079 32	274	1326 16	325	1573 00	376	1819 84	427	2066 88
224	1084 16	275	1331 00	326	1577 84	377	1824 68	428	2071 52
225	1089 00	276	1335 84	327	1582 68	378	1829 52	429	2076 66
226	1093 84	277	1340 68	328	1587 52	379	1834 36	430	2081 20
227	1098 68	278	1345 52	329	1592 36	380	1839 20	431	2086 04
228	1103 52	279	1350 36	330	1597 20	381	1844 04	432	2090 88
229	1108 36	280	1355 20	331	1602 04	382	1848 88	433	2095 72
230	1113 20	281	1360 04	332	1606 88	383	1853 72	434	2100 56
231	1118 04	282	1364 88	333	1611 72	384	1858 56	435	2105 40

STERLING MONEY.

[CONTINUED.]

£	$ cts.	£	$ cts.	£	$ cts.	£	$ cts.
436	2110 24	487	2357 08	538	2603 92	589	2850 76
437	2115 08	488	2361 92	539	2608 76	590	2855 60
438	2119 92	489	2366 76	540	2613 60	591	2860 44
439	2124 76	490	2371 60	541	2618 44	592	2865 28
440	2129 60	491	2376 44	542	2623 28	593	2870 12
441	2134 44	492	2381 28	543	2628 12	594	2874 96
442	2139 28	493	2386 12	544	2632 96	595	2879 80
443	2144 12	494	2390 96	545	2637 80	596	2884 64
444	2148 96	495	2395 80	546	2642 64	597	2889 48
445	2153 80	496	2400 64	547	2647 48	598	2894 32
446	2158 64	497	2405 48	548	2652 32	599	2899 16
447	2163 48	498	2410 32	549	2657 16	600	2904 00
448	2168 32	499	2415 16	550	2662 00	601	2908 84
449	2173 16	500	2420 00	551	2666 84	602	2913 68
450	2178 00	501	2424 84	552	2671 68	603	2918 52
451	2182 84	502	2429 68	553	2676 52	604	2923 36
452	2187 68	503	2434 52	554	2681 36	605	2928 20
453	2192 52	504	2439 36	555	2686 20	606	2933 04
454	2197 36	505	2444 20	556	2691 04	607	2937 88
455	2202 20	506	2449 04	557	2695 88	608	2942 72
456	2207 04	507	2453 88	558	2700 72	609	2947 56
457	2211 88	508	2458 72	559	2705 56	610	2952 40
458	2216 72	509	2463 56	560	2710 40	611	2957 24
459	2221 56	510	2468 40	561	2715 24	612	2962 08
460	2226 40	511	2473 24	562	2720 08	613	2966 92
461	2231 24	512	2478 08	563	2724 92	614	2971 76
462	2236 08	513	2482 92	564	2729 76	615	2976 60
463	2240 92	514	2487 76	565	2734 60	616	2981 44
464	2245 76	515	2492 60	566	2739 44	617	2986 28
465	2250 60	516	2497 44	567	2744 28	618	2991 12
466	2255 44	517	2502 28	568	2749 12	619	2995 96
467	2260 28	518	2507 12	569	2753 96	620	3000 80
468	2265 12	519	2511 96	570	2758 80	621	3005 64
469	2269 96	520	2516 80	571	2763 64	622	3010 48
470	2274 80	521	2521 64	572	2768 48	623	3015 32
471	2279 64	522	2526 48	573	2773 32	624	3020 16
472	2284 48	523	2531 32	574	2778 16	625	3025 00
473	2289 32	524	2536 16	575	2783 00	626	3029 84
474	2294 16	525	2541 00	576	2787 84	627	3034 68
475	2299 00	526	2545 84	577	2792 68	628	3039 52
476	2303 84	527	2550 68	578	2797 52	629	3044 36
477	2308 68	528	2555 52	579	2802 36	630	3049 20
478	2313 52	529	2560 36	580	2807 20	631	3054 04
479	2318 36	530	2565 20	581	2812 04	632	3058 88
480	2323 20	531	2570 04	582	2816 88	633	3063 72
481	2328 04	532	2574 88	583	2821 72	634	3068 56
482	2332 88	533	2579 72	584	2826 56	635	3073 40
483	2337 72	534	2584 56	585	2831 40	636	3078 24
484	2342 56	535	2589 40	586	2836 24	637	3083 08
485	2347 40	536	2594 24	587	2841 08	638	3087 92
486	2352 24	537	2599 08	588	2845 92	639	3092 76

£	$ cts.
640	3097 60
641	3102 44
642	3107 28
643	3112 12
644	3116 96
645	3121 80
646	3126 64
647	3131 48
648	3136 32
649	3141 16
650	3146 00
651	3150 84
652	3155 68
653	3160 52
654	3165 36
655	3170 20
656	3175 04
657	3179 88
658	3184 72
659	3189 56
660	3194 40
661	3199 24
662	3204 08
663	3208 92
664	3213 76
665	3218 60
666	3223 44
667	3228 28
668	3233 12
669	3237 96
670	3242 80
671	3247 64
672	3252 48
673	3257 32
674	3262 16
675	3267 00
676	3271 84
677	3276 68
678	3281 52
679	3286 36
680	3291 20
681	3296 04
682	3300 88
683	3305 72
684	3310 56
685	3315 40
686	3320 24
687	3325 08
688	3329 92
689	3334 76
690	3339 60

STERLING MONEY.

[CONTINUED.]

£	$ cts.	£	$ cts.	£	$ cts.	£	$ cts.	£	$ cts.
691	3344 44	742	3591 28	793	3838 12	844	4084 96	895	4331 80
692	3349 28	743	3596 12	794	3842 96	845	4089 80	896	4336 64
693	3354 12	744	3600 96	795	3847 80	846	4094 64	897	4341 48
694	3358 96	745	3605 80	796	3852 64	847	4099 48	898	4346 32
695	3363 80	746	3610 64	797	3857 48	848	4104 32	899	4351 16
696	3368 64	747	3615 48	798	3862 32	849	4109 16	900	4356 00
697	3373 48	748	3620 32	799	3867 16	850	4114 00	901	4360 84
698	3378 32	749	3625 16	800	3872 00	851	4118 84	902	4365 68
699	3383 16	750	3630 00	801	3876 84	852	4123 68	903	4370 52
700	3388 00	751	3634 84	802	3881 68	853	4128 52	904	4375 36
701	3392 84	752	3639 68	803	3886 52	854	4133 36	905	4380 20
702	3397 68	753	3644 52	804	3891 36	855	4138 20	906	4385 04
703	3402 52	754	3649 36	805	3896 20	856	4143 04	907	4389 88
704	3407 36	755	3654 20	806	3901 04	857	4147 88	908	4394 72
705	3412 20	756	3659 04	807	3905 88	858	4152 72	909	4399 56
706	3417 04	757	3663 88	808	3910 72	859	4157 56	910	4404 40
707	3421 88	758	3668 72	809	3915 56	860	4162 40	911	4409 24
708	3426 72	759	3673 56	810	3920 40	861	4167 24	912	4414 08
709	3431 56	760	3678 40	811	3925 24	862	4172 08	913	4418 92
710	3436 40	761	3683 24	812	3930 08	863	4176 92	914	4423 76
711	3441 24	762	3688 08	813	3934 92	864	4181 76	915	4428 60
712	3446 08	763	3692 92	814	3939 76	865	4186 60	916	4433 44
713	3450 92	764	3697 76	815	3944 60	866	4191 44	917	4438 28
714	3455 76	765	3702 60	816	3949 44	867	4196 28	918	4443 12
715	3460 60	766	3707 44	817	3954 28	868	4201 12	919	4447 96
716	3465 44	767	3712 28	818	3959 12	869	4205 96	920	4452 80
717	3470 28	768	3717 12	819	3963 96	870	4210 80	921	4457 64
718	3475 12	769	3721 96	820	3968 80	871	4215 64	922	4462 48
719	3479 96	770	3726 80	821	3973 64	872	4220 48	923	4467 32
720	3484 80	771	3731 64	822	3978 48	873	4225 32	924	4472 16
721	3489 64	772	3736 48	823	3983 32	874	4230 16	925	4477 00
722	3494 48	773	3741 32	824	3988 16	875	4235 00	926	4481 84
723	3499 32	774	3746 16	825	3993 00	876	4239 84	927	4486 68
724	3504 16	775	3751 00	826	3997 84	877	4244 68	928	4491 52
725	3509 00	776	3755 84	827	4002 68	878	4249 52	929	4496 36
726	3513 84	777	3760 68	828	4007 52	879	4254 36	930	4501 20
727	3518 68	778	2765 52	829	4012 36	880	4259 20	931	4506 04
728	3523 52	779	3770 36	830	4017 20	881	4264 04	932	4510 88
729	3528 36	780	3775 20	831	4022 04	882	4268 88	933	4515 72
730	3533 20	781	3780 04	832	4026 88	883	4273 72	934	4520 56
731	3538 04	782	3784 88	833	4031 72	884	4278 56	935	4525 40
732	3542 88	783	3789 72	834	4036 56	885	4283 40	936	4530 24
733	3547 72	784	3794 56	835	4041 40	886	4288 24	937	4535 08
734	3552 56	785	3799 40	836	4046 24	887	4293 08	938	4539 92
735	3557 40	786	3804 24	837	4051 08	888	4297 92	939	4544 76
736	3562 24	787	3809 08	838	4055 92	889	4302 76	940	4549 60
737	3567 08	788	3813 92	839	4060 76	890	4307 60	941	4554 44
738	3571 92	789	3818 76	840	4065 60	891	4312 44	942	4559 28
739	3576 76	790	3823 60	841	4070 44	892	4317 28	943	4564 12
740	3581 60	791	3828 44	842	4075 28	893	4322 12	944	4568 96
741	3586 44	792	3833 28	843	4080 12	894	4326 96	945	4573 80

STERLING MONEY.

[CONTINUED.]

£	$ cts.	£	$ cts.	£	$	£	$	£	$
946	4578 64	975	4719 00	1400	6776	4300	20812	7200	34848
947	4583 48	976	4723 84	1500	7260	4400	21296	7300	35332
948	4588 32	977	4728 68	1600	7744	4500	21780	7400	35816
949	4593 16	978	4733 52	1700	8228	4600	22264	7500	36300
950	4598 00	979	4738 36	1800	8712	4700	22748	7600	36784
951	4602 84	980	4743 20	1900	9196	4800	23232	7700	37268
952	4607 68	981	4748 04	2000	9680	4900	23716	7800	37752
953	4612 52	982	4752 88	2100	10164	5000	24200	7900	38236
954	4617 36	983	4757 72	2200	10648	5100	24684	8000	38720
955	4622 20	984	4762 56	2300	11132	5200	25168	8100	39204
956	4627 04	985	4767 40	2400	11616	5300	25652	8200	39688
957	4631 88	986	4772 24	2500	12100	5400	26136	8300	40172
958	4636 72	987	4777 08	2600	12584	5500	26620	8400	40656
959	4641 56	988	4781 92	2700	13068	5600	27104	8500	41140
960	4646 40	989	4786 76	2800	13552	5700	27588	8600	41624
961	4651 24	990	4791 60	2900	14036	5800	28072	8700	42108
962	4656 08	991	4796 44	3000	14520	5900	28556	8800	42592
963	4660 92	992	4801 28	3100	15004	6000	29040	8900	43076
964	4665 76	993	4806 12	3200	15488	6100	29524	9000	43560
965	4670 60	994	4810 96	3300	15972	6200	30008	9100	44044
966	4675 44	995	4815 80	3400	16456	6300	30492	9200	44528
967	4680 28	996	4820 64	3500	16940	6400	30976	9300	45012
968	4685 12	997	4825 48	3600	17424	6500	31460	9400	45496
969	4689 96	998	4830 32	3700	17908	6600	31944	9500	45980
970	4694 80	999	4835 16	3800	18392	6700	32428	9600	46464
971	4699 64	1000	4840 00	3900	18876	6800	32912	9700	46948
972	4704 48	1100	5324 00	4000	19360	6900	33396	9800	47432
973	4709 32	1200	5808 00	4100	19844	7000	33880	9900	47916
974	4714 16	1300	6292 00	4200	20328	7100	34364	10000	48400

CALCULATION

OF

FRANCS,

REDUCED INTO DOLLARS AND CENTS, AT THE CUSTOM-HOUSE VALUE OF

$18\tfrac{6}{10}$ CENTS PER FRANC,

AS FIXED BY LAW.

Francs.	$ cts	Francs.	$ cts.	Francs.	$ cts.	Francs.	$ cts.
1	19	39	7 25	77	14 32	1600	297 60
2	37	40	7 44	78	14 51	1700	316 20
3	56	41	7 63	79	14 69	1800	334 80
4	74	42	7 81	80	14 88	1900	353 40
5	93	43	8 00	81	15 07	2000	372 00
6	1 12	44	8 18	82	15 25	2100	390 60
7	1 30	45	8 37	83	15 44	2200	409 20
8	1 49	46	8 56	84	15 62	2300	427 80
9	1 67	47	8 74	85	15 81	2400	446 40
10	1 86	48	8 93	86	16 00	2500	465 00
11	2 05	49	9 11	87	16 18	2600	483 60
12	2 23	50	9 30	88	16 37	2700	502 20
13	2 42	51	9 49	89	16 55	2800	520 80
14	2 60	52	9 67	90	16 74	2900	539 40
15	2 79	53	9 86	91	16 93	3000	558 00
16	2 98	54	10 04	92	17 11	3100	576 60
17	3 16	55	10 23	93	17 30	3200	595 20
18	3 35	56	10 42	94	17 48	3300	613 80
19	3 53	57	10 60	95	17 67	3400	632 40
20	3 72	58	10 79	96	17 86	3500	651 00
21	3 91	59	10 97	97	18 04	3600	669 60
22	4 09	60	11 16	98	18 23	3700	688 20
23	4 28	61	11 35	99	18 41	3800	706 80
24	4 46	62	11 53	100	18 60	3900	725 40
25	4 65	63	11 72	200	37 20	4000	744 00
26	4 84	64	11 90	300	55 80	4100	762 60
27	5 02	65	12 09	400	74 40	4200	781 20
28	5 21	66	12 28	500	93 00	4300	799 80
29	5 39	67	12 46	600	111 60	4400	818 40
30	5 58	68	12 65	700	130 20	4500	837 00
31	5 77	69	12 83	800	148 80	4600	855 60
32	5 95	70	13 02	900	167 40	4700	874 20
33	6 14	71	13 21	1000	186 00	4800	892 80
34	6 32	72	13 39	1100	204 60	4900	911 40
35	6 51	73	13 58	1200	223 20	5000	930 00
36	6 70	74	13 76	1300	241 80	5100	948 60
37	6 88	75	13 95	1400	260 40	5200	967 20
38	7 07	76	14 14	1500	279 00	5300	985 80

FRENCH MONEY.

[CONTINUED.]

Francs.	$ cts.	Francs.	$ cts.	Francs.	Dollars.	Francs.	Dollars.
5400	1004 40	8900	1655 40	33000	6138	67000	12462
5500	1023 00	9000	1674 00	34000	6324	68000	12648
5600	1041 60	9100	1692 60	35000	6510	69000	12834
5700	1060 20	9200	1711 20	36000	6696	70000	13020
5800	1078 80	9300	1729 80	37000	6882	71000	13206
5900	1097 40	9400	1748 40	38000	7068	72000	13392
6000	1116 00	9500	1767 00	39000	7254	73000	13578
6100	1134 60	9600	1785 60	40000	7440	74000	13764
6200	1153 20	9700	1804 20	41000	7626	75000	13950
6300	1171 80	9800	1822 80	42000	7812	76000	14136
6400	1190 40	9900	1841 40	43000	7998	77000	14322
6500	1209 00	10000	1860 00	44000	8184	78000	14508
6600	1227 60	11000	2046 00	45000	8370	79000	14694
6700	1246 20	12000	2232 00	46000	8556	80000	14880
6800	1264 80	13000	2418 00	47000	8742	81000	15066
6900	1283 40	14000	2604 00	48000	8928	82000	15252
7000	1302 00	15000	2790 00	49000	9114	83000	15438
7100	1320 60	16000	2976 00	50000	9300	84000	15624
7200	1339 20	17000	3162 00	51000	9486	85000	15810
7300	1357 80	18000	3348 00	52000	9672	86000	15996
7400	1376 40	19000	3534 00	53000	9858	87000	16182
7500	1395 00	20000	3720 00	54000	10044	88000	16368
7600	1413 60	21000	3906 00	55000	10230	89000	16554
7700	1432 20	22000	4092 00	56000	10416	90000	16740
7800	1450 80	23000	4278 00	57000	10602	91000	16926
7900	1469 40	24000	4464 00	58000	10788	92000	17112
8000	1488 00	25000	4650 00	59000	10974	93000	17298
8100	1506 60	26000	4836 00	60000	11160	94000	17484
8200	1525 20	27000	5022 00	61000	11346	95000	17670
8300	1543 80	28000	5208 00	62000	11532	96000	17856
8400	1562 40	29000	5394 00	63000	11718	97000	18042
8500	1581 00	30000	5580 00	64000	11904	98000	18228
8600	1599 60	31000	5766 00	65000	12090	99000	18414
8700	1618 20	32000	5952 00	66000	12276	100000	18600
8800	1636 80						

CALCULATION

OF

BREMEN RIX DOLLARS,

AND

LOUIS D'OR,

REDUCED INTO DOLLARS AND CENTS, AT THE CUSTOM-HOUSE VALUE OF

78¾ CENTS PER RIX DOLLAR,

AS FIXED BY LAW.

R. Dol.	$ cts	R. Dol.	$ cts.	R. Dol.	$ cts.	R. Dol.	$ cts.
1	78¾	39	30 71	77	60 64	1600	1260 00
2	1 58	40	31 50	78	61 43	1700	1338 75
3	2 36	41	32 29	79	62 21	1800	1417 50
4	3 15	42	33 08	80	63 00	1900	1496 25
5	3 94	43	33 86	81	63 79	2000	1575 00
6	4 73	44	34 65	82	64 58	2100	1653 75
7	5 51	45	35 44	83	65 36	2200	1732 50
8	6 30	46	39 23	84	66 15	2300	1811 25
9	7 09	47	37 01	85	66 94	2400	1890 00
10	7 88	48	37 80	86	67 73	2500	1968 75
11	8 66	49	38 59	87	68 51	2600	2047 50
12	9 45	50	39 38	88	69 30	2700	2126 25
13	10 24	51	40 16	89	70 09	2800	2205 00
14	11 03	52	40 95	90	70 88	2900	2283 75
15	11 81	53	41 71	91	71 66	3000	2362 50
16	12 60	54	42 53	92	72 45	3100	2441 25
17	13 39	55	43 31	93	73 24	3200	2520 00
18	14 18	56	44 10	94	74 03	3300	2598 75
19	14 96	57	44 89	95	74 81	3400	2677 50
20	15 75	58	45 68	96	75 60	3500	2756 25
21	16 54	59	46 46	97	76 39	3600	2835 00
22	17 33	60	47 25	98	77 18	3700	2913 75
23	18 11	61	48 04	99	77 96	3800	2992 50
24	18 90	62	48 83	100	78 75	3900	3071 25
25	19 69	63	49 61	200	157 50	4000	3150 00
26	20 48	64	50 40	300	236 25	4100	3228 75
27	21 26	65	51 19	400	315 00	4200	3307 50
28	22 05	66	51 98	500	393 75	4300	3386 25
29	22 84	67	52 76	600	472 50	4400	3465 00
30	23 63	68	53 55	700	551 25	4500	3543 75
31	24 41	69	54 34	800	630 00	4600	3622 50
32	25 20	70	55 13	900	708 75	4700	3701 25
33	25 99	71	55 91	1000	787 50	4800	3780 00
34	26 78	72	56 70	1100	866 25	4900	3858 75
35	27 56	73	57 49	1200	945 00	5000	3937 50
36	28 35	74	58 28	1300	1023 75	5100	4016 25
37	29 14	75	59 06	1400	1102 50	5200	4095 00
38	29 93	76	59 85	1500	1181 25	5300	4173 75

BREMEN RIX DOLLARS.

[CONTINUED.]

R. Dol.	$ cts.	R. Dol.	$ cts.	R. Dol.	$ cts.	R. Dol.	$ cts.
5400	4252 50	8700	6851 25	12000	9450 00	18000	14175 00
5500	4331 25	8800	6930 00	12100	9528 75	19000	14962 50
5600	4410 00	8900	7008 75	12200	9607 50	20000	15750 00
5700	4488 75	9000	7087 50	12300	9686 25	21000	16537 50
5800	4567 50	9100	7166 25	12400	9765 00	22000	17325 00
5900	4646 25	9200	7243 00	12500	9843 75	23000	18112 50
6000	4725 00	9300	7325 75	12600	9922 50	24000	18900 00
6100	4803 75	9400	7402 50	12700	10001 25	25000	19687 50
6200	4882 50	9500	7481 25	12800	10080 00	26000	20475 00
6300	4961 25	9600	7560 00	12900	10158 75	27000	21262 50
6400	5040 00	9700	7638 75	13000	10237 50	28000	22050 00
6500	5118 75	9800	7717 50	13100	10316 25	29000	22837 50
6600	5197 50	9900	7796 25	13200	10395 00	30000	23625 00
6700	5276 25	10000	7875 00	13300	10473 75	31000	24412 50
6800	5355 00	10100	7953 75	13400	10552 50	32000	25200 00
6900	5433 75	10200	8032 50	13500	10631 25	33000	25987 50
7000	5512 50	10300	8111 25	13600	10710 00	34000	26775 00
7100	5591 25	10400	8190 00	13700	10788 75	35000	27562 50
7200	5670 00	10500	8268 75	13800	10867 50	36000	28350 00
7300	5748 75	10600	8347 50	13900	10946 25	37000	29137 00
7400	5827 50	10700	8426 25	14000	11025 00	38000	29925 00
7500	5906 25	10800	8505 00	14100	11103 75	39000	30712 50
7600	5985 00	10900	8583 75	14200	11182 50	40000	31500 00
7700	6063 75	11000	8662 50	14300	11261 25	41000	32287 50
7800	6142 50	11100	8741 25	14400	11340 00	42000	33075 00
7900	6221 25	11200	8820 00	14500	11418 75	43000	33862 50
8000	6300 00	11300	8898 75	14600	11497 50	44000	34650 00
8100	6378 75	11400	8977 50	14700	11576 25	45000	35437 50
8200	6457 50	11500	9056 25	14800	11655 00	46000	36225 00
8300	6536 25	11600	9135 00	14900	11733 75	47000	37012 50
8400	6615 00	11700	9213 75	15000	11812 50	48000	37800 00
8500	6693 75	11800	9292 50	16000	12600 00	49000	38587 50
8600	6772 50	11900	9371 25	17000	13387 50	50000	39375 00

CALCULATION

OF

PRUSSIAN RIX DOLLARS,

REDUCED INTO DOLLARS AND CENTS, AT THE CUSTOM-HOUSE VALUE OF

69 CENTS PER RIX DOLLAR,

AS FIXED BY LAW.

Thalers.	$ cts.	Thalers.	$ cts.	Thalers.	Dollars.
1	0 69	60	41 40	1100	759
2	1 38	70	48 30	1200	828
3	2 07	80	55 20	1300	897
4	2 76	90	62 10	1400	966
5	3 45	100	69 00	1500	1035
6	4 14	110	75 90	1600	1104
7	4 83	120	82 80	1700	1173
8	5 22	130	89 70	1800	1242
9	6 21	140	96 60	1900	1311
10	6 90	150	103 50	2000	1380
11	7 59	160	110 40	3000	2070
12	8 28	170	117 30	4000	2760
13	8 97	180	124 20	5000	3450
14	9 66	190	131 10	6000	4140
15	10 35	200	138 00	7000	4830
16	11 04	300	207 00	8000	5520
17	11 73	400	276 00	9000	6210
18	12 42	500	345 00	10000	6900
19	13 11	600	414 00	20000	13800
20	13 80	700	483 00	30000	20700
30	20 70	800	552 00	40000	27600
40	27 60	900	621 00	50000	34500
50	34 50	1000	690 00	100000	69000

POUNDS SPANISH,

REDUCED TO POUNDS AVOIRDUPOIS.

lb. S.	lb. Av'd	lb. S.	lb. Av'd	lb. S.	lb. Av'd	lb. S.	lb. Av'd	lb. S.	lb. Av'd
1	1 01	43	43 62	85	86 22	19000	19273 60	61000	61878 40
2	2 03	44	44 63	86	87 24	20000	20288 00	62000	62892 80
3	3 04	45	45 65	87	88 25	21000	21302 40	63000	63907 20
4	4 06	46	46 66	88	89 27	22000	22316 80	64000	94921 60
5	5 07	47	47 68	89	90 28	23000	23331 20	65000	65936 00
6	6 09	48	48 69	90	91 30	24000	24345 60	66000	66950 40
7	7 10	49	49 71	91	92 31	25000	25360 00	67000	67964 80
8	8 12	50	50 72	92	93 32	26000	26374 40	68000	68979 20
9	9 13	51	51 73	93	94 34	27000	27388 80	69000	69993 60
10	10 14	52	52 75	94	95 35	28000	28403 20	70000	71008 00
11	11 16	53	53 76	95	96 37	29000	29417 60	71000	72022 40
12	12 17	54	54 78	96	97 38	30000	30432 00	72000	73036 80
13	13 19	55	55 79	97	98 40	31000	31446 40	73000	74051 20
14	14 20	56	56 81	98	99 41	32000	32460 80	74000	75065 60
15	15 22	57	57 82	99	100 43	33000	33475 20	75000	76080 00
16	19 23	58	58 84	100	101 44	34000	34489 60	76000	77094 40
17	17 24	59	59 85	200	202 88	35000	35504 00	77000	78108 80
18	18 26	60	60 86	300	304 32	36000	36518 40	78000	79123 20
19	19 27	61	61 88	400	405 76	37000	37532 80	79000	80137 60
20	20 29	62	62 89	500	507 20	38000	38547 20	80000	81152 00
21	21 30	63	63 91	600	608 64	39000	39561 60	81000	82166 40
22	22 32	64	64 92	700	710 08	40000	40576 00	82000	83180 80
23	23 33	65	65 94	800	811 52	41000	41590 40	83000	84195 20
24	24 35	66	66 95	900	912 96	42000	42604 80	84000	85209 60
25	25 36	67	67 96	1000	1014 40	43000	43619 20	85000	86224 00
26	26 37	68	68 98	2000	2028 80	44000	44633 60	86000	87238 40
27	27 39	69	69 99	3000	3043 26	45000	45648 00	87000	88252 80
28	28 40	70	71 01	4000	4057 60	46000	46662 40	88000	89267 20
29	29 42	71	72 02	5000	5072 00	47000	47676 80	89000	90281 60
30	30 43	72	73 04	6000	6086 40	48000	48691 20	90000	91296 00
31	31 45	73	74 05	7000	7100 80	49000	49705 60	91000	92310 40
32	32 46	74	75 07	8000	8115 20	50000	50720 00	92000	93324 80
33	33 48	75	76 08	9000	9129 60	51000	51734 40	93000	94339 20
34	34 49	76	77 09	10000	10144 00	52000	52748 80	94000	95353 60
35	35 50	77	78 11	11000	11158 40	53000	53763 20	95000	96368 00
36	36 52	78	79 12	12000	12172 80	54000	54777 60	96000	97382 40
37	37 53	79	80 14	13000	13187 20	55000	55792 00	97000	68396 80
38	38 55	80	81 15	14000	14201 60	56000	56806 40	98000	99411 20
39	39 56	81	82 17	15000	15216 00	57000	57820 80	99000	100425 60
40	40 58	82	83 18	16000	16230 40	58000	58835 20	100000	101440 00
41	41 59	83	84 20	17000	17244 80	59000	59849 60	200000	202880 00
42	42 60	84	85 21	18000	18259 20	60000	60864 00	300000	304320 00

100 lbs. Spanish equal to 101$\frac{44}{100}$ lbs. Avoirdupois.

AUSTRIAN POUNDS

REDUCED TO CONFEDERATE STATES POUNDS.

A. P.	C. S. Pounds.	A. P.	C.S.P.	A. P.	C.S.P.	A. P.	C.S.P.
1	1 23.60	20	24.72	300	370.80	4000	4944
2	2 47.20	30	37.08	400	494.40	5000	6180
3	3 70.80	40	49.44	500	618.00	6000	7416
4	4 94.40	50	61.80	600	741.60	7000	8650
5	6 18.00	60	74.16	700	865.20	8000	9888
6	7 41.60	70	86.52	800	988.80	9000	11124
7	8 65.20	80	98.88	900	1112.40	10000	12360
8	9 88.80	90	111.24	1000	1236.00	20000	24720
9	11 12.40	100	123.60	2000	2472 00	30000	37080
10	12 36.00	200	247.20	3000	3708.00	50000	61800

POUNDS OF ANTWERP,

ALSO,

BELGIUM, BRUSSELS, GHENT, LIEGE, BRUGES, MONS, NAMUR, TOURNAY, LOUVAIN,

MALINES, COURTRAY, ST. NICHOLAS AND OSTEND,

REDUCED TO CONFEDERATE STATES POUNDS.

A. P.	C.S.P.	A. P.	C. P S.	A. P.	C.S.P.	A. P.	C. S. P.
1	1 03.35	20	20 67.00	300	310.05	4000	4134.00
2	2 06.70	30	31 00.50	400	413.40	5000	5167.50
3	3 10.05	40	41 34.00	500	516.75	6000	6201.00
4	4 13.40	50	51 67.50	600	620.10	7000	7234.50
5	5 16.75	60	62 01.00	700	723.45	8000	8268.00
6	6 20.10	70	72 34.50	800	826.80	9000	9301.50
7	7 23.45	80	82 68.00	900	930.15	10000	10335.00
8	8 26.80	90	93 01.50	1000	1033.50	20000	20670.00
9	9 30.15	100	103 35.00	2000	2067.00	30000	31005.00
10	10 33.50	200	206 70.00	3000	3100.50	50000	51675.00

TONS REDUCED TO POUNDS.

TONS.	POUNDS.	TONS.	POUNDS.	TONS.	POUNDS.	TONS.	POUNDS.
1	2240	44	98560	87	194880	130	291200
2	4480	45	100800	88	197120	131	293440
3	6720	46	103040	89	199360	132	295680
4	8960	47	105280	90	201600	133	297920
5	11200	48	107520	91	203840	134	300160
6	13440	49	109760	92	206080	135	302400
7	15680	50	112000	93	208320	136	304640
8	17920	51	114240	94	210560	137	307880
9	20160	52	116480	95	212800	138	309120
10	22400	53	118720	96	215040	139	311360
11	24640	54	120960	97	217280	140	313600
12	26880	55	123200	98	219520	141	315840
13	29120	56	125440	99	221760	142	318080
14	31360	57	127680	100	224000	143	320320
15	33600	58	129920	101	226230	144	322560
16	35840	59	132160	102	228480	145	324800
17	38080	60	134400	103	230720	146	327040
18	40320	61	136640	104	232960	147	329280
19	42560	62	138880	105	235200	148	331520
20	44800	63	141120	106	237440	149	333760
21	47040	64	143360	107	239680	150	336000
22	49280	65	145600	108	241920	151	338240
23	51520	66	147840	109	244160	152	340480
24	53760	67	150080	110	246400	153	342720
25	56000	68	152320	111	248640	154	344960
26	58240	69	154560	112	250880	155	347200
27	60480	70	156800	113	253120	156	349440
28	62720	71	159040	114	255360	157	351680
29	64960	72	161280	115	257600	158	353920
30	67200	73	163520	116	259840	159	356160
31	69440	74	165760	117	262080	160	358400
32	71680	75	168000	118	264320	200	448000
33	73920	76	170240	119	266560	300	672000
34	76160	77	172480	120	268800	400	896000
35	78400	78	174720	121	271040	500	1120000
36	80640	79	176960	122	273280	600	1344000
37	82880	80	179200	123	275520	700	1568000
38	85120	81	181440	124	277760	800	1792000
39	87360	82	183680	125	280000	900	2016000
40	89600	83	185920	126	282240	1000	2240000
41	91840	84	188160	127	284480	2000	4480000
42	94080	85	190400	128	286720	3000	6720000
43	96320	86	192640	129	288960	5000	11200000

CWTS. REDUCED TO POUNDS.

CWTS	POUNDS	CWTS	POUNDS	CWTS	POUNDS	CWTS	POUNDS	CWTS	POUNDS
1	112	53	5936	105	11760	157	17584	209	23408
2	228	54	6048	106	11872	158	17696	210	23520
3	336	55	6160	107	11984	159	17808	211	23632
4	448	56	6272	108	12096	160	17920	212	23744
5	560	57	6384	109	12208	161	18032	213	23856
6	672	58	6496	110	12320	162	18144	214	23968
7	784	59	6608	111	12432	163	18256	215	24080
8	896	60	6720	112	12544	164	18368	216	24192
9	1008	61	6832	113	12656	165	18480	217	24304
10	1120	62	6944	114	12768	166	18592	218	24416
11	1232	63	7056	115	12880	167	18704	219	24528
12	1344	64	7168	116	12992	168	18816	220	24640
13	1456	65	7280	117	13104	169	18928	221	24752
14	1568	66	7392	118	13216	170	19040	222	24864
15	1680	67	7504	119	13328	171	19102	223	24976
16	1792	68	7616	120	13440	172	19264	224	25088
17	1904	69	7728	121	13552	173	19376	225	25200
18	2016	70	7840	122	13664	174	19488	226	25312
19	2128	71	7952	123	13776	175	19600	227	25424
20	2240	72	8064	124	13888	176	19712	228	25536
21	2352	73	8172	125	14000	177	19824	229	25648
22	2464	74	8288	126	14112	178	19936	230	25760
23	2576	75	8400	127	14224	179	20048	231	25872
24	2688	76	8512	128	14336	180	20160	232	25984
25	2800	77	8624	129	14448	181	20272	233	26096
26	2912	78	8736	130	14560	182	20384	234	26208
27	3024	79	8848	131	14672	183	20496	235	26320
28	3136	80	8960	132	14784	184	20608	236	26432
29	3248	81	9072	133	14896	185	20720	237	26544
30	3360	82	9184	134	15008	186	20832	238	26656
31	3472	83	9296	135	15120	187	20944	239	26768
32	3584	84	9408	136	15232	188	21056	240	26880
33	3696	85	9520	137	15344	189	21168	241	26992
34	3808	86	9632	138	15456	190	21280	242	27104
35	3920	87	9744	139	15568	191	21392	243	27216
36	4032	88	9856	140	15680	192	21504	244	27328
37	4144	89	9968	141	15792	193	21616	245	27440
38	4256	90	10080	142	15904	194	21728	246	27552
39	4368	91	10192	143	16016	195	21840	247	27664
40	4480	92	10304	144	16128	196	21952	248	27776
41	4592	93	10416	145	16240	197	22064	249	27888
42	4704	94	10528	146	16352	198	22176	250	28000
43	4816	95	10640	147	16464	199	22288	251	28112
44	4928	96	10752	148	16576	200	22400	252	28224
45	5040	97	10864	149	16688	201	22512	253	28336
46	5152	98	10976	150	16800	202	22624	254	28448
47	5264	99	11088	151	16912	203	22736	255	28560
48	5376	100	11200	152	17024	204	22848	256	28672
49	5488	101	11312	153	17136	205	22960	257	28784
50	5600	102	11424	154	17248	206	23072	258	28896
51	5712	103	11536	155	17360	207	23184	259	29008
52	5824	104	11648	156	17472	208	23296	260	29120

CWTS. REDUCED TO POUNDS.

[CONTINUED.]

CWTS.	POUNDS.	CWTS.	POUNDS.	CWTS.	POUNDS.	CWTS.	POUNDS.	CWTS.	POUNDS.
261	29232	293	32816	324	36288	355	39760	386	43232
262	29344	294	32928	325	36400	356	39872	387	43344
263	29456	295	33040	326	36512	357	39984	388	43456
264	29568	296	33152	327	36624	358	40096	389	43568
265	29680	297	33264	328	36736	359	40208	390	43680
266	29792	298	33276	329	36848	360	40320	391	43792
267	29904	299	33488	330	36960	361	40432	392	43904
268	30016	300	33600	331	37072	362	40544	393	44016
269	30128	301	33712	332	37184	363	40656	394	44128
270	30240	302	33824	333	37296	364	40768	395	44240
271	30352	303	33936	334	37408	365	40880	396	84352
272	30464	304	34048	335	37520	366	40992	397	44464
273	30576	305	34160	336	37632	367	41104	398	44576
274	30688	306	34272	337	37744	368	41216	399	44688
275	30800	307	34384	338	37856	369	41328	400	44800
276	30912	308	34496	339	37968	370	41440	450	50400
277	31024	309	34608	340	38080	371	41552	500	56000
278	31136	310	34720	341	38192	372	41664	550	61600
279	31248	311	34832	342	38304	373	41776	600	67200
280	31360	312	34944	343	38416	374	41888	650	72800
281	31472	313	35056	344	38528	375	42000	700	78400
282	31584	314	35168	345	38640	376	42112	750	84000
283	31696	315	35280	346	38752	377	42224	800	89600
284	31808	316	35392	347	38864	378	42336	850	95200
285	31920	317	35504	348	38976	379	42448	900	100800
286	32032	318	35616	349	39088	380	42560	950	106400
287	32144	319	35728	350	39200	381	42672	1000	112000
288	32256	320	35840	351	39312	382	42784	2000	224000
289	32368	321	35952	352	39424	383	42896	3000	336000
290	32480	322	36064	353	39536	384	45008	4000	448000
291	32592	323	37176	354	39648	385	43120	5000	560000
292	32704								

QRS. REDUCED TO POUNDS.

QRS.	POUNDS.	QRS.	POUNDS.	QRS.	POUNDS.	QRS.	POUNDS.	QRS.	POUNDS.
1	28	14	392	27	756	40	1120	53	1484
2	56	15	420	28	784	41	1148	54	1512
3	84	16	448	29	812	42	1176	55	1540
4	112	17	476	30	840	43	1204	56	1568
5	140	18	504	31	868	44	1232	57	1596
6	168	19	532	32	896	45	1260	58	1624
7	196	20	560	33	924	46	1288	59	1652
8	224	21	588	34	952	47	1316	60	1680
9	252	22	616	35	980	48	1344	61	1708
10	280	23	644	36	1008	49	1372	62	1736
11	308	24	672	37	1036	50	1400	63	1764
12	336	25	700	38	1064	51	1428	64	1792
13	364	26	728	39	1092	52	1456	65	1820

POUNDS OF AMSTERDAM AND THE NETHERLANDS,

ALSO,

CURACOA, FLANDERS, HOLLAND, BELGIUM, SURINAM, ROTTERDAM, THE HAGUE, UTRECHT, LEYDEN, GRONINGEN, LENWARDEN, HAARLEM, DORT, MAESTRITCH, NIMEGUEN, DELFT, ZEVOLLE,

REDUCED TO CONFEDERATE STATES POUNDS.

A. P.	C. S. P.	A. P.	C. S. P.	A. P.	C. S. P.	A. P.	C. S. P.
1	1 08.93	20	21 78.60	300	326.79	4000	4357.20
2	2 17.86	30	32 97.90	400	435.72	5000	5446.50
3	3 26.79	40	43 57.20	500	544.65	6000	6535.80
4	4 35.72	50	54 46.50	600	653.58	7000	7625.10
5	5 44.65	60	65 35.80	700	762.51	8000	8714.40
6	6 53.58	70	76 25.10	800	871.44	9000	9803.70
7	7 62.51	80	87 14.40	900	980.37	10000	10893.00
8	8 71.44	90	98 03.70	1000	1089.30	20000	21786.00
9	9 80.37	100	108 93.00	2000	2178.60	30000	32679.00
10	10 89.30	200	217 86.00	3000	3267.90	40000	43572.00

SPANISH AROBAS

REDUCED TO CONFEDERATE STATES POUNDS.

S. A.	C. S. P.	S. A.	C. S. P.	S. A.	C. S. P.	S. A.	C. S. P.
1	25.36	20	507.20	300	7608	4000	101440
2	50.72	30	760.80	400	10144	5000	126800
3	76.08	40	1014.40	500	12680	6000	152160
4	101.44	50	1268.00	600	15216	7000	177520
5	126.80	60	1521.60	700	17752	8000	202880
6	152.16	70	1775.20	800	20288	9000	228240
7	177.52	80	2028.80	900	22824	10000	253600
8	202.88	90	2282.40	1000	25360	11000	278960
9	228.24	100	2536.00	1100	27896	12000	304320
10	253.60	110	2789.60	1200	30432	13000	329680
11	278.96	120	3043.20	1300	32968	14000	355040
12	304.32	130	3296.80	1400	35504	15000	380400
13	329.68	140	3550.40	1500	38040	16000	405760
14	355.03	150	3804.00	1600	40576	17000	431120
15	380.40	160	4057.60	1700	43112	18000	456480
16	405.76	170	4311.20	1800	45648	19000	481840
17	431.12	180	4564.80	1900	48184	20000	507200
18	456.48	190	4818.40	2000	50720	30000	760800
19	481.84	200	5072.00	3000	76080	50000	1268000

FRENCH KILLOGRAMMES
REDUCED TO CONFEDERATE STATES POUNDS.

F. K.	C. S. P.	F. K.	C. S. P.	F. K.	C. S. P.	F. K.	C. S. P.	F. K.	C. S. P.
1	2.21	20	44.20	300	663	3000	6630	30000	66300
2	4.42	30	66.30	400	884	4000	8840	40000	88400
3	6.63	40	88.40	500	1105	5000	11050	50000	110500
4	8.84	50	110.50	600	1326	6000	13260	60000	132600
5	11.05	60	132.60	700	1547	7000	15470	70000	154700
6	13.26	70	154.70	800	1768	8000	17680	80000	176800
7	15.47	80	176.80	900	1989	9000	19890	90000	198900
8	17.68	90	198.90	1000	2210	10000	22100	100000	221000
9	19.89	100	221.00	1100	2431	11000	24310	110000	243100
10	22.10	110	243.10	1200	2652	12000	26520	120000	265200
11	24.31	120	265.20	1300	2873	13000	28730	130000	287300
12	26.52	130	287.30	1400	3094	14000	30940	140000	309400
13	28.73	140	309.40	1500	3315	15000	33150	150000	331500
14	30.94	150	331.50	1600	3536	16000	35360	160000	353600
15	33.15	160	353.60	1700	3757	17000	37570	170000	375700
16	35.36	170	375.70	1800	3978	18000	39780	180000	397800
17	37.57	180	397.80	1900	4199	19000	41990	190000	419900
18	39.78	190	419.90	2000	4420	20000	44200	200000	440000
19	41.99	200	442.00						

FRENCH LITRES
REDUCED TO CONFEDERATE STATES PINTS.

LITRES.	C. S. P.	LITRES.	C. S. P.	LITRES.	C. S. P.	LITRES.	C. S. P.
1	2.11	20	42.20	300	633	3000	6330
2	4.22	30	63.30	400	844	4000	8440
3	6.33	40	84.40	500	1055	5000	10550
4	8.44	50	105.50	600	1266	6000	12660
5	10.55	60	126.60	700	1477	7000	14770
6	12.66	70	147.70	800	1688	8000	16880
7	14.77	80	168.80	900	1899	9000	18990
8	16.88	90	189.90	1000	2110	10000	21100
9	18.99	100	211.00	1100	2321	11000	23210
10	21.10	110	232.10	1200	2532	12000	25320
11	23.21	120	253.20	1300	2743	13000	27430
12	25.32	130	274.30	1400	2954	14000	29540
13	27.43	140	295.40	1500	3165	15000	31650
14	29.54	150	316.50	1600	3376	16000	33760
15	31.65	160	337.60	1700	3587	17000	35870
16	33.76	170	358.70	1800	3798	1800	37980
17	35.87	180	379.80	1900	4009	19000	40090
18	37.98	190	400.90	2000	4220	20000	42200
19	40.09	200	422.00				

PORTUGUESE ARROBAS
REDUCED TO CONFEDERATE STATES POUNDS.

P. A.	C. S. P.	P. A.	C. S. P.	P. A.	C. S. P.	P. A.	C. S. P.
1	32.38	20	647.60	300	9714	3000	97140
2	64.76	30	971.40	400	12952	4000	129520
3	97.14	40	1295.20	500	16190	5000	161900
4	129.52	50	1619.00	600	19428	6000	194280
5	161.90	60	1942.80	700	22666	7000	226660
6	194.28	70	2266.60	800	25904	8000	259040
7	226.66	80	2590.40	900	29142	9000	291420
8	259.04	90	2914.20	1000	32380	10000	323800
9	291.42	100	3238.00	1100	35618	11000	356180
10	323.80	110	3561.80	1200	38856	12000	388560
11	356.18	120	3885.60	1300	42094	13000	420940
12	388.56	130	4209.40	1400	45332	14000	453320
13	420.94	140	4533.20	1500	48570	15000	485700
14	453.32	150	4857.00	1600	51808	16000	518080
15	485.70	160	5180.80	1700	55046	17000	550460
16	518.08	170	5504.60	1800	58284	18000	582840
17	550.46	180	5828.40	1900	61522	19000	615220
18	582.84	190	6152.20	2000	64760	20000	647600
19	615.22	200	6476.00				

FRENCH FEET
REDUCED TO CONFEDERATE STATES FEET.

F.F.	C. S. F.	F.F.	C. S. F.	F. F.	C. S. F.	F. F.	C. S. F.	F. F.	C. S. F.
1	1 06.6	21	22 38.6	180	191 88	1500	1599.00	12000	12792
2	2 13.2	22	23 45.2	190	202 54	1600	1705.60	13000	13858
3	3 19.8	23	24 51.8	200	213 20	1700	1812.20	14000	14924
4	4 26.4	24	25 58.4	210	223 86	1800	1918.80	15000	15990
5	5 33.0	25	26 65.0	220	234 52	1900	2025.40	16000	17056
6	6 39.6	30	31 98	230	245 18	2000	2132.00	17000	18129
7	7 46.2	40	42 64	240	255 84	2100	2238.60	18000	19188
8	8 52.8	50	53 30	250	266 50	2200	2345.20	19000	20254
9	9 59.4	60	63 96	300	319 80	2300	2451.80	20000	21320
10	10 66.0	70	74 62	400	426 40	2400	2558.40	30000	31980
11	11 72.6	80	85 28	500	533 00	2500	2665.00	40000	42640
12	12 79.2	90	95 94	600	639 60	3000	3198	50000	53300
13	13 85.8	100	106 60	700	746 20	4000	4264	60000	63960
14	14 92.4	110	117 26	800	852 80	5000	5330	70000	74620
15	15 99.0	120	127 92	900	959 40	6000	6396	75000	79950
16	17 05.6	130	138 58	1000	1066 00	7000	7462	80000	85280
17	18 12.2	140	149 24	1100	1172 60	8000	8528	85000	90610
18	19 18.8	150	159 90	1200	1279 20	9000	9594	90000	95940
19	20 25.4	160	170 56	1300	1385 80	10000	10660	95000	101270
20	21 32.0	170	181 22	1400	1492 40	11000	11726	100000	106600

RATES OF FOREIGN MONEY OR CURRENCY,

IN WHICH INVOICES OF IMPORTED MERCHANDISE ARE MADE OUT.

The law requires invoices of merchandise imported into the Confederate States, and subject to an ad valorem duty, to be made out in the currency of the country or place from which the importation is made.

In the estimation of the value of imports in order to the assessment of duties, the currency of the invoice must be converted into money of the Confederate States, at the following rates.

	$ cts.	FRACTIONAL PARTS OF THE CURRENCY.		ACT PASSED.
Dollar of United States..	1 00	100		
Ducat of Naples.........	80	100 grani		May 22, 1846
Franc of France, Belgium and Switzerland......	0 18 6/10	100 centimes		do 22, do
Florin of the Netherlands	40	100 do		do 22, do
Florin of the Southern States of Germany....	40	60 kreutzers	4 pfennings	do 22, do
Florin of Austria.......	48½	60 do	4 do	do 22, do
Florin of Trieste.......	48½	60 do	4 do	do 22, do
Florin of Nuremburg....	40	60 do	4 do	do 22, do
Florin of Frankfort.....	40	60 do	4 do	do 22, do
Florin of Bohemia......	48½	60 do	4 do	do 22, do
Florin of the city of Augsburg...............	48½	60 do	4 do	do 22, do
Guilder of Netherlands and other places—same as Florins............				
Lira of the Lombardo and Venetian Kingdom....	16	100 centisimi	100 millessemi	do 22, do
Livre of Leghorn.......	16	20 soldi	12 denair	do 22, do
Livre Tournois of France	18½			March 2, 1799
Lira of Tuscany........	16	20 soldi	12 do	May 22, 1846
Lira of Sardinia........	18 6/10	4 reali	20 soldi	do 22, do
Livre of Genoa.........	18 6/10	20 soldi	12 denair	do 22, do
Milrea of Portugal......	1 12	1000 reas		March 3, 1843
Milrea of Madeira......	1 00	1000 do		do 3, do
Milrea of Azores........	83¼	1000 do		do 3, do
Marc Banco of Hamburg	35	16 shillings	12 pfennings	do 3, do
Ounce of Sicily.........	2 40	30 tari	20 grani	May 22, 1846
Pound Stl. of G. Britain	4 84	20 shillings	12 pence	July 27, 1842
Pound Stl. of Jamaica...	4 84			
Pound Sterling of British Provinces of Nova Scotia, New Brunswick, Newfoundland, & Canada...............	4 00	20 do	12 do	May 22, 1846
Pagoda of India........	1 94	36 fanams	48 jittas	March 3, 1801
Pagoda Star of Madras..	1 84	36 fanams	48 jittas	do 2, do

RATES OF FOREIGN MONEY OR CURRENCY

[CONTINUED.]

	$ cts.	FRACTIONAL PARTS OF THE CURRENCY.		ACT PASSED.
Real Vellum of Spain...	5	34 Maravedis		March 2, 1799
Real Plate of Spain.....	10	34 do		do 2, do
Rupee Company........	44½	16 annas	12 pice	do 3, 1843
Rupee British India.....	44½	16 do	12 do	do 3, do
Rix Dollar (or Thaler) of Prussia and the Northern States of Germany	69	30 groschen	12 pfennings	May 22, 1846
Rix Dollar of Bremen...	78¾	72 grotes	5 swares	March 3, 1842
Dollar Thaler of Bremen, of 72 grotes.........	71	72 grotes	5 swares	do 3, 1843
Rix Dollar (or Thaler) of Berlin	69	30 groschen	12 pfennings	May 22, 1846
Rix Dollar (or Thaler) of Saxony	69	30 do	12 do	do 22, do
Rix Dollar (or Thaler) of Leipsic	69	30 do	12 do	do 22, do
Rouble, silver, of Russia	75	100 kopecks		March 3, 1843
Specie Dollar of Denmark	1 05	6 marks	16 skillings	May 22, 1846
Specie Dollar of Norway	1 06	6 do	16 do	do 22, do
Specie Dollar of Sweden	1 06	48 skillings	12 ore	do 22, do
Tael or Tale of China...	1 48	10 mace	100 candareins	March 2, 1799
Tael of Japan.........	1 40	10 do	100 do	

CURRENCIES BY USAGE,

When a Consular Certificate of the real value of Exchange is not attached to the Invoice.

	$ cts.	FRACTIONAL PARTS OF THE CURRENCY.	
Banco Rix dollar, Sweden....	36¾		
" " Norway....	39¾		
" " Denmark...	53		
Guilder, Brabant............	33¾		
Crown of Tuscany..........	1 05	20 soldi	12 denari
Curacoa Guilder............	40	20 stivers	12 pfennings
Ducat of Sicily.............	80		
Dollar of Sicily.............	96		
Dollar Macquina of Porto Rico	92 6/10		
Francisconi	1 06		
Kobang of Japan...........	1 38 76/100	4 itzebou	1600 seni
Leghorn Dollar or Pezzo.....	90/100	20 soldi	12 denari
Livre of Catalonia.........	53½	20 sueldos	12 dineros
Livre of Neufchatel........	26¼	20 sols	12 deniers
Rihs Daler or Rix Mynth Dollar of Sweden................	26¼		
Rix ral Thaler of Gottenburg	27¾		
Swiss Livre................	27	100 centimes	
Scudi of Malta.............	40	12 tair	20 grani
Scudi, Roman............:	99 a 99½		
St. Gall Guilder............	40 36/100	60 kreutzers	4 pfennings
Rix Dollar of Batavia.......	75	48 stivers	
Roman Dollar..............	1 05		

CURRENCIES BY USAGE

[CONTINUED.]

	$ cts.	FRACTIONAL PARTS OF THE CURRENCY.	
Rouble, paper of Russia......	....	100 kopecks	Varies from 4 roubles 65 copecks to 4 roubles 84 copecks to the dollar.
Tical of Siam...............	61		
Turkish Piastre.............	5	100 aspers	
Current Mark...............	28		
Florin of Prussia............	22¾		
Florin of Basle.............	41		
Genoa Livre.................	21		
Livre Tournois of France....	18½		
Pound Sterling, depreciated of Nova Scotia..............	3 84		

FOREIGN COINS MADE CURRENCY,

AND

RECEIVABLE FOR THE PAYMENT OF ALL DEBTS AND DEMANDS,

By act 14th March, 1861,

GOLD COIN.

Doubloons of Spain or Mexico, not less weight than 17 dwts., 8¼ grs. and fineness 899..........c... $15 53
Napoleon of France, weight not less than 4 dwts., 3½ grs., and fineness not less than 899.. 3 82
Sovereign of England, not less weight than 5 dwts., 3 grs., and fineness of 915½.. 4 82

SILVER COINS.

Half Dollars of the United States, issued in conformity with act 21st Feb'y, and 3d March, 1853*... $ 50
Quarter Dollars* " " " " " " " " " 25
Dimes* " " " " " " " " 10
Half Dimes* " " " " " " " " 05
Dollar of United States 412½ grs................................. 1 02
" of Mexico 415 grs., fineness 897........................... 1 02
Five Franc piece of France, 384 grs., fineness 900................ 95

*Legal tender in payment of debts, for all sums not exceeding ten dollars.

TABLE OF WEIGHTS AND MEASURES,

REDUCED TO THE STANDARD OF THE CONFEDERATE STATES.

ALEXANDRIA, (EGYPT.)

Cantaro of 100 rottoli farforo of 15 oz. (avoirdupois).........●.93½ lbs.
100 rottoli zaydino 21½ oz...133¼ "
100 " zaura of 33 oz....207 "
100 " mina of 26¾ oz....167 "
1 oke 400 drams of 16 carats each 43⅔ oz.

ALICANT, (SPAIN.)

Arroba.................27.39 lbs. av.
Quintal ....109¼ lbs.
100 varas.... ....83.22 im. yds.

AMSTERDAM.

100 lbs. 1 centner........ 108.93 lbs.
Last of grain............83.25 bush.
Ahm of wine............41.00 gall.
Amsterdam foot.............0.93 ft.
Antwerp foot..............0.94 ft.
Rhinland foot..............1.03 ft.
Amsterdam ell.............2.26 ft.
Ell of Hague...............2.28 ft.
Ell of the Brabant..........2.30 ft.
Medden or measure of coal...2¾ bus.

Ahm or Ohm, a German wine measure, varies in different places.
Of Dantzic...........33.00 im. galls.
" Hamburg........31.75 " "
" Hanover..........34.25 " "
" Rotterdam.......33.25 " "

ANCONA, (ITALY.)

100 lbs. Roman equal .102.75 Ancona.
100 lbs. Ancona...........73.75 lbs.
The braccio...............25.33 in.
" wine soma, 2 barili 24 boccali, 18.90 im. galls.
The rubbio of corn, 8 coppi. 7.87 im. bush.

ARRAGON, (SPAIN.)

Libras of 100 lbs..........77.01 lbs.
Quintal, 4 arrobas of 36 lbs.112.00 "

AUSTRIA.

The ell of Vienna........3.06 im. in.
" klafter, 6 Vienna feet.6.23 "
" Vienna wine eimas of 70 klofpen, 40 maases, or 4 viertels, 12.46 im galls

The fuder................32 eimers.
" dreyling ....30 "
" corn metzen of 4 viertels, or 8 achtels, 1.69 im. bush.
100 metzen..............21⅙ im. qrs.
30 mutzen..................1 mutti.
The Vienna lb. 4 qu. 16 oz., or 32 loths, 8645 Troy grains.
100 lbs. 1 centner...........123¼ lbs.
20 lbs....................1 stone.
The oil oma, 107 Vienna lbs., 14.17 im. galls.
The woolen ell of Trieste.26.6 im. in.
" silk " " .25.22 " "
" wine oma or cimer 12.45 im. galls.
" barile...........114⅓ " "
100 staji of corn.........28⅔ im. qrs.

BASSORA, (PERSIAN GULF.)

Maund attary, 25 vakias tary.28.05 lbs.
One vakia................19 oz.

BATAVIA, (E. INDIES.)

Large Bahar.............4½ peculs.
Small Bahar..............3 "
1 pecul.................100 catties.
1 catty..................16 tales.
1 pecul..............135 lbs. 10 oz.

BAVARIA.

The ell...............32 4-5 im. in.
" Wine cimer of 60 maas 8.12 im galls
" Scheffel of 6 metzen or 12 viertels, 9.98 im. bush.
" centner or quintal, of 5 stones, or 100 lbs., 56 kilos or....123½ lbs. av.
" traders' or long ell..24.00 im. in.
" fustian or short ell .23.32 " "
" muid of 48 maas...15.08 im galls.
" schaff of 8 metzen...5.65 im. bush.
100 lbs. heavy weight...108.30 lbs. av.
100 lbs. light ' " ..104.23 " "

BELGIUM.

The Antwerp silk ell.....27.32 im. in.
" woolen ell..........26.97 " "
" Brabant ell.........27.58 " "
" oam of 50 stoops.32 2-5 im. galls.
" velte............4.1 "
" last of 37½ viertels...10¼ im. qrs.
100 lbs. Brabant weight 103.35 lbs. av.

BERGEN, (NORWAY.)

Shippond, 20 lisponds......320 lbs.
Centner 6¼ lisponds..........100 "
Lispond....................16 "
Waag, 3 bismar pounds......36 "
1 lb. 2 marcs, 16 oz. 32 loths.
100 Norway pounds......110.23 "

(CHRISTIANA, (NORWAY.)

Shippond................352 lbs.

LAURWIG. (NORWAY.)

Shippond................352 lbs.

BOMBAY.

Candy equal to..............560 lbs.
Maund   "   ....28 "
Seer   "   ....11 1-5 oz.
Candy   "   ....20 maunds.
Maund   "   ....10 seers.
Seer   "   ....30 pice.

BRAZIL.

5 varas...................6 im. yds.
4 cavados.................3 " "
99 Brazilian lbs.............100 av.

AT RIO JANEIRO.

100 medidas, 61 1-10 im galls., or 73¼
  C. S. galls.
12 alqueires..............13½ bush.

AT MARANHAM.

1 alqueire................1¼ bush.

AT BAHIA.

1 canada.................1¾ im. galls.
7 alqueires...............6 bush.

BREMEN.

Shipfund.................2½ centners.
Centner..................127.44 av.
Waag of iron..............120 "
Stone of flax.............20 "
Stone of wool.............10 "
Lispund...................11 "
100 lbs...................110 12-100 "
The ell of 2 feet........22.76 im. in.
100 ells..................63.25 im. yds.
The ahm of 20 viertels, 15 stubchen, or
   180 quarts..............31½ im. galls.
1 fuder Rheinish wine......6 ahms.
1 ahm French wine......44 stubchens.
1 tonne of beer...........45 "
10 lbs. Bremen......nearly 11 lbs. av.

CADIZ. (SPAIN.)

Quintal of 4 arrobas........100 lbs.
1 lb. 2 marcs 16 oz., or...256 adarms.
100 lbs. equal to........101.43 lbs.

CAIRO, (EGYPT.)

Cantaro. 100 rottoli.........95 lbs.
One rottoli is............144 drachms.
Occa equal to 100 drams, or 26.39 lbs.
36 occas equal to..........1 cantaro.

CHINA.

Tail.........................1¼ oz.
16 tails, 1 catty..............1¼ lbs.
100 catties, 1 picul..........133⅓ "
The covid of 10 punts...14.625 im in.
32 covids..................13 im. yds.
The li of 180 fathoms....632 "   "
200 lis........................1 degree.
Liquids and grain are sold by weight.
3 peculs...................400 lbs. av.
84 catties..................1 cwt.
12 taels....................1 lb.

CHILI.

100 varas................100 im. yds.
96 Chilian, 100 lbs Spanish 101.44 lbs av.
In all other respects, same as Spain.

CALCUTTA.

Maund equal to.............40 seers.
Seer   "   ....16 chattacks.
English factory maund..71 lbs. 10 oz.
Seer.....................1 lb. 13 oz.
Chattack....................1 oz.
Bengal bezar maund is 10 per cent.
  heavier than the factory maund.
Bezar maund equal to 82 lbs., 2 oz.
                     2.4-13 drams.
Seer equal to......2 lbs. 13.2-3 drams.
Chattock...........2 oz. 5 6 drams.

CONSTANTINOPLE.

Quintal equal to..........100 rottolis.
   "   "   ....45 okes.
   "   "   ....176 cheques.
   "   "   ....127 lbs.
1 " oke. " ..2 lbs. 13 oz. 4 drams.

CUBA.

Measures and Weights.

The standards of Spain are those
generally in use.
In trade the following proportions
are commonly observed:
108 varas...............100 im. yds.

1 vara..................33¼ im. in.
The fanega............2.90 im bush.
" arroba of wine or spirits, 3.42 im.
gals., or............4.10 gals. C. S.
The quintal of 4 arrobas each 25 lbs.
or 101¾ lbs. av.
1 arroba................25 lbs. 7 oz.
The varas of Neuritas 81 superficial feet.
" ton of wood estimated at 20 Spanish Quintals.

DENMARK.

100 lbs. 1 centner......110.28 pounds.
Barrel or toende of corn...3.95 bush.
Viertel of wine..........2.04 galls.
Copenhagen or Rhineland foot 1.03 foot
Centner or 100 lbs. Denmark equal to 110.28 lbs.
1 lispund..................16 "
1 bismerpund...............12 "
1 waag, 3 bismerpunds or.....36 "
The ell of 2 Rhineland feet 24.75 im in.
" viertel of 4 kans or 8 pots. 1.70 im. galls.
" hhd. of 30 viertels...51 " "
100 viertels..........170.08 " "
The ahm of 4 ankers..33.14 " "
60 bbls.................29 im. qrs.
The toende or bbl.......3.83 im bush
" last of corn, 12 toendes, 45.91 im bush
The shippond of 20 lisponds, or 320 lbs Danish, 3 1-7 cwt....352 lbs av
The ship last 4000 lbs Dan, or 4400 lbs av

ENGLAND.

Old ale gallon.............1.22 galls
Imperial gallon............1.20 "
Old wine " ....1.00 "
Quarter of grain, or 8 imperial bushels, 8.25 bush
Imperial corn bushel, or 8 imperial gallons, 1.03 bush
Old Winchester do.........1.00 "
Imperial yard................36.00 in
Troy lb........144-175ths of a lb av
Newcastle chaldron..........53 cwt
Stone........................16 lbs
Tun of wine............256 im galls

The Wine Measure is

the gal, 4 qts, 8 pints or 32 gills, and contains 231 cubic inches of these gallons.
The anker contains..........10 galls
" rundlet " ....18 "
" tierce " ....42 "

The hhd " ....63 galls
" puncheon " ....84 "
" pipe " ....126 "
" butt " ....126 "
" ton " ....252 "

The wine gallon is ¼ less than the imperial, or 5 imperial gallons equal to 6 wine gallons.
The standard guages of wine recognized in the trade are:
The pipe of port........115 im galls
" " of Lisbon......117 " "
" " of Cape or Madeira 92 " "
" " of Teneriffe....100 " "
" butt of sherry.....108 " "
" hhd of claret........46 " "
" anme of hock........30 " "

Ale and Beer Measure.

The gallon divided in the same manner as the wine gallon, equal to 282 cubic inches of these gallons.
The firkin...................9 galls.
" kilderkin..............18 "
" barrel.................36 "
" hhd....................54 "
" puncheon...............72 "
" butt..................108 "
" tun...................216 "
59 galls of ale are equal to 60 im "

The Fodder of Lead.

At London and Hull........19½ cwt.
" Newcastle..............21 "
" Chester................20 "
" Stocton................22 "
" Derby..................22½ "
The London chaldron coal...25½ "

FRANCE.

Metre.....................3.28 feet.
Decimetre (1-10th metre)..3.94 inches.
Velt......................2.00 galls.
Hectolitre................26.42 "
Decalitre.................2.64 "
Litre.....................2.11 pints.
Kilolitre.................35·32 feet.
Hectolitre................2.84 bush.
Decalitre.................9.08 quarts.
Millier...................2.205 lbs.
Quintal...................220.54 "
Killogramme...............2.21 "
100 pounds................107.93 "
100 feet..................106.60 feet.
Tun (of wine).............240 galls.

FLORENCE AND LEGHORN.

100 lbs. or 1 cantaro.......74.86 lbs.

Moggio of grain..........16.59 bush.
Barile of wine...........12.04 galls.

GENOA.

100 lbs. peso grosso........76.86 lbs.
100 lbs. or peso sotile......68.89 "
Mina of grain..............3.43 bush.
Mezzarola of wine........39.22 galls.
The oil barile of 4 quarti or 64 quarteroni..............11.23 im. galls.
The barile of wine....16.34 " "
100 Rottoli of 1½ lbs. 104.83 lbs. avoir.
The palmas, a measure for marble, ½ cubic foot.
The braccio................2¼ palmi

GIBRALTAR.

British weights and measures are employed; also the following Spanish:
The pipe of 117 galls—105 im. galls, or 126 C. S. galls.
The arroba (l'q'd meas.) 2.77 im. g. 3¼ galls.
The arroba (weight)........26 lb avoir.
" quintal of 100 lbs..101¾ " "
" 5 fanegas of grain.......8 bush
" 2 "   " maize or beans. 1¼ "

GUIANA, (BRITISH,) includes Berbice, Demerara, and Esequibo.

Measures and weights chiefly British.
The Dutch ell of 26 inches 27 inches C S

GUIANA OR SURINAM.

Partly the property of the city of Amsterdam. Measures and weights. chiefly those of Holland, under the old system.

GUIANA (FRENCH,) OR CAYENNE.

Measures, weights and moneys, same as France.

HAYTI OR ST. DOMINGO.

The measures and weights are chiefly those of the old French system.
The old English wine gallon is used.
The quintal of 100 livres 107.928 lbs C S, toise (of 6 pieds de roi) 19490 metres 2.1315 im yds, or 6 feet 1¾ inches 100 pieds........106 60 feet
100 lbs Haytien.....107 95 lbs avoir.

HAMBURG.

Last of Grain...........89.64 bush.
Ahm of wine...........38.25 galls.

Hamburg foot..............0.96 feet
Ell.......................1.22 "
Shipfund, 2½ centners or......280 lbs
Hamburg, equal to..........299 "
1 centner equal to 8 lispunds, or 112 lbs Hamburg
1 lispund equal to.... 14 lbs   do
1 stone of flax equal to.20 "   do
1 stone of wool   " .10 "   do
1 stone of feathers " .10 "   do
100 lbs of Hamburg equal to 110 4-1000 lbs.
The ell of 2 feeet or 6 palms 22.58 im in
" Brabant ell........27.58 " "
4 ankers, 5 eimers, 20 viertels, 40 stubgen or 160 quarters.....1 ahm
6 ahms....................1 fuder
The faas of wine is 4 oxhofts or 6 tierces.
The wispel, corn measure, of 10 scheffels, 20 faas or 40 himstens 29 im bush
3 wispels=1 last of wheat or rye—1 stock of barley or oats=10⅞ im qrs 89.61 bush
The centner of 112 Hamburg lbs, or 8 lispunds..........119.64 lbs avoir
A small tonne of butter 224 lbs Hamburg
A great tonne of butter 280 lbs Hamburg
A quartel of train oil, of 2 tonnes or 64 stubgen, is 4 centners, or 48 Hamburg lbs, or..........478.56 lbs C S
A pipe of oil is....820 lbs Hamburg

ITALY.

100 rottoli of 31 3-7 oz each, equal to 196¼ lbs
1 cantaro grosso equal to....196¼ lbs

LUBECK, (HANSEATIC STATES.)

The ell of 2 feet......22.70 im inches
The ahm of 20 viertels, 40 stubgen or 80 kannes, 51.87 im galls, or 38.25 C S galls
The last of wheat or rye..11.04 im qrs
The last of oats.........11.95 " "
1 centner. 8 lispunds, 112 lbs 119.67 lbs C S
100 Lubec lbs.........106.85 lbs C S

MADRAS.

Candy, equal to..............500 lbs
Candy, equal to..........20 maunds
Maund, equal to........ .....8 bis
Bis, equal to............ ....8 seers

MALACCA.

Pecul, equal to..............135 lbs

A pecul. equal to 100 catties, or 1660 tales

MALTA

100 lbs 1 cantaro......... 174.50 lbs
Salma of grain............ 8.22 bush
Cantaro, equal to.........100 rottoli
Rottoli, equal to............. 30 oz
One cantaro equal to (mercantile usage)................... 175 lbs
The barile of wine......9.35 im galls
" caffiso of oil........4.50 " "
" canna of 8 palmi....82.40 inches
3½ palmi.....................1 yard
64 rottoli..............1 cwt 112 lbs

MAURITIUS, (OR ISLE OF FRANCE.)

The quintal of 100 lbs French poids de marc...................108 lbs C S
20 quintals—1 French ton 2160 "   "
1 velt...................2 galls "
30 velts................1 cask "

NAPLES.

Cantaro grosso............196.50 lbs
Cantaro Picolo............106.00 "
Carro of grain............52.24 bush
Carro of wine............264.00 galls
The canna or ell of 8 palmi 83.05 inches
The passo is 7½ palmi
" barile (wine or brandy measure) of 60 Caraffi..........9.60 im galls
The carro is 2 botte or 24 barile
" pipe is 14 barile
" salma (oil measure of 16 staja, or 256 quarti) weighs 324½ lbs 34.91 im galls
At Gallipoli,
The oil salma of 10 staja, or 230 piquatte..........34.11 im galls
At Bari,
The salma.............36.42 im galls
The tomolo (corn measure) of 2 mezzette or 4 quarti, is..1,519 im bush
The 100 tomoli........19 im quartes
" carro of 36 tomoli...6.84 im qrs

NETHERLANDS.

Ell.....................3.28 feet
Mudde of Zak..............2.84 bush
Vat hectolitre............26.42 galls
Kan litre.................2.11 pints
Pond killogramme..........2.21 lbs
100 pounds:..............108.93 "

Measures and Weights.

The modern system introduced in 1820, is the same as France, but with the old Dutch nomenclature

The ell or metre of 10 palms
100 elles
The vat or hectolitre of 100 kans or litres
The kan is divided into 10 maatjes or 100 vingerhords
The mudde, zak or hectolitre (dry measure) of 10 schepels, or 100 kops or litres, 100 mudden
The pond or killogramme,
100 ponden

The old measures and weights still retained in many places, are as follows:
The Amsterdam foot
" Rhineland foot
" Amsterdam ell
" Brabant or Flemish ell
" wine stekan of 8 stoops 4.27 im gls
" brandy " • "   " 4.13 " "
" beer   "   "   " *4.32 " "
" Amsterdam ahm of 4 ankers, 8 wine stekans, 64 stoops, 128 mingels, 256 pintes, 512 mutjes 34.16 im galls
The velt contains 3 stoops
" oxhoft "   96 "
" legger "   240 "
" vat, 6 ahms, or 384 stoops
" Amsterdam corn last, 27 mudden, 36 sacks, or 108 chepels 82.62 im bush
The Rotterdam ahm....33.32 im galls
The centner of 100 lbs.108.93 lbs. C. S.
A last for freight is estimated at 4000 lbs.

NICE, (SARDINIA.)

The ell ....46,77 inches.
" charge (liquid measure) of 12 rubbi, 20.75 im. galls.
The charge (corn measure) of 4 setiers, 4.40 im. bush.
The quintal of 6 rubbi or 150 lbs.
103.14 lbs. C. S.

PORTUGAL.

100 lbs ....101.19 lbs.
32 lbs. (1 arroba).........32.38 "
4 arrobas of 32 lbs. (1 quintal)
129.52 "
Alquiere ....4.75 bush.
Mojo of grain .... 23.06 "
Last of salt............70.00 "
Almude of wine ....4.37 galls.
The moyo (dry measure) of 15 fanegas, 60 Lisbon alquieres, or 240 quartos, 22.39 im bush., or
23.06 C. S. bush.
100 Lisbon alquieres..37.32 im. bush.
100 Oporto   "   ..46.50   "
The tonelada............54 arrobas.
The palmo of 8 inches....8.62 inches

The pe or foot .... 1½ palmos.
The vara, 5 palmos .... 43.11 in
The covado, 3 palmos, is 21¾ Portuguese, or 26.67 im. inches.
The braca .... 10 palmos.
The Lisbon almude (liquid meas.) of 2 pots, 12 canadas, or 48 quartillos, 3.64 im. galls., or 4.37 galls. C. S.
The barile .... 18 almudes.
The pipe .... 26 "
The tonelado .... 52 "
The Oporto almude is 5.61 im. galls. or 6.73 galls. C. S.
On March 8, 1850, the U. S. Consul reports the almude of Portugal at 7½ galls. U. S.

PRUSSIA.

100 lbs of 2 Cologne marks each, 103.11 lbs
Quintal, of 110 lbs .... 113.42 "
Sheffel of grain .... 1.56 bush.
Eimar of wine .... 18.14 galls
Ell of cloth .... 2.19 feet
Foot .... 12.356 inches
The ell of 25½ Prussian inches, 26 26 inches
100 ells .... 72.94 yards
The ohm of 2 eimers, 4 ankers, or 120 qts., 30.23 im galls, or 36.28 galls. C. S.
The ohm of Dantzic ..39.60 galls "
The oxhoft .... 3 merise
The tun (beer meas) 100 qts, or 25.19 im galls
The scheffel (corn measure) of 16 metzen, or 48 qts ... 1.512 im bush
5½ scheffels .... 1 im qr
100 " .... 18.89 im qr
60 " .... 1 last
The ship last .... 4000 Prussian lbs
The last of timber .... 80 cubic feet

ROME.

Rubbio of grain .... 8.36 bush
Barile of wine .... 15.41 galls
100 Roman lbs, equal to ... 74.77 lbs
The foot .... 11.72 inches
The mercantile canna of 8 palmi 78.35 inches
The tavola censuale, 1000 square metres .... 11.96 square yards
The rubbio .... 18.484 tavoli
The wine barile, 32 boccali, 128 foglilette, 12.84 im. galls, or 15.41 C S galls
16 barile .... 1 botte
The soma of oil, 80 boccali, 36.14 im galls
The oil barile of 28 boccali, 12.65 im galls

The rubbio of corn, 4 quarts, 22 scorzi, or 88 quartucci, 8.10 im bu, or 8.34 C S bu

RUSSIA.

100 lbs of 32 loths each .... 90.26 lbs
Chertwort of grain .... 5.95 bush
Vedro of wine .... 3.25 galls
Pood .... 36 lbs
The Russian foot .... 13.75 im inches
The Moscow foot .... 13.17 "
Archine (cloth meas).28.00 "
100 archines, " ...77.77 yards
The sagine or fathom .... 7 feet
The anker .... 2 stekars or 3 vedros
The oxhoft .... 6 ankers
10 poods .... 1 berkovitz

SICILY.

Cantaro grosso .... 192.53 lbs C S
Cantaro sottile .... 175.03 " "
100 lbs .... 70.01 " "
Salma grossa of grain ..9.77 bush "
Salma generale .... 7.84 " "
Salma of wine .... 23.06 galls "
The canna, 8 palmi, 96 inches, or 81.35 in
The tonna, 4 barile, or 31.24 im galls
The pipe, 12 barile .... 93.72 "
The cafliso of oil, in Messina,258 "
Or by weight .... 24 lbs avoir
In Palermo, oil is sold by the cantaro grosso.

SPAIN.

Quintal, or 4 arrobas .... 101.44 lbs
Arroba .... 25.36 "
Arroba of wine .... 4.13 galls
Fanega of grain .... 1.60 bush
The fanega (corn meas) of 12 celemines, or 48 quartillos..1.55 im bu
100 fanegas .... 19¾ im qrs
The cahiz 12 fanegas ... 18 3 5 im bu
The burgos foot of 12 pulgados or 16 dedos .... 11.128 inches
The varo or Castile Ell, 3 feet or 4 palmos .... 33 38 inches
100 varas .... 92.73 yards
The cantara, or quarter arroba (wine meas) of 8 azumbres, 32 quartillos, 3.54 im. galls
16 wine arrobas. 1 moyo, 56.64 "
The lesser arroba (oil meas) of 4 quartillos, or 100 quarterones, 2.77 im. galls
The botta, 30 wine arrobas, or 38½ oil arrobas
The pipe, 27 wine arrobas, or 34½ oil arrobas
The botta .... 95½ im galls

The preceding are the Castillian standards, which are the general or official standards of Spain, but the local variations are numerous, viz:

ALICANT.

100 varas .... 83.52 im yards
The tonelado, 2 pipes, 80 arrobas, 100 cantars .... 254½ im galls
The caffiso .... 6¾ im bush
The arroba of 24 great lbs,
        27.39 lbs avoir.
The arroba of 36 small lbs.
        27.39 lbs avoir
The quintal .... 4 arrobas
The carga .... 10 "

BARCELONA.

The canna, 2 varas ...... 62.25 inches
The carga, 16 cortanas, 12 arrobas,
        27¼ im galls
The pipe .... 4 cargas
The oil carga is divided into 11 arro's
The salma, 4 quartuas ... 7.53 im bush
The carga of corn ...... 2½ quartuas
The arroba of 26 lbs, each 12 oz
        21.37 lbs avoir
The quintal .... 4 arrobas

BILBOA.

The fanega (corn meas), 1.65 im bush
The quintal of 100 lbs..108 lbs avoir
The quintal macho, used in weighing iron, is 146 lbs, or 157⅔ lbs avoir

MALAGA.

The arroba (weight) ...... 36 lbs C S
The cantara, or arroba, of 8 azumbres
        3.49 im galls
The pipe of wine .... 118½ "
The botta of oil..43 Castilian arrobas
The carga of raisins, 7 arrobas, or
        177½ lbs avoir

VALENCIA.

The varra .... 36.16 im inches
Arroba (liquid meas) ...2.59 im galls
Carga of wine .... 15 arrobas
Carga of oil .... 12 "
Cahiz .... 5.65 im bush
Arroba (weight) .... 28¼ lbs avoir
4 arrobas .... 1 quintal
3 quintals .... 1 carga

SAXONY.

The ell .... 22.30 inches
100 ells .... 61.96 yards

The eimer of 72 kannes.
        17.81 galls C S
The ahm, 2 eimers..... 35.62 "
The oxhoft. 3 " ..... 53.43 "
The fass, 5 " ..... 89.05 "
The fuder. 12 " ... 213.72 "
The corn scheffel is 2.859 im bush, or 2.945 bushel C S
The wispel, 2 mattus, 24 scheffel, 8.58 im qrs
The last of wheat or rye oontains 6 wispels
The last of barley or oats...2 wispels
The centner of 110 lbs...113.23 lbs av

ST. GALL.

100 heavy lbs equal to .... 128 lbs
100 light lbs equal to .... 102 lbs

SURAT.

20 Surat maunds or 10 Bengal factory maunds .... 1 candy
One candy .... 746 lbs 10 oz

SWEDEN.

The aln or ell of two feet.23.38 im in
100 ells .... 64.94 yards
The fathom .... 3 ells
The kann (liquid meas), 2 stoops, or 8 quarters .... 2.76 pints C S
100 kannes .... 69.0720 galls C S
Anker, 15 kannes, or 10.3608 "
Eimer, 30 " 20.7216 "
Tunna, 48 " 33.1545 "
Ahm, 60 " 41.4432 "
Oxhufond, 90 " 62.1648 "
Pipe, 180 " 124.3296 "
Fuder, 360 " 248.6592 "
The tunna (corn measure) of 2 spann, 8 fjerdingar, 32 kappar, or 56 kannes, 4.029 bush; but, as 4 kappa are allowed to each tunna of wheat, oats, barley or rye, for good measure, the tunna of corn is 4½ im bushs
The commercial weight is termed victualie weight.
100 lbs victualie ...... 93.76 lbs avoir
The lispund .... 20 lbs vict. weight
The sten .... 32 " "
The centner ...... 120 " "
The waag .... 165 " "
The skeppund of 20 lispunds is 100 lbs vict wt, or 375.04 lbs avoir
  The iron or metal is 4-5 of the vict weight
Skeppund for metal .... 300 lbs avoir
  The Gefle weight exceeds Stockholm weight 5 per cent.

TRIESTE.

100 ....125.60 lbs
Stajo of grain ....4.34 bush
Orna or eimer of wine....11.91 galls
Ell for woolens...........2.22 feet
Ell for silk ....2.10 feet

TUSCANY.

Grand Duchy of Florence and Leghorn.

The quintal of 100 Tuscan lbs,
                        74.86 lbs avoir
The cantaro, 100 rotoli of 30 oz each,
                        175 lbs avoir
16 cantars ....30 bush, or 1 chaldron
The pissata, 330 rottoli, 5772 lbs avoir
12.80 rottoli............1 ton British
The braccio of 20 soldi, 22.979 inches
100 braccia ....63.83 yards
The passetto ....2 braccia
The canna ....5 "
The Tuscan mile.......28.33 "
The barril (wine meas) of 20 flasci
                    12.04 galls C S
The oil barril..........7.36 im galls
The soma.................2 barrili
The cogna ....10 "
The stajo [corn measure], 2 mine,
                    2.676 im pecks
100 staja ....66 9-00 im bushs
The sacca of 3 staja......2 "
The moggio of 24 staja,
    2 im qrs, or 16.50 bush C S

TURKEY.

The pik or ell is of two kinds, the quarter pik, called halebi or archim, used in the measurement of silks and woolens, is ....27.90 inches
The lesser pik, termed endasse, used in the measurement of cottons and carpets, is.............27.06 inches
The pik in trade is reckoned at 27 ins
The almude [liquid meas]
                    1 1-7 im galls
100 almudes ....115.10 "
The almude of oil weighs .....8 okes
The oke of 4 chequers, or 400 drams,
    2 lbs, 13 oz, 1½ drams avoir
The fortin [corn measure], 4 killows,
                    3.84 im bush

100 killows ....12 im qrs
The cantar or quintal of 44 okes, or 100 rotoli...........125 lbs avoir
The preceding are Constantinople weights. In Smyrna,
100 killows ....17¾ im qrs
2 killows of Smyrna equal to 3 of Constantinople
The cantar..........127.29 lbs avoir
One cantar..............7½ batmans
  "   ....45 okes
  "   ....100 rotoli
The batman of Persian silk...6 okes
The cantar of cotton yarn....45 okes
The taffee of busa silk....610 drams
The cheque of goat wool..800 "
The cheque of opium .....250 "
The tchekis of Smyrna......1⅜ avoir

SERVIA,

A Province of European Turkey.

The rottoli of 180 drams, ..1.27 lbs av
The oke of 400 drams..2.83 lbs avoir
The almude [liquid meas] 1.15 im galls
The killow of corn ....96 im bush
The pike................26⅝ inches

TURIN, SARDINIA.

The rasso or ell ....23.60 inches
The mile of 800 trabucchi, 2697 yards
The Piedmontese mile....2771 "
The brenta of 6 rubbi, 14.41 im galls
The carso of oil is ....10 brenti
The corn stacco of 3 staja'is
                    3.17 im bush
The pound of 1½ marks is
                  5693 Troy grs
4 rubby or 100 lbs....81.33 lbs avoir

VENICE.

100 libre peso groso, 105,17 lbs avoir
100 libbre peso sottile, 66.41 "
100 secchi ....236.19 "
Moggio of grain............9.08 bush
100 braccia [woolen measure],
                    74.17 yards
100 braccia [silk measure],69.81 "
Anfora [liquid measure].
    111 im galls, or 136.80 galls C S

MISCELLANEOUS TABLE

OF

FOREIGN WEIGHTS AND MEASURES.

Arroba of Brazil..............	equal to	32.38 pounds	Confederate States.
Arroba of Buenos Ayres..........	do	25.36 do	do
Amir or Emir, of Stuttgard........	do	78 gallons	do
Ahm of Hanover.................	do	41.43 do	do
Ahm of Leipsic..................	do	40 do	do
Balsam Copavia, 8 lbs...........	do	1 do	do
Butt of wine....................	do	130 do	do
Canado of Balsam Copavia.......	do	30 pounds	do
Chaldron of Coal, British Provinces	do	36 bushels	do
do do Cumberland....	do	53 do	do
Coal, last of Hamburg............	do	5100 pounds	do
Cheki of opium [from Smyrna]....	do	1 76-100 do	do
Coal, a railway wagon load, Pictu	do	62 cwt.	do
Fax, a head, of about............	do	6 3-4 pounds	do
Foot, 100 cubic, of St. Domingo....	do	121-13 feet	do
Honey, one gallon weighs.........		12 pounds	do
Imperial gallon..................	equal to	1-20 gallons	do
do quarter.................	do	8.25 bushels	do
do bushel	do	1.03 do	do
do yard....................	do	36 inches	do
Linseed, one bushel..............	do	47 pounds	do
Mudd or Maud, of Rotterdam......	do	148 do	do
Mudde of Augsburg..............	do	14.92 gallons	do
Moyo of Salt [Spain].............	do	70 bushels	do
Modius of salt [from Ivica, Spain]	do	40 do	do
do do [Oporto and St Ubes]	do	23 do	do
Mass [of Antwerp,] ⅟ of ohm ...	do	10 gallons	do
Ohm "	do	40 do	do
Besado of Buenos Ayres..........	do	35 pounds	do
do of dry hides of Montevideo	do	40 do	do
do of dry salt hides of do	do	40 do	do
do of wet salt hides of do	do	60 do	do
Picul of Hemp, of Manilla........	do	139-50 pounds	do
Pounds of Austria........100 lb..	do	123 50-100	do
do Antwerp...... do ...	do	103 35-100	do
do Bavaria......... do ..	do	123 50-100	do
do Belgium....... do ..	do	103 35-100	do
do Brussels .... do ..	do	103 35-100	do
do Bremen........ do ..	do	110 12-100	do
do Berlin......... do ..	do	103 11-100	do
do Hamburg...... do ..	do	110 4-10,000	do
do Malaga........ co ..	do	101 44-100	do
do Netherlands.... do ..	do	108 93-100	do
Pounds of Portugal.......100 lb..	equal to	101 19-100	do
do Prussia........ do ..	do	103 11-100	do
do Rotterdam..... do ..	do	108 93-100	do
do Spain......... do ..	do	101 44-100	do
do St. Domingo... do ..	do	107 93-100	do
do Trieste........ do ..	do	123 60-100	do
do Vienna........ do ..	do	123 50-100	do

Palm of Italy, of marble.........	equal to	6 inches......	Confederate States.
Quintal of France...............	do	220 54-100	do
Salma of oil...	do	42.16 gallons	do
Skippond of Gottonburg.........	do	300 pounds	do
do of Getle...............	do	314 1-10 pounds	do
Salt, one barrel................	do	3½ bushels	do
Vara, Spanish.....	do	8 feet	do
Vara of Baracoa................	do	20 feet	do
Oils, Linseed, 1 gallon...........	do	7 pounds 12 oz.	do
do Rapeseed, do	do	7 do 12 oz.	do
do Cocoanut, do	do	7 do 8 oz.	do
do Olive, do	do	7 do 9 oz.	do
do Groundnut, do	do	7 do 9 oz.	do
do Palm, do	do	7 do 8 oz.	do

The palm of Marble from Carrara 5 $\frac{57}{100}$ cubic or 9 $\frac{6}{100}$ in inches by actual measurement.

LIST OF TARES

ALLOWED BY LAW AND CUSTOM.

Articles.		By Law.	By Custom.
Almonds	in cases		8 per cent.
"	in casks		15 "
"	in double bales,		8 lb. each.
"	in bales		4 lb "
"	in frails		10 per cent.
"	in ceroons		10 "
"	in bags		4 "
Alum	in bags		5 lb. each.
"	in casks		10 per cent.
Anvils	in casks		90 lb. each.
Bristles	in casks		10 per cent.
Butter, weighing from 80 to 100 lb in kegs			18 lb. each.
Black plate	in boxes		8 lb. "
Candles	in boxes	8 per cent.	
Candy, sugar	in boxes	10 "	
Cheese	in hampers	10 "	
"	in baskets	10 "	
"	in boxes	20 "	
"	in casks or tubs		15 per cent.
Cassia	in boxes		actual.
"	in mats		{ 9 per cent. or 1 1-2 lb. for 4 mats.
Chocolate	in boxes	10 per cent.	
Coffee	in bags	2 "	
"	in bales	3 "	
"	in casks	12 "	
"	in ceroons		6 per cent.
"	in boxes		15 "
Cinnamon	in boxes		actual.
"	in bales		6 per cent.
Cocoa	in bags	1 per cent.	
"	in casks	10 "	
"	in ceroons		8 "
"	in baskets		2 lb. each.
Cloves	in casks		12 lb. "
"	in bags		4 lb. "
Cotton	in bales	2 per cent.	
"	in ceroons	6 "	
Composition spikes or nails	in casks	8 "	
Copper	in casks	8 "	
Copperas	in casks		10 per cent.
Corks	in small bales		5 lb. each.
"	in large bales		8 lb. "
"	in double bales		16 lb. "
Cordage, Twine	in boxes		15 per cent.
" "	in casks	12 per cent.	
" "	in bales	3 "	
Currants	in casks		12 "
"	in boxes		10 "

Articles.		By Law.	By Custom.
Figs	in boxes		10 per cent.
"	in mats		4 "
"	in frails		4 "
"	in drums		8 "
"	in casks		12 "
Fish, Dry	in casks		12 "
" "	in boxes		12 "
Flax	in bobbins		3 to 3½ lb each.
Gunpowder	in casks		23 lbs each.
"	in ½ casks		9 "
"	in ¼ casks		5 "
Glue	in boxes		15 per cent.
"	in casks		20 "
" from Canton	in boxes		11 "
Hemp, Manilla	in bales		6 lbs. each.
" Hamburg, Leghorn, Trieste, in bales			no allowance.
Indigo	in cases		15 per cent.
"	in barrels	12 per cent.	
"	in other casks	15 "	
"	in ceroons	10 "	
"	in bags	3 "	
"	in mats	3 "	
Iron, Sheet	in boxes		8 "
" Hoop	in boxes		8 "
" Russia Sheet	in packs		14 to 28 lb each.
Jalap	in yellow mats		12 lbs. each.
Lead, pigs, bars, sheets	in casks		3 per cent.
" White, in oil	in kegs		8 "
" " "	in hhds		100 lbs. each.*
" " dry	in casks		6 per cent.
" Red, dry	in casks		5 "
" " in oil	in casks		10 "
" Shot	in casks		3 "
Nails	in casks	8 per cent.	
"	in bags		3 "
Ochre, dry	in casks		10 "
" in oil	in casks		12 "
Paris white	in casks		10 "
Pepper	in casks	12 per cent.	
"	in bales	5 "	
"	in bags	2 "	
"	in doub. bags		4 lbs. each.
Pimento	in casks	16 per cent	
"	in bags	3 "	
Plums	in boxes		8 per cent.
"	in casks		12 "
Prunes	in boxes		8 "
Paper	in bales		5, 6, 7 & 8 lb. ea.
Raisins	in jars		18 lbs. each.
"	in boxes		15 per cent.
"	in casks		12 "
"	in frails		4 "
"	in drums		10 "
Rice	in casks		10 "

*Extra allowance for hogsheads.

Articles		By Law.	By Custom.
Salts, Glauber	in casks	8 per cent	
" Epsom	in casks		11 per cent.
Segars	in boxes	18 per cent	
"	in casks	18 "	
Shot	in casks	3 "	
Snuff	in casks		12 "
"	in boxes		15 "
Soap	in boxes	10 per cent	actual tare.
Spanish Brown, dry	in casks		12 "
" " in oil	in casks		12 "
Spikes	in casks		8 "
"	in bags		3 "
Steel	in casks		8 "
"	in cases		8 "
"	in bundles		3 "
" from Trieste, in large size	in boxes		11 lbs. each.
" " in 2d size	in boxes		10¾ lb. "
Sheet iron	in casks		15 per cent.
Sugar, Candy	in boxes	10 per cent	
" "	in tubs		15 "
"	in bags	5 per cent	
"	in boxes	15 "	
"	in casks	12 "	
"	in barrels		10 "
"	in mats	5 per cent	
"	in ceroons		8 "
"	in canisters		40 lbs. each.
Starch, from Bremen, weighing 62 lbs each	in boxes		13 lb. "
Tallow	in bales		8 per cent.
"	in casks		12 "
"	in ceroons		8 "
"	in tubs		15 "
Tea, Bohea	in chests*		22 lbs. each.
" Green, 70 lbs and over	in boxes	20 lb each	
" other, between 50 and 70 lb.	in boxes	18 lb each	
" " of 80 lb	in boxes	20 lb each	
" " over 80 lb	in boxes	22 lb each	
Tobacco, Leaf	in bales		8 lb each.
" " with extra cover	in bales		10 lb "
" "	in boxes		15 per cent.
Twine	in casks	12 per cent	
"	in boxes		15 "
"	in bales	3 per cent	
Whiting	in casks		10 "
Wire	in casks		8 "
Wool	in bales		3 "

*Chest, so called, as now imported, but in reality quarter chest.

ACTS OF CONGRESS.

AN ACT
TO CONTINUE IN FORCE CERTAIN LAWS OF THE UNITED STATES OF AMERICA.

Be it enacted by the Confederate States of America in Congress assembled, That all the laws of the United States of America, in force and in use in the Confederate States of America on the first day of November last, and not inconsistent with the constitution of the Confederate States, be and the same are hereby continued in force until altered or repealed by the Congress.

ADOPTED, February 9, 1861.

AN ACT
TO DEFINE THE LIMITS OF THE PORT OF NEW ORLEANS, AND FOR OTHER PURPOSES.

The Congress of the Confederate States of America do enact, That the Port of New Orleans, in the State of Louisiana, shall embrace and include all the waters, inlets and shores, on both sides of the Mississippi river within the whole parish of Orleans, that part of the parish of Jefferson on the right bank of said river to the upper line of the Destrehans canal, and that portion of the said parish of Jefferson on the left bank of the river Mississippi to the upper limits of the town or faubourg of Hurtsville. That the ports of delivery known as Bayou St. John's, Lake Port, and Port Pontchartrain, and the customs officers authorised therefor, be and the same are hereby abolished and discontinued, and all the waters, inlets and shores, embraced within the limits of said ports be added to and included in the port of New Orleans.

APPROVED, May 14, 1861.

AN ACT

TO PROHIBIT THE EXPORTATION OF COTTON FROM THE CONFEDERATE STATES, EXCEPT THROUGH THE SEAPORTS OF SAID STATES; AND TO PUNISH PERSONS OFFENDING THEREIN.

SECTION 1. *The Congress of the Confederate States of America do enact,* That from and after the first day of June next, and during the existence of the blockade of any of the Ports of the Confederate States of America by the government of the United States, it shall not be lawful for any person to export any raw cotton or cotton yarn from the Confederate States of America, except through the seaports of the said Confederate States; and it shall be the duty of all the marshals and revenue officers of the said Confederate States to prevent all violations of this act.

SEC. 2. If any person shall violate or attempt to violate or evade the provisions of the foregoing section, he shall forfeit all the cotton or cotton yarn thus attempted to be illegally exported, for the use of the Confederate States; and in addition thereto, he shall be guilty of a misdemeanor, and on conviction thereof shall be fined in a sum not exceeding five thousand dollars, or else imprisoned in some public jail or penitentiary, for a period not exceeding six months, at the discretion of the court, after conviction upon trial by a court of competent jurisdiction.

SEC. 3. Any person informing as to a violation or attempt to violate the provisions of this act, shall be entitled to one-half the proceeds of the articles forfeited by reason of his information.

SEC. 4. Any justice of the peace, on information under oath from any person of a violation or attempt to violate this act, may issue his warrant and cause the cotton or cotton yarn specified in the affidavit to be seized and retained until an investigation can be had before the courts of the Confederate States.

SEC. 5. Every Steamboat or railroad car which shall be used with the consent of the owner or person having the same in charge, for the purpose of violating this act, shall be forfeited in like manner to the use of the Confederate States. But nothing in this act shall be so construed as to prohibit exportation of cotton to Mexico through its co-terminous frontier.

Approved, May 21, 1861.

AN ACT
TO DECLARE AND ESTABLISH THE FREE NAVIGATION OF THE MISSISSIPPI RIVER.

Section 1. *The Congress of the Confederate States of America do enact,* That the peaceful navigation of the Mississippi River is hereby declared free to the citizens of any of the States upon its borders, or upon the borders of its navigable tributaries; and all ships, boats, rafts or vessels may navigate the same, under such regulations as may be established by authority of law, or under such police regulations as may be established by the States within their several jurisdictions.

Sec. 2. *Be it further enacted,* All ships, boats or vessels which may enter the waters of said river within the limits of this Confederacy, from any port or place beyond the said limits, may freely pass with their cargoes to any other port or place beyond the limits of this Confederacy, without any duty or hindrance, except light-money, pilotage, and other like charges; but it shall not be lawful for any such ship, boat or vessel, to sell, deliver, or in any way dispose of her cargo, or land any portion thereof for the purpose of sale and delivery within the limits of this Confederacy; and in case any portion of such cargo shall be sold or delivered, or landed for that purpose in violation of the provisions of this act, the same shall be forfeited, and shall be seized and condemned by a proceeding in admiralty before the court having jurisdiction of the same in the district in which the same may be found; and the ship, boat or vessel, shall forfeit four times the amount of the value of the duties chargeable on the said goods, wares, or merchandise so landed, sold or disposed of in violation of the provisions of this act, to be recovered by a proper proceeding in admiralty before the said court, in the district in which such ship, boat or vessel may be found, one-half for the use of the collector of the district who shall institute and conduct such proceeding, and the other half for the use of the Government of the Confederate States; *Provided*, That if any such ship, boat or vessel shall be stranded, or from any cause become unable to proceed on its voyage, the cargo thereof may be landed and the same be entered at the nearest port of entry, in the same manner as goods, wares and merchandise regularly consigned to said port; and the person so entering the same shall be entitled to the benefit of drawback of duties or of warehousing said goods, wares and merchandise, as provided by law in other cases.

Sec. 3. *And be it further enacted,* If any person having the charge of or being concerned in the transportation of any goods, wares or merchandise, upon the said river, shall, with intent to defraud the revenue, break open or unpack within the limits of the Confederate States, any part of the merchandise entered for transportation beyond the said limits, or shall exchange or consume the same, or with like intent shall break or deface any seal or fastening placed thereon by any officer of the revenue, or if any person shall deface, alter or forge any certificate granted for the protection of merchandise transported as aforesaid, each and every person so offending shall forfeit and pay five hundred dollars, and shall be imprisoned not less than one nor more than six months, at the discretion of the court before which such person shall be convicted.

Sec. 4. *Be it further enacted,* In case any ship, boat or vessel shall enter the waters of the said river within the limits of the Confederate States, having on board any goods, wares and merchandise subject to the payment of duties, and the master, consignee or owner shall desire to land the same for sale or otherwise, it shall be lawful to enter the said goods, wares and merchandise at any port of entry, in the same manner as goods, wares and merchandise regularly consigned to the said port, or to forward them under bond or seal, according to the regulations customary in such cases, when consigned to any port or place beyond the limits of this Confederacy; and on payment of the duties on said goods, to obtain from the collector a license to land the same at any point on the river; and when goods, wares or merchandise shall be entered as aforesaid, the owner, importer or consignee shall be entitled to the benefit of drawback of duties or of warehousing the said goods, wares and merchandise, as is provided by law, upon complying with all the laws and regulations which apply to cases of entry for drawback or warehousing respectively.

SEC. 5. *Be it further enacted*, When any such ship, boat or vessel, having on board goods, wares and merchandise subject to the payment of duties, as set forth in the fourth section, shall arrive at the first port of her entry of the Confederate States, the master or person in command of such ship, boat or vessel shall, before he pass the said port, and immediately after his arrival, deposit with the collector a manifest of the cargo on board subject to the payment of duties, and the said collector shall, after registering the same, transmit it, duly certified to have been deposited, to the officers with whom the entries are to be made, and the said collector may, if he judge it necessary for the security of the revenue, put an inspector of the customs on board any such ship, boat or vessel, to accompany the same until her arrival at the first port of entry to which her cargo may be consigned; and if the master or person in command shall omit to deposit a manifest as aforesaid, or refuse to receive such inspector on board, he shall forfeit and pay five hundred dollars, with costs of suit, one-half to the use of the officer with whom the manifest should have been deposited, and the other half to the use of the collector of the district to which the vessel was bound: PROVIDED, HOWEVER, That until ports of entry shall be established above the city of Vicksburg, on the Mississippi River, the penalties of this act shall not extend to the delivery of goods above that port by vessels or boats descending said river.

APPROVED, February 25, 1861.

AN ACT
TO MODIFY THE NAVIGATION LAWS AND REPEAL ALL DISCRIMINATING DUTIES ON SHIPS OR VESSELS.

SECTION 1. *The Congress of the Confederate States of America do enact,* That all laws which forbid the employment in the coasting trade of all ships or vessels not enrolled or licensed, and also all laws which forbid the importation of goods, wares and merchandise from one port of the Confederate States to another port of the Confederate States, or from any foreign port or place, in a vessel belonging wholly or in part to a subject or citizen of any foreign state or power, are hereby repealed.

SEC. 2. All laws which impose any discriminating duty on the tonnage of ships or vessels owned by any subject or citizen of any foreign state or power, or upon goods, wares or merchandise imported in any such ship or vessel, are hereby repealed.

APPROVED, February 26, 1861.

AN ACT
TO AUTHORIZE THE SECRETARY OF THE TREASURY TO ESTABLISH ADDITIONAL PORTS AND PLACES OF ENRTY AND DELIVERY, AND APPOINT OFFICERS THEREFOR.

SECTION 1. *The Congress of the Confederate States of America do enact,* That the Secretary of the Treasury be and he is hereby authorized and empowered to establish such ports of entry and delivery of goods, wares and merchandise as in his judgment may be necessary for the proper collection of the customs and the enforcement of the revenue laws of the Confederate States; and that he have power to change, alter and abolish such ports and places of entry and delivery at any time when the public interests may require it.

SEC. 2. *Be it further enacted,* That the Secretary of the Treasury be and he is hereby authorized and empowered to appoint suitable persons as collectors of the customs at such ports and places of entry and delivery, under such regulations and with such salaries as he may from time to time prescribe and establish.

APPROVED, February 28, 1861.

EXPORT DUTY ON COTTON.

AN ACT
TO RAISE MONEY FOR THE SUPPORT OF THE GOVERNMENT, AND TO PROVIDE FOR THE DEFENCE OF THE CONFEDERATE STATES OF AMERICA.

SEC. 5. From and after the first day of August, 1861, there shall be levied and collected and paid, a duty of one-eighth of one cent per pound on all cotton in the raw state exported from the Confederate States, which duty is hereby specially pledged to the due payment of interest and principal of the loan provided for in this act; and the Secretary of the Treasury is hereby authorized and required to establish a sinking fund to carry into effect the provisions of this section: PROVIDED, HOWEVER, That the interest coupons, issued under the second section of this act, when due, shall be receivable in payment of the export duty on cotton: PROVIDED, ALSO, That when the debt and interest thereon herein authorized to be contracted shall be extinguished, or the sinking fund provided for that purpose shall be adequate to that end, the said export duty shall cease and determine.

APPROVED, February 28, 1861.

AN ACT
TO REPEAL SO MUCH OF THE LAWS OF THE CONFEDERATE STATES OF AMERICA AS PROHIBIT THE INTRODUCTION OF LIQUORS, EXCEPT IN CASKS OR VESSELS OF OR ABOVE CERTAIN NAMED CAPACITY, AND FOR OTHER PURPOSES.

SECTION 1. *The Congress of the Confederate States of America do enact,* That all laws and parts of laws which prohibit the importation into this Confederacy of beer, ale or porter, or distilled spirits, except in casks or vessels not below certain prescribed capacities; also, all laws requiring loaf and refined sugars to be brought in, in vessels of a certain tonnage, and in packages of certain sizes, be and the same are hereby repealed. And hereafter it shall be lawful to import the same, subject to the payment of the duties prescribed by law, in such quantities as the importer shall choose.

APPROVED, March 5, 1861.

AN ACT

TO PROVIDE FOR THE REGISTRATION OF VESSELS OWNED IN WHOLE OR IN PART BY CITIZENS OF THE CONFEDERATE STATES.

The Congress of the Confederate States of America do enact, That all vessels, wherever built, one-fourth or more of which shall be owned by a citizen or citizens of the Confederate States, and commanded by a citizen thereof, shall be registered as a vessel of the Confederacy at the custom-house thereof: PROVIDED, That a majority in interest of the owners shall consent to such registration, and such vessels be not registered elsewhere.

APPROVED, March 6, 1861.

AN ACT

TO REGULATE FOREIGN COINS IN THE CONFEDERATE STATES.

SECTION 1. *The Congress of the Confederate States of America do enact,* That all laws and parts of laws now in force for the regulation of the mint and branch mints of the United States, and for the government of the officers and persons employed therein, and for the punishment of all offences connected with the mint or coinage of the United States, shall be and they are hereby declared to be in full force in relation to the mints of New Orleans and Dahlonega.

SEC. 2. That all laws now in force in reference to the coins of the United States, and the striking and coining of the same, shall, as far as applicable, have full force and effect in relation to the coins therein authorized, whether the said laws are penal or otherwise, and whether they are for preventing counterfeiting or debasement; for protecting the currency; for regulating and guarding the process of striking and coining and the preparations therefor; or for the security of the coin, or for any other purpose.

SEC. 3. That the silver coins issued in conformity with the law of the United States of twenty-first of February and third of March, eighteen hundred and fifty-three, shall be legal tenders in payment of debts for all sums not exceeding ten dollars, all laws to the contrary notwithstanding.

*Sec. 4. That the following foreign gold coin shall pass current as money within the Confederate States of America, and be receivable for the payment of all debts and demands at the following rates, that is to say: The sovereign of England, of no less a weight than five pennyweights and three grains, and of the fineness of (915½) nine hundred fifteen and one-half thousandths, shall be deemed equal to four dollars and eighty-two cents; the Napoleon, of the weight of not less than (4 dwts., 3½ grs.) four pennyweights three grains and one-half, and of a fineness of not less than (899) eight hundred ninty-ninth thousandths, shall be deemed equal to three dollars and eighty-two cents; the Spanish and Mexican doubloons, of no less a weight than (17 dwts., 8½ grs.) seventeen pennyweights eight grains and one-half, and of the fineness of not less than (899) eight hundred ninty-ninth thousandths, shall be deemed equal to fifteen dollars and fifty-three cents.

Sec. 5. That the following silver coins shall pass current as money within the Confederate States of America, and be received in payment for all debts and demands at the following rates, that is to say: The American dollar, (412½ g.) four hundred twelve and one-half grains, and the dollar of Mexico, of not less than (897) eight hundred ninty-seventh thousandths in fineness, and (415 g.) four hundred fifteen grains in weight, shall be deemed equal to one dollar and two cents; the five-franc piece, of not less than (900) nine hundred thousandths in fineness and (384) three hundred eighty-four grains in weight, shall be deemed equal to ninty-five cents.

Be it further enacted, That all laws and parts of laws inconsistent with this act be and the same are hereby repealed.

Approved, March 14, 1861.

---
*Since repealed.

AN ACT
TO PROVIDE FOR THE PAYMENT OF LIGHT MONEY IN THE CONFEDERATE STATES.

The Congress of the Confederate States of America do enact, That a duty of five cents per ton, to be denominated "Light Money," shall be levied and collected on all ships or vessels which, after the first day of May next, may enter the seaports of the Confederate States from any seaport, to be collected in the manner heretofore provided by law as to tonnage duties: PROVIDED, HOWEVER, That on all vessels trading regularly between ports of the Confederate States, the said duties shall not be levied and collected oftener than once in every three months.

APPROVED, March 16, 1861.

AN ACT
TO EXEMPT FROM DUTY CERTAIN ARTICLES OF MERCHANDISE THEREIN NAMED.

SECTION 1. *The Congress of the Confederate States of America do enact,* That the Secretary of the Treasury is hereby authorized and empowered to remit the duty in all cases where commodities were bona fide purchased or contracted for on or before the 18th of February last, within the late United States, where the importer has not been able to comply with the provisions of the act to define more accurately the exemption of certain goods from duty, which required that the goods, wares and merchandise should have been actually laden on board of the exporting vessel or conveyance destined for any port in this Confederacy on or before the 15th day of March in the present year: PROVIDED, Such testimony is furnished the Secretary of the Treasury by the importer, that it was impossible to comply with the provisions of said act, and also that the demand and collection of said duty has operated injuriously to him or them beyond the commercial effect upon articles of consumption by the imposition of duties.

SEC. 2. *And be it further enacted,* That all books, pamphlets, and tracts, and other publications printed and published by any church or benevolent society, whose organization extends to and embraces citizens of the Confederate States, shall be free and exempt from duty.*

SEC. 3. *And be it further enacted,* That all facts herein required to exist in order to entitle a party to the benefits of this act, shall be established to the satisfaction of the Secretary of the Treasury, in a manner to be prescribed by him.

APPROVED, March 15 1861.

---

* Repealed by Tariff Act of 21st May, 1861.

AN ACT
TO AUTHORIZE THE TRANSIT OF MERCHANDISE THROUGH THE CONFEDERATE STATES.

SECTION 1. *The Congress of the Confederate States of America do enact,* That goods, wares and merchandise imported from any foreign country, into the Confederate States, destined for any foreign country, may be entered and have transit through the Confederate States free of duty, subject to such regulations as the Secretary of the Treasury from time to time shall make; and the said Secretary of the Treasury shall have power to make such regulations as he may deem expedient for the safety of the revenue and for the public convenience, which regulations may be enforced in the manner prescribed by law as to other regulations in relation to the revenue.

APPROVED, March 15, 1861.

RECENT CIRCULAR INSTRUCTIONS

OF THE

TREASURY DEPARTMENT,

RELATIVE TO

COMMERCE, NAVIGATION, AND THE REVENUE.

CIRCULAR INSTRUCTIONS NO. 1.

REGULATIONS RELATIVE TO IMPORTATIONS FROM PLACES ABOVE THE CONFEDERATE STATES, BY VESSELS NAVIGATING THE MISSISSIPPI AND OTHER RIVERS.

All steamboats or other vessels navigating the River Mississippi, destined for ports or places within the Confederate States, on arrival within the territory of the Confederate States of America, from any port or place beyond the northern limits thereof, shall come to at the port of Norfolk,* otherwise known as Nelm's landing, in the State of Mississippi, and the master or person in command of every such vessel, shall make due report of the arrival of the said vessel, by exhibiting to the Revenue officer at said port, duplicate manifests of the whole cargo, declaring the name of the vessel, name of master, where from, the port of destination, and a full particular description of said cargo; and shall obtain from the Revenue officer a certificate endorsed on one of the said

---

* By the extension of the Confederacy, in lieu of the port of Norfolk, these regulations will apply to the port established on the river nearest the frontier of the Confederate States.

manifests, of the fact of its exhibition, and shall leave with the said officer the duplicate of the same.

It shall be the duty and is hereby required of the Collector or chief revenue officer at the port of Norfolk, to board at all hours of the day and night, either in person or by deputy, in the person of a customs officer, all vessels entering the Confederate States by the river Mississippi from any place above the limits of the Confederacy on said river or its tributaries, for the purpose of receiving the report of the master or commander, as hereinbefore required to be made to him, and to demand of said master or commander duplicate manifests containing the particulars before mentioned, and on a compliance with this demand to certify on each of such manifests as follows:

Port of

day of 18

I certify this to be the original (or duplicate as the case may be) manifest of the of master, bound for exhibited to me this date.

A. B.

Revenue officer,

and to return to the said master or commander the original manifest, retaining the duplicate, which shall be forwarded by him, by the shortest route, to the Collector of the port of final destination of said vessel, having first registered the same in a book to be kept by him for that purpose, in the following form:

BOARDING AND MANIFEST REGISTER.

DATE WHEN BOARDED.	CLASS AND NAME OF VESSEL.	NAME OF MASTER.	WHERE FROM.	WHERE BOUND.	GENERAL CARGO.	REMARKS.

Should the whole or any portion of the cargo of any vessel entering the waters of the Confederate States as aforesaid, being composed of goods, wares or merchandise exempted by law from the payment of duty, be intended to be landed at places other than ports of entry or delivery within the limits of the Confederacy, such landing shall be permitted on the commander or master exhibiting to the first revenue officer, in addition to the manifest before required, a schedule, in duplicate, of the articles intended to be so landed, which shall describe the goods, the quantity and value, the name of the consignee, and the place where they are to be landed; and receiving a permit endorsed on the original schedule, (which it is hereby made the duty of the boarding officer to furnish on the foregoing requisites being complied with,) and this permit shall be in the following form:

Port of

day of   18

Permission is hereby given to land the goods described, by   entries in this schedule at the places designated therein.

A. B.

Revenue officer.

The original schedule, with the permit endorsed, being returned to the master, the duplicate shall be retained and filed in the office of the revenue officer, after having been first recorded, in a book to be kept by him for that purpose, detailing all the particulars stated in the original schedule; and a copy of this record, rendered to the Treasury Department monthly, shall form an abstract of the free goods imported through the port of Norfolk.

FLATBOATS.

All flatboats with coal in bulk, intended to be landed at places within the limits of the Confederate States other than ports of entry or delivery, may be permitted to land said cargo, on the master or commander complying with the following regulations, to-wit:

A schedule setting forth the name of the boat, name of the

owners, master, where from, quality, quantity and value of the coal, and the fact of its being intended to be landed at places other than ports of entry or delivery, shall be prepared by the master or commander in duplicate, and presented to and verified by oath before the Collector or chief revenue officer at the port of Norfolk, whose duty it shall be to estimate on both the original and duplicate, the duties due on the quantity declared and further ascertained by the cubic measurement, to be made by a competent officer appointed for that purpose, residing at said port, and on the duty thus assessed and ascertained being paid to the said revenue officer, this officer shall endorse on the original schedule a certificate of such payment and a permit to land the cargo at any place other than ports of entry or delivery.

It shall be the duty of the revenue officer at the port of Norfolk to retain in his office the duplicate schedule received, to record the same, detailing all the particulars, and to render monthly a copy of the record as an abstract to the Treasury Department, and also to account for and deposit all moneys received by him for duties from this source in accordance with the provisions of existing laws and the instructions of the Secretary of the Treasury.

OTHER VESSELS WITH CARGOES FOR INTERMEDIATE PORTS.

Should any portion of the cargo of vessels arriving as aforesaid, composed of dutiable or free articles be destined to ports of entry or delivery within the Confederate States, other than the port of final destination of said vessel, permission may be obtained to land the same under the following regulations, viz:

The master or commander shall present to the revenue officer at the port of Norfolk, a schedule in triplicate of said goods, describing them by marks and numbers, number of packages and contents, corresponding with the description in the general manifest of the vessel, also stating the consignee and name of the port of destination of the merchandise.

Should the merchandise as aforesaid be intended to be landed at more than one intermediate port, then separate schedules of the goods destined for each port, to be made out in triplicate, with all the particulars hereinbefore required, shall be presented as aforesaid. And it shall be the duty of the revenue officer to certify on each of said schedules the fact of presentation, and also on the original to endorse his permission for the vessel to proceed to and land at the port or ports designated, the goods described in said schedule. The original shall be then returned to the master or commander, the triplicates forwarded as promptly as possible by the shortest route to the principal revenue officer of each port at which the goods are intended to be landed, and the duplicate retained in his office and recorded in a book prepared for that purpose, in the following form:

DATE.	CLASS AND NAME OF VESSEL.	MASTER.	WHERE FROM.	PORT OF LANDING.	MARKS AND NUMBERS.	DESCRIPTION OF MERCHANDISE.

and a transcript of this record shall be rendered monthly to the Treasury Department.

ON ARRIVAL AT INTERMEDIATE PORTS.

On the arrival of the vessel at each port designated in the schedule as aforesaid, the master or commander shall present to the chief revenue officer the original schedule, and receive a general permit to land the goods, upon their being duly entered and special landing permits issued as now provided by law for the landing of imported merchandise. Should, however, the vessel arrive at said ports after or before the business hours of the Custom-House, or should other circumstances render it necessary, the master or commander shall be permitted to deposit the goods intended to be landed either in a bonded warehouse or in the custody of a customs officer, on receiving a receipt from either the Government officer in charge of the warehouse in which they are deposited, or of the customs officer into whose custody they are delivered, which receipt shall contain all the particulars detailed in the schedule; and the said original schedule shall be surrendered to the person with whom the merchandise is deposited, and by him be delivered to the chief revenue officer as soon as the opening of the Custom House will admit.

It shall be the duty of the chief revenue officer at such intermediate ports at which goods may be landed on the schedule endorsed by the revenue officer at the port of Norfolk, as hereinbefore provided, to keep a correct and particular record of the same, shewing the date of importation, class and name of the vessel, name of the master, where from, marks, numbers and description of merchandise, the value and duty assessed thereon, and whether the same has been entered for consumption or warehousing, and to render monthly to the Treasury Department a transcript of this record as an abstract of such importations; and in case any of the goods deposited in warehouse under the provisions of these regulations shall remain unclaimed, a return of the same with the foregoing particulars shall be rendered as a supplement to such monthly return. And all moneys received for duties shall be accounted for and deposited as now provided by law, or as the Secretary of the Treasury may direct.

ON ARRIVAL AT PORT OF FINAL DESTINATION.

On the arrival of the vessel at the port of final destination, the master or commander shall make due entry at the Custom House by delivering his original manifest, together with all schedules endorsed with the permits to land at intermediate ports, and the receipts of officers to whom any goods may have been delivered, or any other documents shewing the disposition of any portion of the cargo, and the residue of the cargo shall be landed on permits similar to those provided by law for the landing of imported merchandise; and the total cargo, as shown by the original manifest, shall be delivered at this port, with the exception of such as is shown by the documents presented at time of entry to have been landed elsewhere, under the penalties now provided by law for discrepancies existing in the cargoes of vessels arriving from foreign ports.

In order to relieve vessels in this branch of importing trade from embarassments, all goods imported therein remaining unclaimed, or for which no entry shall be made or permit granted within twenty-four hours after arrival, may be taken possession of by the Collector and deposited in a bonded warehouse on a general permit to be issued by him for that purpose.

To afford further facilities in the event of vessels in this trade arriving at the port of final destination before the opening, or after the closing of the Custom House for the day, and a necessity exist for discharging the cargo, it shall be lawful to deposit the same or any part thereof, at the risk and expense of said vessel, on the levee, in the charge of the inspection service of the customs, or in any bonded warehouse at the port, such portion of said cargo as may be practicable, the master or commander of the vessel obtaining for the goods so deposited a receipt from the inspection officer on the levee, or the customs officer in charge of the warehouse, which receipt shall be delivered to the Collector of customs as soon thereafter as the business hours of the Custom House at said port will permit.

Any goods, wares or merchandise imported as aforesaid, may be entered at the port of destination on the presentation to the Collector of the bill or bills of lading, together with the other documents now required by law on the entry of imported merchandise, before and in anticipation of the arrival of the importing vessel, and the necessary permits for the landing shall issue on the completion of these entries.

And on the presentation of these permits to the surveyor, it shall be his duty and is hereby required of him, (if the vessel by which the goods are imported shall have arrived at the port,) to detail an inspector of the customs to superintend the landing of the merchandise described therein, and such landing is authorized before entry has been made by the importing vessel at the Custom

House, when the interest of commerce or circumstances attending such arrival shall render it necessary. It must, however, be distinctly understood, that it is unlawful to discharge any portion of the cargoes of these vessels, except under the supervision and inspection of a customs officer.

APPRAISERS' SAMPLES, EXAMINATIONS, &c.

In discharging the cargoes of these vessels, it shall be the duty of the discharging officer to either send all the samples as designated on permit to the appraisers' store, or retain the same on the levee for examination, in accordance with the directions to this effect declared in the permit.

And for the convenience of commerce, it is hereby required that all distilled spirits and wines in casks, imported from any foreign port or place shall be examined by samples taken from the number of packages designated on the invoice, entry and permit, for examination, which samples shall not exceed in quantity four ounces each.

And the examination of all other goods as may be deemed practicable by the Collector, shall be made by the appraisers on the levee or place of landing, and such examination shall have the same validity as if made at the appraisers' store.

The quantities of dutiable merchandise shall be ascertained as provided by law, by either gauge, weight or measure, but the quantities of all goods exempt by law from the payment of duty shall be taken as that declared in the entry of the same at the Custom House.

IMPORTATIONS BY RIVERS AND WATER COURSES OTHER THAN THE MISSISSIPPI.

The master or commander of all vessels entering the territorial limits of the Confederate States of America, by rivers other than the Mississippi, shall be obliged to come to at the first port on the river by which the said vessel enters the territorial limits, and to report to the chief revenue officer residing thereat, and there to comply with all the regulations heretofore provided for vessels entering by way of the river Mississippi and arriving at the port of Norfolk, and the duties required by these regulations to be performed by the Collector or revenue officer at the said port of Norfolk, shall be performed in all particulars by the revenue officers at the said frontier ports on such other rivers.

CLEARANCES.

Before the departure of any vessel navigating the Mississippi or other rivers, destined to a foreign port or place beyond the northern limits of the Confederate States of America, the master or person having charge thereof shall deliver to the Collector or chief officer of the customs, at the port from which such vessel is about to depart, a manifest of the cargo on board the same, in the form and verified in the manner now provided by law for vessels to a foreign port, and obtain from the said Collector a clearance in the following form:

         Confederate States of America,
  District of
  Port of   18

These are to certify to all whom it doth concern, that
            master or commander of the
        , of   bound for
        , hath entered and cleared his said vessel according to law.
          Given under my hand and seal, at
          the Custom House of
          this   day of   18
                Collector.

It shall be permitted to vessels engaged in the navigation and commerce provided for by these regulations, after clearance, to take on board, at the port of original departure or any other port or place within the limits of the Confederacy, any goods, wares or merchandise, and to proceed therewith to a destination beyond the Confederate limits, on delivering to the Collector or chief revenue officer at the port of Norfolk, on the river Mississippi, or at the port nearest the frontier of the Confederacy on any other river, a schedule describing all the goods on board, the quantity, value and destination, not declared in the manifest delivered at the time of clearance at the Custom House of the original port of departure; and the schedule thus received shall be transmitted by the revenue officer receiving the same, by the shortest route, to the Collector of customs at the port from which the vessel may have originally cleared.

In order that the service herein provided for may be properly rendered, it shall be the duty, and it is hereby required, of the Collector or chief revenue officer at the port of Norfolk, or at the other frontier ports at which masters of outward bound vessels are required to deliver schedules, to board all vessels bound for places beyond the Confederate limits, in the same manner and at the hours as is hereinbefore provided for inward bound vessels.

Treasury Department, March 6th, 1861.

CIRCULAR INSTRUCTIONS No. 8,

SUPPLEMENTARY TO CIRCULAR INSTRUCTIONS No. 1.

REGULATIONS relative to the Entry of Dutiable Merchandise, imported by the River Mississippi, from places above the limits of the Confederate States, and intended to be landed at places other than Ports of Entry or Delivery.

1. Dutiable merchandise, imported from any foreign port or place beyond the northern limits of the Confederate States, by the River Mississippi, into said Confederate States, and intended to be landed at plantations or places on said river, other than ports of entry or delivery, may be entered for the payment of duties, and be delivered at the places of destination, under the following regulations:

2. The master or person in command of any steamer or other vessel, entering the Confederate States of America by way of the River Mississippi, having on board any goods, wares or merchandise, subject to duty, bona fide purchased for the use of, and destined for plantations, or persons located on or near the coast of said river, and intended to be landed at such plantations, or other places, the same not being either ports of entry or delivery, shall, in addition to the manifest now required by the Circular Instructions of this Department, to be exhibited to the Collector at the Port of Norfolk,* deliver to the said Collector in duplicate, an account and entry in the following form, together with the original bills or invoices of the purchase of said goods:

ACCOUNT AND ENTRY.

Account and entry of dutiable merchandise, purchased and intended to be landed at the places herein stated, having been

---

* In lieu of the port of Norfolk, these regulations, since the extension of the Confederate limits, will apply to the port established on the river nearest the frontier.

imported in the   of
whereof   is master, bound
for
   Delivered this   day of   18

MARKS AND NUMBERS.	PACKAGES AND CONTENTS.	QUANTITY.	VALUE.	RATE OF DUTY.	DUTY.	OWNER OR CONSIGNEE.	PLACE OF DESTINATION.

3. On the delivery of this account to the said Collector, it shall be his duty to examine the same, by the bills or invoices of the purchases presented, and, finding the description, quantity and value of the goods to be correctly stated, to assess and estimate the duty on both the original and duplicate, and on the payment to him of the amount of such duty, to return to the master the original of such account and entry, with a certificate and permit endorsed thereon in the following form:

                    Port of
                    day of   18

I certify that this account and entry was delivered to me on this date, and the duties assessed on the goods therein described having been paid, permission is hereby given to land the same at the places therein designated.

                                              A. B.,
                                                Collector.

4. The duplicate of this account and entry shall be filed in the office of said Collector, after being first recorded in a book to be kept for that purpose, in the following form:

REGISTER OF ACCOUNTS AND ENTRIES OF WAY GOODS.

DATE OF RECEIPT.	MARKS AND NUMBERS.	PACKAGES AND CONTENTS.	QUANTITY.	VALUE.	RATES OF DUTY.	DUTY PAID.	IMPORTING VESSEL.	NAME OF MASTER.	WHERE FROM.	WHERE BOUND.	OWNER OR CONSIGNEE.	PLACE OF DESTINATION.

ABSTRACTS.

5. A copy of this register shall be rendered monthly, to this Department, as Abstract of Dutiable Goods, for "Way Delivery," imported through said port.

ACTION AT FINAL PORT.

6. On the arrival at the port of final destination of the vessel importing the goods as aforesaid, it shall be required of the master, on entrance of his vessel at the Custom House, to deliver to the Collector the original account and entry of merchandise landed as aforesaid, together with the receipts of the overseer or other person, at the plantations or other places, to whom such merchandise has been delivered, and these receipts, after being carefully compared with the aforesaid account, shall be returned to the master.

7. In cases where the merchandise intended to be landed at places other than ports of entry or delivery, as hereinbefore provided, shall be composed of both dutiable and free goods, then, instead of the delivery of a separate schedule for the free goods, as provided for by Circular Instructions No. 1, the articles exempt from duty may be described on the account and entry herein directed, stating all the particulars required by the form, with the exception of "Rate" and "Amount of Duty," and the columns headed "Rate of Duty" and "Duty" may be filled by writing the word "Free," in which case, the permit endorsed on such account shall be sufficient for the delivery of all the merchandise described therein.

8. On the receipt of accounts including both of these three classes of merchandise, the separate records and abstracts shall be kept and made in the same manner, as if the free schedule and the account and entry of dutiable merchandise were delivered separately.

9. All moneys received for duties on these entries shall be accounted for and deposited as now provided by law, and by the instructions of this Department, concerning moneys received for duties on direct importation.

Treasury Department, April 11, 1861.

REGISTRATION OF VESSELS.

CIRCULAR INSTRUCTIONS No. 2.

CONFEDERATE STATES OF AMERICA,
TREASURY DEPARTMENT, MARCH 8th, 1861.

Collectors of customs at the several ports of entry, on issuing certificates of registry to vessels under the provisions of the act of 4th March, 1861, entitled "An Act to provide for the Registration of vessels owned, in whole or in part, by citizens of the Confederate States," shall require of the applicant for such certificate, if the vessel is in part owned by persons not citizens of the Confederate States of America, an instrument in writing describing and identifying the vessel to be registered, signed by all the owners, (not citizens of the Confederate States,) declaring clearly and distinctly their consent to the proposed change in the nationality of the vessel, which document shall be attested before a Notary Public or other officer qualified under the laws of the nations which may have issued the same, to make attestations of public documents.

And before the new register shall be issued, the Collector to whom the application is made, shall require the former register of the said vessel to be surrendered to him, and it shall be his duty on such being done, to endorse on the face thereof the following certificate:

Confederate States of America,
District of   Port of
Collectors' Office,   18

I hereby certify, that this register has this day been surrendered to me for cancellation, and that a register of the Confederate States

of America, number has issued from this office on this date.
Given under my hand and
[L. S.] official seal the day and
year above written
A. B.,
Collector.

And the certificate of register thus surrendered or cancelled, shall be transmitted by the Collector to the consul of the nation by whom it was issued, if there be one residing at the port, or if there is no such resident consul, then to the representative of the said nation at the seat of government of this Confederacy.

Collectors of the several ports are hereby required to keep separate and distinct records of all vessels registered under the provisions of this act, and to render to the Register of the Treasury quarterly, an abstract of the same, which abstract, in addition to other particulars, shall state the date and manner of disposing of the register surrendered.

On application for certificates of registry to vessels wholly owned by citizens of the Confederate States, it shall be the duty of the several Collectors to issue the same conformably to the provisions of existing laws and Treasury regulations; and until otherwise provided, Collectors are authorized and directed to conform the oaths and bonds required in all cases arising under these regulations to the provisions of the act of 4th March, 1861.

All former regulations of the treasury in respect to the revenue and collection laws, which were of force at the secession of the several States from the Federal Union, are continued of force in the Confederate States, so far as they are applicable, substituting, in all cases, the words Confederate States, for United States.

C. G. MEMMINGER,
Secretary of the Treasury.

TREASURY CIRCULAR No. 3.

Regulation governing the introduction of goods, wares and merchandise into the Confederate States of America by Railroad on inland routes.

1. All goods, wares and merchandise introduced into the Confederate States of America from any foreign territory contiguous to that of the said Confederate States, by means of railway conveyances, must be introduced over the following rail road lines, and through the following revenue posts, until otherwise provided for by this department, and shall be subject to the provisions of these regulations.

RAIL ROAD LINES.

2. The rail road lines by which goods may be introduced as aforesaid, are those named in the list hereunto annexed.

REVENUE STATIONS.

3. For the protection of the revenue and the execution of these regulations, there shall, at the following named points, (and such others as this department may hereafter deem proper,) nearest to the frontier of the Confederate States, on rail road lines before named, be organized revenue establishments, to be known as "REVENUE STATIONS," at which shall reside an officer of the customs, known as a REVENUE GUARD, whose duties shall be of a supervisory nature over all merchandise introduced, as hereinafter provided. These revenue stations shall be at the points named in the list hereunto annexed.

REVENUE DEPOTS.

4. There shall be established at the places hereinafter named revenue ports, to be known as Revenue Depots, at which shall reside a chief revenue officer, with all the powers, and to discharge all the duties and exercise the control now exercised by collectors of customs over importations by sea at ports of entry; which powers and duties are hereinafter defined in these regulations.

These revenue depots shall be at the points stated in the list attached hereto.

ACTION ON ARRIVAL AT REVENUE STATIONS.

5. Immediately on the arrival of any rail road carrriage or train from any foreign territory contiguous to the Confederate States, at any of the revenue stations before referred to, the conductor or other person in charge shall be required to produce to the revenue guard at said first revenue station, a manifest in triplicate of all the goods, wares and merchandise brought into the Confederate States on board such railway carriage or train, and this manifest shall be in the following form:

MANIFEST.

Report and manifest of merchandise laden on board the cars of the   rail road, whereof   is conductor, which merchandise was taken on board at the several places specified therein in the contiguous territory.

NO. CARS.	MARKS AND NO.	DESCRIPTION OF PACKAGES & CONTENTS.	WHERE TAKEN ON BOARD.	BY WHOM FORWARDED.	TO WHOM CONSIGNED.	PLACE OR PORT OF DESTINATION.

Date.   A. B.,
                                      Conductor.

6. It shall be the duty of the revenue guard at the revenue station aforesaid, to board all railway trains arriving at said station, from said foreign territory, at all hours of the day and night, to receive the manifest hereinbefore required, and on its presentation, to see that the goods described therein are placed in separate cars from those in which mails or passengers are conveyed, and to place on each of said freight cars revenue locks of the Confederate States of America, (it being required of the railroad company transporting such goods, to provide cars suitable for such goods, and so constructed as to admit of such locks being placed thereon,) and to certify on the original and duplicate manifest the fact of its presentation, in the following form:

CERTIFICATE OF MANIFEST.

Revenue Station at

day of   18

I certify this to be the original (or duplicate as the case may be) manifest, exhibited to me on the above date.

A. B.,
Revenue Guard.

The original manifest, thus certified, shall be returned to the conductor; the duplicate forwarded under seal to the revenue officer at the first revenue depot to which the cars are destined, by the shortest route, and the triplicate filed in his office, after being first recorded in a book to be kept by him for that purpose, in the following form:

MANIFEST REGISTER.

DATE OF RECEIPT.	NAME OF RAILWAY.	NUMBER OF CAR.	MARKS, NUMBERS AND DESCRIPTION OF PCKGS. AND CONTENTS.	PLACE OF DESTINATION.	REMARKS.

A transcript of this register shall be rendered monthly to the chief revenue officer, at the revenue depot within his jurisdiction on the railroad line in which such station is established.

ACTION ON ARRIVAL AT REVENUE DEPOTS.

On the arrival of the railway train or cars at the first revenue depot within the limits of the Confederate States, the conductor, or other person in charge of such train, shall deliver to the chief revenue officer residing thereat, the original manifest presented to, and endorsed with the certificate of, the revenue guard at the station aforesaid, and also to deliver to the said chief revenue officer all the merchandise described in said manifest, by either leaving at said depot all the locked cars containing the same, or depositing said goods in a warehouse of deposit, at said depot, to be provided for that purpose, under the regulations now governing bonded warehouses, or as may be otherwise provided. On such delivery being made, and an examination being instituted of the train by said revenue officer, he shall, if satisfied that all the merchandise has been delivered, furnish to the Conductor, or other person in charge of the train, a permit in the following form:

Revenue Depot at
day of   18

The conductor of the train on   rail road, arriving at this depot at hour minutes this date, having delivered to me all the merchandise on board said train, has permission to proceed to a further destination.

A. B.,
Chief Revenue Officer.

8. The aforesaid chief revenue officer shall be furnished with duplicate keys to the revenue locks placed on said cars by the revenue guard at the frontier revenue station, and should the cars containing such goods not be left at said depot, it shall be his duty to unlock the cars containing such goods, and, either in person or by deputy, superintend the unloading of said goods, and their deposit in the warehouse of deposit before referred to.

FREE GOODS.

9. Should any portion of the merchandise thus transported on said cars be composed of articles exempted by law from the payment of duty, and of a character to admit of a speedy and satisfactory examination at the revenue depots, and such goods are intended to be landed at interior places on said rail road or its connections beyond the aforesaid first revenue depots, it shall be permitted for such merchandise to remain on board said train and pass to such further destination, on the conductor furnishing to said chief revenue officer at the revenue depot a schedule in duplicate, in the following form :

Schedule of free goods introduced into the Confederate States of America, over the   rail road from

NUMBER OF CARS.	MARKS AND NUMBERS.	PACKAGES AND CONTENTS.	QUANTITY IN WEIGHT.	VALUE.	TO WHOM AND WHERE CONSIGNED.

And on the examination being satisfactory, the aforesaid revenue officer shall return the schedule to the conductor, with a permit endorsed thereon, to deliver the same in the following form :

FORM OF PERMIT.

Revenue Depot at
              day of   18

The goods described in the within schedule, having been examined by me and found to be exempted by law from the payment of duty, permission is hereby given to deliver the same at the places stated therein :

A. B.,
Chief Revenue Officer.

The duplicate of the schedule shall be filed in the office of said chief revenue officer, and recorded by him in a book to be kept for that purpose, in the following form :

Register of free goods brought into the Confederate States of America, through the revenue depot at

DATE.	NAME OF RAILROAD.	PACKAGES AND CONTENTS.	QUANTITY.	VALUE.	DESTINATION.

A copy of the above register shall be rendered monthly to the Treasury Department, as an abstract of the free goods introduced through said revenue depot. Should, however, from the character of the goods, such examinations be impracticable, they will be required to be left at said revenue depot and disposed of under proper permits, to issue for the same on entry, under the provisions of these regulations.

DUTIABLE MERCHANDISE.

10. Dutiable merchandise arriving on said trains may also be immediately forwarded to their destination on permits for the same, as hereinafter provided, being in the possession of said chief revenue officer at the time of arrival of said cars, and on so doing, he shall furnish to said conductor a permit in the following form:

Revenue Depot at
day of   18

Permission is hereby given to transfer the following described goods to their destination within the territory of the Confederate States of America.

(Here describe the goods by marks, numbers and description of packages and general contents :)

A. B.,
Chief Revenue Officer.

11. The manifests presented by the conductor of all cars arriving at said revenue depot, shall be consecutively numbered and recorded by the revenue officer, in a book kept by him for that purpose, in the following form:

REGISTER OF MANIFEST.

DATE OF REGISTER	NUMBER OF MANIFEST.	RAIL-ROAD. [NAME.]	MARKS, NUMBERS, DESCRIPTION OF PACKAGES AND CONTENTS.	FREE.	DUTIABLE.	TIME AND MODE OF DISPOSITION.

In this register the time and mode of disposition shall explain when the goods passed from the custody of said revenue officer, and whether forwarded by the same train by which they arrived, or at some other period, and by other conveyance; and a copy of this register shall be monthly rendered to the Treasury Department, as a record of the transactions at said revenue depot.

12. For the proper discharge of the aforesaid duties, the chief revenue officer at the revenue depots shall board all trains on arrival, at all hours of the day and night, either in person or by dep-

uty, and shall be accessible at all hours by having his office constantly opened.

PASSENGER BAGGAGE.

13. The baggage of all passengers passing over the railroad routes before named, on arrival at the aforesaid revenue station or depots, shall be subject to the inspection and examinations of either the revenue guard at such stations, or revenue officer at such revenue depots, and any baggage that may be intended to be landed at places between the revenue stations and first revenue depots, may be examined by the revenue guard, and if containing no articles subject to duty, shall be landed at the intermediate place named, by having the following permit, signed by the said revenue guard, pasted permanently on the trunk, valise, carpet-bag, or other envelop of such baggage, and the permit shall be in the following form:

BAGGAGE PERMIT.

Revenue Station, at

18

Passenger baggage examined, and may be delivered.

A. B.,
Revenue Guard.

BAGGAGE CONTAINING DUTIABLE MERCHANDISE.

14. Should, however, dutiable articles be found in such baggage, the trunk or other package containing the same must be placed in the car with the merchandise, and under the revenue lock, as before required, and the fact noticed in the manifest; and such baggage shall be delivered with the other merchandise, to the chief revenue officer at the revenue depot, under the foregoing regulations.

DISPOSITION OF BAGGAGE AT REVENUE DEPOTS.

15. Passenger baggage destined for places beyond or more interior than the revenue depot, must be examined by the chief revenue officer at said revenue depot, and if they are found not to

contain any merchandise subject to duty, may pass to their destination by having a permit in the same form as that provided for revenue stations, signed by the chief revenue officer, pasted thereon.

Should, however, such baggage contain dutiable merchandise, the trunks or other package in which said baggage is contained, shall be deposited at said revenue depot, as hereinbefore provided for regular merchandise.

DISPOSITION OF MERCHANDISE AT REVENUE DEPOTS.

16. All merchandise delivered into the custody of the chief revenue officer, at revenue depots, as aforesaid, and not disposed of as heretofore provided, may be disposed of in accordance with the following regulations:

Entries may be made of merchandise arriving at revenue depots, under all the provisions of existing laws, and the regulations of the Department, for consumption and payment of duties or warehousing and withdrawals, and on these entries, as full compliance shall be required of all laws and regulations relating thereto, as if such were made at ports of entry or delivery.

17. In addition to the delivery of merchandise on such entries, it shall be permitted to deliver the same, on entries being made under the provisions of the following regulations, viz:

Entry of merchandise at port of destination, imported or brought in the Confederate States through a revenue depot.

Importers of merchandise, residing at any port of entry or port of delivery within the Confederate States of America, may be permitted to introduce goods into said Confederacy, from any foreign territory contiguous thereto, through and by way of any revenue depot provided for in the foregoing regulations, on presenting to the collector at such depot all the documents (with the exception of substituting the railway receipt for bill of lading) now required by law and treasury regulations, for the entry of imported merchandise, and making due entry of the same for either consumption or warehousing, stating therein the fact of importation through a revenue depot, and substituting in the form of entry now provided for, the name of such revenue depot, and State where located, for the name of vessel and master; also, furnishing a schedule describing the goods as described in the invoice and entry, and executing, in addition to the bonds now required by law, a bond in a penal sum equal to double the invoice value of the goods, conditioned to produce the said goods and deliver them to the collector with whom such entries shall be made, within a period of time to be stated in such bond; and this bond shall be in the following form:

IMPORTATION BOND.

Know all men by these presents, that we, as principals, and   as sureties, are held bound unto the Confederate States of America, in the sum of   dollars, for the payment whereof to the Confederate States we firmly bind ourselves, our heirs, executors, administrators and assigns, jointly and severally.

As witness our hands and seals, this   day of   eighteen hundred and

The condition of this obligation is such, that if the above bounden principals, or either of them, or either of their heirs, executors, administrators or assigns, shall, within   days from the date hereof, or within such further time as the Secretary of the Treasury may, on application of any of them before said day, allow, or in case of delay from unavoidable accident, within a reasonable time thereafter, transport from the revenue depot of the Confederate States, at   in the State of   by (here name the route) the merchandise described in an entry made at the Custom House at   this date, for (here name the class of entry) as per margin, (describe on the margin the merchandise,) and shall deliver the same to the Collector at said port of (here name the port where the bond is executed,) in the same condition, and in the identical packages as brought into the Confederate States, and delivered to the revenue officer at the said revenue depot, at   or, failing so to do, shall pay to the Collector, or proper collecting officer of the Confederate States, at the port of (here name the port where the entry is made) the full sum stated in the bond, then this obligation is to be void, otherwise it shall remain in full force and virtue, and be enforced by due process of law.

Sealed and delivered in presence of

On the execution of this bond, the Collector at the port of entry shall issue a permit directed to the revenue officer at the revenue depot through which the goods are to be introduced for transportation, which shall be in the following form:

PERMIT FOR INWARD TRANSPORTATION.

District of
Port of
day of   18

To the chief revenue officer
of the revenue depot at

Bond having been given to me at this office for the delivery to me at this port, of the following merchandise here entered, for (state kind of entry,)   viz:

(Here describe the goods by marks, numbers and description, as on the entry)

Imported through your revenue depot by
          from   you will deliver the
same.

Witness my hand and official seal, the date
[L. S.]
above written.

A. B.,
Collector.

This permit shall be delivered to the importer, and on its

presentation to the chief revenue officer at the revenue depot at which said goods are to arrive, they shall be delivered by him, for forwarding to the person presenting the permit, as heretofore provided, and the schedule furnished with said bond shall be, by the Collector with whom the entry is made, forwarded by mail to the chief revenue officer at the revenue depot through which the goods are introduced, and on its receipt by said revenue officer, it shall be his duty to compare it with the permit for said goods, (if such permit has been received, or immediately on its being received,) and to notify the Collector forwarding the same of any discrepancies between said schedule and permit.

DISPOSITION OF GOODS ON ARRIVAL AT DESTINATIONS.

18. On arrival at the port of destination of goods brought into the Confederate States through revenue depots, and entered under the provisions of these regulations, they shall be delivered to the Collector at said port, by depositing the same in warehouse, and taking the receipt of the custom officer in charge of the same, if the goods have been entered for warehousing; or if the entry be for consumption, by notifying the surveyor of the port of the fact of arrival, and placing the same in charge of an inspection officer of the customs, (which it shall be the duty of the surveyor to detail for that purpose,) taking his receipt for the same.

19. Delay attending a delivery to an inspection officer may be avoided on entries for consumption, by the importer notifying the Collector of the arrival of such goods, and requesting him to select the packages required for examination, which it shall be the duty of said Collector to do, by designating the same on the invoice and entry, and issuing a permit to the surveyor to deliver said packages to the appraisers' store, which permit shall be in the following form:

PERMIT FOR SAMPLES.

District of
Port of
day of 18

To the surveyor
20

You will cause to be sent to the appraisers' store for examination the following merchandise:

imported by   through the revenue
depot at   for
landed at

A. B.,
Collector.

20. If all the packages are not required for samples, the residue may be delivered to the importer on his paying the duty estimated on the entry, executing a bond in the form and manner now required by law and treasury regulations, on the delivery of other than sample packages on entry of merchandise imported from foreign ports by sea.

CANCELLATION OF IMPORTATION BONDS.

21. The bonds executed for the transportation of goods from revenue depots, shall be cancelled on the receipt of the assistant store-keeper in charge of the warehouse in which they are deposited, and the completion of all examinations and final liquidation of warehouse entries, or if the entry be for consumption, on the final liquidation of said entry.

EXAMINATIONS AND APPRAISEMENTS.

22. All examinations necessary to ascertain the quantities and value of goods imported through the revenue depots, as herein provided, shall be conducted in the same manner as is now required for merchandise imported directly by sea.

ABSTRACTS, RECORDS AND RETURNS.

23. The abstracts, records and returns of all goods introduced by way of revenue depots, shall be the same as those on importations by sea, substituting the word "inland," and name of revenue depot, for that of vessel and master.

24. On the establishment, by the Department, of inland revenue posts, for the entry of merchandise and other revenue purposes, all

the provisions of these regulations shall apply to such, in the same manner as hereinbefore provided for ports of entry or delivery, and the duties hereinbefore required to be discharged by surveyors shall, at places where there are no surveyors, be performed by the chief revenue officer at such posts, or such other officer as he, or this Department, may designate for that duty.

BONDS FROM RAIL ROAD COMPANIES.

25. All rail road companies over whose lines goods are intended to be introduced into the Confederate States, from foreign contiguous territory, shall be authorized to do so, on filing in the Treasury Department a bond executed to the Confederate States of America, in a sum to be fixed by the Secretary of the Treasury, obligating themselves to the faithful execution of the revenue laws of the Confederate States, and the regulations of the Treasury Department, so far as relates to the correctness of manifest, and their custody of the merchandise transported; and under said bond, they shall be responsible for all frauds committed or attempted by conductors or other persons in their employ, and while the merchandise is in their custody; and the form of this obligation shall be fixed and determined by this Department.

DELIVERY OF GOODS BETWEEN THE FRONTIER AND THE FIRST REVENUE DEPOT.

26. Where goods are to be delivered by railroad at any place between the frontier and the first revenue depot, the Collector at such depot may authorize the rail road company in possession of such goods to receive entries and to collect the duties chargeable upon the same; and in such cases, the manifest delivered to the revenue guard shall declare the goods so to be delivered, and the rail road company shall account for the entries and pay over the duties to the said Collector, of all goods delivered, or shall warehouse the same at their depots, according to the warehousing regulations.

PASSENGERS' BAGGAGE TO BE DELIVERED BETWEEN THE FRONTIER AND THE FIRST REVENUE DEPOT.

27. Such baggage as is above described may be examined on the train before it reaches the place at which it is to be delivered, by an agent of the rail road company, to be approved by the Collector at the revenue depot; and in case dutiable goods are found therein, the baggage must be taken to the revenue depot, and dealt with according to law.

RAILROADS WHERE NO REVENUE STATION IS LOCATED.

28. On lines where no revenue station is located, the duties required to be discharged by conductors and by the revenue guard, at such station shall, as far as the change of circumstances require, be discharged at the revenue depot, by the conductors and officers there.

Treasury Department, March 12, 1861.

NOTE.—The lists of rail road lines, revenue stations and revenue depots, referred to in the foregoing regulations, are not added, as the change in the frontiers, by the extension of the Confederacy, will require the issue of new lists instead of those originally accompanying this Circular.

TREASURY CIRCULAR No. 4.

CONFEDERATE STATES OF AMERICA,

Montgomery, March 23, 1861.

The following regulations have been adopted in relation to Express Carriers, and must be carefully executed by all persons engaged in the collection of the revenues.

C. G. MEMMINGER,
Secretary of the Treasury.

AS TO EXPRESS CARRIERS.

March 23, 1861.

The Express Carriers authorized by this Department may enter the Confederate States, and deliver goods, under the following regulations:

1. The owners of such express shall file in this Department a bond to the Confederate States of America, with sufficient sureties, in a sum to be fixed by the Secretary of the Treasury, obligating themselves to the faithful execution of the revenue laws of the Confederate States of America and the regulations of the Treasury Department; and that they shall account for all frauds and omissions of their agents or persons in their employment, affecting the interests of the Confederate States of America.

2. A commission shall then issue, appointing the said express company agents to collect the revenue upon all goods imported in their express carriages into the Confederate States, and thereupon, the owners and all agents of the express companies in the Confederate States shall take an oath faithfully to discharge the duties assigned them by the regulations of the Treasury, and by the laws of the Confederate States.

3. At the first revenue station or depot, the express agent shall

produce to the revenue guard, in triplicate, separate schedules of all goods to be left at each revenue depot, and at the final destination of the goods, and of all goods to be delivered on the way, before arrival at such revenue depot, and one of these schedules shall be delivered to the express agent, certified by the revenue guard; another shall be kept by the revenue guard, and entered in his book; the third shall be forwarded, under seal, by the revenue guard, by the speediest route, to the revenue depot at or next to the point of delivery of the said goods; whereupon, the said express carrier shall be authorized to carry on the said goods, and to levy and collect the duties chargeable thereon, and to deliver the said goods to the consignee or owner upon the road before reaching the revenue depot; and for all goods so delivered, the express carrier shall be bound to pay the duties.

4. Upon arrival at the revenue depot, the express carrier shall pay over to the Collector all such duties, and shall deliver to him sworn invoices of all the goods which have been delivered on the way, upon which shall be entered the duties charged; and all the goods consigned to said revenue depot shall be regularly entered therein, or placed in a bonded warehouse, according to law, and as to any goods destined for places beyond such revenue depot, the same arrangements shall take effect as have been already directed before and at reaching such depot.

5. Goods in transit by express from one part of the Confederate States through foreign territory, returning into the Confederate States, may pass free under the following regulation:

6. The express agent shall produce at the revenue depot or station nearest the frontier at which the goods are to pass out, a manifest in triplicate of the said goods, in the form required in Treasury Circular No. 3, page 485, one of which shall be delivered to the officer, to be entered by him; one to the express agent, certified by the officer of the customs; and the third shall be sent to the revenue station or depot nearest the point at which the said express carriage shall return into the Confederate States; and

upon production of the said manifest, certified, as aforesaid, to the revenue officer at the station or depot at which they return, as aforesaid, the goods mentioned in said manifest shall be permitted to enter free of duty.

7. Where goods in charge of an express carrier are in transit to and from different places in foreign territory through the Confederate States, the free transit may be allowed under the following regulations:

The express agent shall produce, at the station or depot nearest the point where the train enters the Confederate States, a manifest as in cases of transit out of the Confederate States, which shall be forwarded and produced to the custom house officer nearest the point at which the express carriage goes out of the Confederate States, and if the revenue officer is satisfied that all the goods in the manifest remain in the carriage and are there taken out of the Confederate States, he shall certify accordingly on the manifest, and if there be any parcels not produced, the express company shall be liable to pay the duties thereon; and, to the end that the examination may be satisfactory, the invoices of all the parcels must be exhibited, if required.

TREASURY CIRCULAR No. 6.

CONFEDERATE STATES OF AMERICA,

TREASURY DEPARTMENT, Montgomery, April 5th, 1861.

The following regulations are established for the entry and transportation of goods and passengers by rail road companies, which have duly been admitted as agents of the revenue service in the Confederate States.

C. G. MEMMINGER,
Secretary of Treasury.

---

1. The rail road companies chartered by any of the Confederate States, may be appointed agents in the revenue service by the Secretary of the Treasury, on filing a bond with sufficient sureties in such amount as shall be approved by said Secretary, with condition to account for all goods, wares and merchandise placed in their possession as such agents, and for all duties chargeable thereon; and also that said company will, by its agents and officers, faithfully observe and execute the revenue laws of the Confederate States of America, enacted or to be enacted, and the rules and regulations of the Treasury Department of said Confederate States, established or to be established, so far as the same may be applicable to the duties required or to be required of said rail road company, and to account for all frauds and omissions of their agents, or of persons in their employment affecting the interests of the Confederate States of America; and furthermore, to cause all written or printed orders to or from any officers of the Treasury Department, or from any revenue officer or station, to be forthwith forwarded to the person or place, to whom or to which it shall or may be addressed or directed, without delay.

2. Upon filing such bond, the company shall cause each and every of its officers, who shall have charge of dutiable goods and

baggage of passengers, to take an oath, faithfully to execute the revenue laws of the Confederate States, and the regulations of the Treasury Department; whereupon, a commission shall be issued from the Treasury Department, authorizing the said company to become an agent in the revenue service of the Confederate States.

3. On the arrival from a foreign port or place of any goods intended for immediate transportation to any foreign place, and which goods shall appear by the invoice, bills of lading and manifest, or other satisfactory evidence, have been shipped to the Confederate States in transit, and for exportation, the consignee or agent may make entry in triplicate, setting forth the route by which the goods are to be forwarded. The form of entry shall be as follows:

FORM.

Entry for exportation in bond to
        Custom House   186
Entry of Merchandise imported into this district by
        on the   day of
186   , in the   Master,
from   to be exported in bond
to   in   by
way of

MARKS.	NUMBERS.	PACKAGES AND CONTENTS.	QUANTITY.	PER CENT.	PER CENT.	PER CENT.	PER CENT.	PER CENT.	TOTAL.	DUTIABLE VALUE OF EACH PACKAGE.

4. This entry shall be verified by the oath or affirmation of the consignee or agent, in the form prescribed by the 107th section of the act of 1799, in the form following:

FORM.

I,   do solemnly, sincerely and truly swear, that the entry now subscribed with my name, and delivered by me to the Collector of the district of   , contains a just and true account of all the goods, wares and merchandise contained in the several packages therein mentioned; that they are brought into this district solely for the purpose of being transported by way of   , with the intention of being immediately carried without the limits of the Confederate States of America, and are not intended, directly or indirectly, to be sold, exchanged or consumed within the limits of the Confederate States of America; and I do further swear that if I shall hereafter know that the whole, or any part of said goods, wares or merchandise shall have been sold, alienated, exchanged or consumed within the limits of the Confederate States of America, I will immediately report the same with the circumstances thereof, truly, to the Collector of this district.

So help me God.

    Sworn before me, this   day of
        186   .

                                                     Collector.

5. The entry having been compared with the invoice, and the duties estimated, the Collector shall issue a permit directing the inspector having charge of the vessel in which the goods may have been imported, to deliver the same to the rail road company authorized to act as revenue agent at the said port; and the Collector shall dispatch a duplicate copy of the entry to the revenue officer at the revenue station on the frontier.

6. The rail road company shall, under the permit of the Collector, receive the goods from the vessel in which they are imported, and shall become immediately answerable for their actual transit through the Confederate States to a foreign territory, and shall immediately place the same in a closed warehouse, under their own

charge, or in the cars, to be immediately forwarded to their destination beyond the Confederacy, and they shall be bound in no event to allow the goods to pass out of their possession, except it be into the possession of another rail road company, on the same continuous route, which company shall also be a duly admitted agent in the revenue service.

7. Whenever the said goods shall commence their transit from the said port, the rail road company shall prepare a manifest thereof in duplicate, one of which shall be delivered to the conductor of the train, and the other to the Collector, who shall compare the same with the entry, and if found correct, shall certify and forward the same to the revenue officer at the revenue station on the frontier, and within thirty days from the date of such manifest, the said company shall produce to the Collector of said seaport, a certificate from the revenue officer at the revenue station nearest the frontier, on the route by which the transit was made, showing that the identical parcels or packages of goods had passed over the frontier, into the adjacent territory: in default whereof, the said company shall be bound to pay to the Confederate States the invoice value of any parcel or package of goods which shall not be so certified, as aforesaid, within the said thirty days.

8. A consignee of goods consigned to a place beyond the frontier, after their entry as aforesaid, and before they are loaded, may transfer his permit, with the consent of the Collector of the port, to any rail road company which has been appointed a revenue agent at said port, and such transfer shall charge upon the said rail road company the same duties in all respects, as if the permit had originally been given to such company.

9. Rail road companies which shall be duly commissioned as revenue agents, as aforesaid, and whose officers and agents have been duly sworn, shall be admitted to the same privileges in respect to goods to be delivered at way stations, as are allowed the express carriers by Treasury Circular No. 4. Upon the arrival of any rail road train at the frontier, the conductor shall produce

to the revenue guard, in duplicate, a schedule of all goods to be delivered between the frontier and the first revenue depot; also, a schedule of all goods to be delivered at, and beyond, such revenue depot; and if, on the continuous route of the said rail road, or its connections, there shall be, further on, another revenue depot, or place of delivery, at which it is desired to deliver goods, a further schedule shall be added of the goods to be delivered on the way, and at such other depot or place of delivery. One set of these schedules shall be delivered to the revenue guard, and shall be forwarded by him to the Collector, with whom such rail road company is required by these regulations to account; the other set of schedules shall be certified by said revenue guard, and delivered to the conductor, to be produced by him as a permit to pass the goods to the point named in the schedule.

10. The said rail road company shall thereupon be authorized to levy and collect all duties which may be chargeable upon all goods to be delivered by them at the way stations as aforesaid, and to that end they shall require sworn invoices to be delivered with every parcel of goods, and they and their agents are required to open and examine any goods which they have reason to suspect as not being fairly invoiced, and they shall assess the true value, at the same rates with the seaports, and detain the goods until the duties are paid.

11. The rail road company which shall bring the dutiable goods across the frontier into the Confederate States shall be liable for the duties on all goods set forth in the schedules aforesaid, which shall not have been delivered to the Collector at some revenue depot, or place of delivery. Such rail road company is to be held charged with the liability of other rail road companies which may be connected with it on any through route, and shall be bound to settle with the Treasury Department in the same manner as though the other railroad companies were its authorised agents.

12. On the 1st and 15th days of every month, each rail road company shall account with, and pay over to such revenue officer

as the Secretary of the Treasury may appoint, the amount of all duties which have been chargeable, on any goods delivered by them at any other place than a revenue depot or place of delivery, whether they may have been paid or not; and they shall produce to the accounting officer the invoices of all the goods, showing the duties as assessed, and also, copies of their own freight lists for the period of accounting, verified by the oath or certificate of the rail road officer whose duty it was to make out said lists, and on all moneys paid over by the said rail road companies to the said Collector, they shall be entitled to receive a commission of one per cent.

13. The baggage of passengers brought into the Confederate States, by any of the said rail road companies, if to be delivered on the way, shall be examined by the conductor of the train in any way that shall be found most convenient; and if dutiable goods be found therein, it shall be detained and delivered over to the next revenue depot, to be dealt with according to law.

14. Passenger's baggage intended to pass through to some revenue depot, or place of delivery, shall be placed in a car, or portion of a car, which shall be under the lockof the company, and shall not be opened until it shall reach such depot, or place of delivery.

15. The revenue officers at such revenue depot, or place of delivery, shall take charge of the baggage brought through from the frontier to such depot, and shall be at the rail road station at the moment of the arrival of the train, and shall promptly examine and deliver the same, if no dutiable goods are found therein; and all agents are expressly charged to use courtesy and dispatch, and to make no useless examinations into mere personal baggage.

16. For the greater convenience of passengers, whenever rail road companies can make proper arrangements for the examination of baggage before its arrival at the points of delivery, they are at liberty to do so; and in that case, the conductor or agent

shall paste a label on the trunk or other envelop of the baggage examined, in the following form:

BAGGAGE PERMIT.

This baggage examined, and may be delivered.

A. B.,
Conductor.

17. The Treasury Department cannot require its officers to surrender the privileges of Sunday beyond the demands of absolute necessity. The revenue guard must receive and forward the schedules of trains passing the frontier on that day; but trains which require any other duties to be performed by revenue officers on Sunday, must remain over until the next day, in the same manner as vessels are now required to do at seaports.

18. The regulations contained in Circular No. 3 must be observed by all rail road companies who have not been admitted revenue agents under the provisions of the present Circular; and such of those regulations as are not changed by this Circular, must be observed by all rail road companies.

TREASURY CIRCULAR No. 7.

CONFEDERATE STATES OF AMERICA,

TREASURY DEPARTMENT, Montgomery, April 5, 1861.

The following supplemental regulations are established in relation to express carriers.

C. G. MEMMINGER,
Secretary of the Treasury.

SUPPLEMENTAL TO CIRCULAR No. 6, IN RELATION TO EXPRESS CARRIERS.

1. The express carriers who are commissioned under Circular No. 4 may, instead of the schedules required by the said Circular, produce to the revenue guard a manifest or schedule, in duplicate, of all the goods which enter the Confederate States by the same express train, exhibiting all the particulars following:

NO. CARS.	MARKS AND NUMBERS.	DESCRIPTION OF PACKAGES AND CONTENTS.	TO WHOM CONSIGNED.	PLACE OF DESTINATION.

One of these manifests shall be certified by the revenue guard and returned to the express carrier, and shall have the effect of a permit to pass the goods mentioned therein to their final destination; the other manifest shall be retained by the revenue guard, and forwarded by the speediest route to such Collector as shall be designated by the Secretary of the Treasury.

2. Instead of accounting at the revenue depots for duties received, the express carriers shall account, on the 1st and 15th days of every month, with the Collector to be appointed by the

Secretary of the Treasury, for the duties on all goods delivered during the previous half month; and to that end, the said carrier shall cause to be forwarded daily to the said Collector, a copy of his own freight or forwarding list, for that day, of all goods which entered the Confederate States, and at the time of accounting, shall produce invoices of every parcel of goods which have been delivered in the Confederate States to the owner, agent or consignee.

STEAMER EXPRESS GOODS.

3. Goods which are imported at a port of entry on the sea-coast by steamer express, may be delivered to the express carrier in whose charge they were imported, under the same regulations as entries by inland routes. The express carrier shall produce to the Collector at the port of entry, a duplicate manifest of the said goods, one of which shall be certified by the Collector and delivered to the carrier, and the other shall be retained by the Collector; and the Collector shall thereupon deliver a permit to the express carrier to receive the goods, and the said express carrier shall proceed to collect the duties on the same, and shall account for the same in the manner directed as to goods which have been entered inland, and the Collector shall distinguish between express goods and those which are, or should have been, consigned. In the latter case, he shall require the goods to be entered as usual.

TREASURY CIRCULAR No. 9.

CONFEDERATE STATES OF AMERICA,
TREASURY DEPARTMENT, Montgomery, May 11th, 1861.

In enforcing the act of Congress approved March 16th, 1861, authorizing the collection of light money, and to avoid the difficulty of satisfying Collectors of the customs that coasting vessels had regularly paid their dues, Collectors of the customs will have attached hereafter, to the registers, enrollments and licenses of vessels, the subjoined certificate.

C. G. MEMMINGER,
Secretary of the Treasury.

CERTIFICATE TO BE ATTACHED TO REGISTERS, ENROLLMENTS AND LICENSES OF VESSELS.

Custom House,
Collector's Office,   186

This is to certify, that the   , called the
            , whereof
is at present master, measuring   tons, trading regularly between the ports of the Confederate States, has this day paid, at this office, light money, amounting to
dollars, as provided by the act of 16th March, 1861.

Collector.

TREASURY CIRCULAR No. 11.

CONFEDERATE STATES OF AMERICA,
TREASURY DEPARTMENT, Richmond, Aug. 8, 1861.

RELATIVE TO TREASURY NOTES.

The treasury notes issued under date of July 25th, 1861, per act of 16th May, 1861, will be received, as expressed on their face, in payment of all public dues except export duties. The several Assistant Treasurers, and designated depositaries of the Confederate States are instructed to receive them on deposit, and to re-issue the same as money, upon warrants. They will in no case be cancelled. C. G. MEMMINGER,
Secretary of the Treasury.

TREASURY CIRCULAR

RELATIVE TO ARRIVAL OF VESSELS FROM FOREIGN COUNTRIES DURING THE EXISTENCE OF [THE BLOCKADE, ETC.

Vessels of foreign countries engaged in trade, passing in the neighborhood of the coast of the Confederate States, and deeming it advisable, in view of what may appear to be the inefficiency of the blockade, to enter any port on said coast where there is no Collector nor custom house, for the purpose of discharging their cargoes, and it being advisable that this should be effected without inconvenient delay to the parties concerned, the following regulation is established, to-wit:

When a vessel has thus made port, such port shall be considered the proper port of entry for such vessel, if the master or owner shall, without delay, dispatch a messenger to the nearest collection district, in order that a proper revenue officer may be sent by the Collector, or the Surveyor acting as such, to take charge of the cargo. This officer will be invested, for the time being, by the Collector, or Surveyor acting as such, in writing, with power to execute the formalities required in connection with the entry of goods at a regular port.

Treasury Department, August 22, 1861.

WAREHOUSE SYSTEM.

That branch of the revenue system of the Confederate States known as the warehousing system rests upon the U. S. Warehousing Acts of 6th August, 1846, and 28th March, 1854, the Act 3d March, 1849, the Inland Transportation and Exportation Acts of 28th September, 1850 and 30th August, 1852, the Drawback System of Act 2d March, 1799, and the act of 20th April, 1818, "for the Deposit of Distilled Spirits in Public Warehouse"—and provides for the entry of imported merchandise without the immediate payment of duties, on securing such to the Government by satisfactory bonds, and for the deposit of merchandise in bonded warehouses under the control and supervision of the Government, with the privilege of so remaining for a period of *three years from the date of original importation*, and during that period, at any time in the option of the importer, of being withdrawn, for either *consumption and the payment of duty, for transportation in bond, or for exportation to foreign countries without the payment of duties.*

BONDED WAREHOUSES.

The warehouses in which unclaimed and bonded merchandise are stored under this system are divided into four classes.

CLASS 1.—Stores owned or leased by the Government.

CLASS 2.—Stores bonded by importers for the sole purpose of storing merchandise imported by or consigned to them, which may be entered for warehousing.

CLASS 3.—Stores bonded by the occupant for the general storage of bonded goods.

CLASS 4.—Yards or sheds bonded for the storage of bonded goods of a heavy and bulky character.

The warehouses thus known and designated and the goods deposited therein are subject to the following regulations, viz.:

Class 1.

Stores owned by the Confederate States or hired by them.

UNCLAIMED GOODS.

All unclaimed goods must be stored in these stores, when there are such at the port available for the purpose; and they are also to be used for the storage of other foreign merchandise, as hereinafter provided.

All the labor in these stores shall be performed under the superintendence of the officer in charge, at the expense of the owner or importer of the merchandise, and all charges for storage, labor, and other expenses, accruing on the goods, shall not exceed the regular rates for such objects at the port.

Class 2.

Stores in the possession of an importer and in his sole occupancy, which he may desire to place under the customs lock, in addition to his own lock, (said locks to be of a different character,) for the purpose of storing dutiable merchandise imported by himself only.

The entire store shall be appropriated to this sole purpose, under the regulations hereinafter provided; and for the time of the customs officer necessarily required in attendance at such store, the proprietor shall pay, monthly, to the collector of the port, a sum equivalent to the pay of such officer. All the labor on goods so stored must be performed by the importer at his own expense, under the supervision of the officer in charge.

BOND.

Before any importer shall be permitted to use his own store for such purpose, he shall enter into a bond, according to the following form, in such sum and with such sureties as may be approved by the Collector and the Treasury Department.

FORM OF BOND FOR WAREHOUSE OF CLASS 2.

Know all men by these presents, that we,   as principals, and   as sureties, are held and firmly bound unto the Confederate States of America in the sum of   dollars; for the payment of which, well and truly to be made to the Confederate States, we bind ourselves, our heirs, executors, administrators, and assigns, jointly and severally, by these presents. As witness our hands and seals, this   day of   eighteen hundred and

The condition of this obligation is such, that if the above bounden   , the principal, shall comply in all respects with the provisions and requirements of the warehousing laws, and the regulations of the Treasury Department in pursuance thereof, and shall not store in the store or premises known as   street, any other goods, wares, or merchandise, than those imported by or consigned to him, and duly entered and bonded for warehousing, and ordered by the proper officer of the customs to be deposited therein, and shall pay to the collector, monthly, the salary of the officer or officers of the customs in charge of said goods, wares, and merchandise, or such part of said salary as may be required in pursuance of the regulations of the Treasury Department, and shall not remove, nor suffer to be removed, any goods, wares, or merchandise, from said store, without lawful permit and without the presence of the customs officer in charge, or, in case of such removal, shall pay to the proper collecting officer at the port the value of the merchandise so removed, and five thousand dollars as liquidated damages for each removal, then this obligation is to be void; otherwise, in full force and virtue.

Sealed and delivered in presence of

[SEAL.]
[SEAL.]

Class 3.

Stores in the occupancy of persons desiring to engage in the business of storing dutiable merchandise under the warehouse acts, and of performing the labor on such goods, in what is usually termed the storage business. The labor performed on the goods in stores of this class shall be under the control and at the expense of the owner or occupant; and the store shall be subject to such further rules as the Department may deem necessary, from time to time, for the safe-keeping of the goods and protection of the revenue, and to be discontinued as a bonded warehouse when the public interest may require. All arrangements as regards the rates of storage and the price of labor in these stores must be made between the importer and the owner or occupant of the store, and all amounts due for storage and labor must be collected by the latter, the Collector looking only to the safe custody of the merchandise for the security of the revenue.

Before any person shall be permitted to open a store of this description, he shall enter into bond according to the following form, in such sum and with such sureties as may be approved by the Collector and the Treasury Department:

FORM OF BOND OF WAREHOUSES OF CLASS 3.

Know all men by these presents, that we,   as principals, and   as sureties, are held and firmly bound unto the Confederate States of America in the sum of   dollars; for the payment of which, well and truly to be made to the Confederate States, we bind ourselves, our heirs, executors, administrators and assigns, jointly and severally, by these presents, as witness our hands and seals, this   day of eighteen hundred and

The condition of this obligation is such, that if the above bounden principals, or either of them, or either of their heirs, executors, administrators or assigns, shall comply in all respects with the provisions and requirements of the warehousing laws and the regulations of the Treasury Department, and exonerate and hold the Confederate States and its officers harmless from or on account of any risk, loss or expense, of any kind or description, connected with or arising from the deposit or keeping of imported merchandise, under the provisions of the several acts of Congress concerning warehousing, in the store or premises known as   , and shall also pay to the Collector, monthly, the salary of the officer or officers in charge of said goods, wares and merchandise; and if the proprietor or occupant of said store shall receive for storage therein such unclaimed and seized goods as the Collector of the customs may order to be deposited in said store, and shall safely keep and deliver the same to the order of the Collector, looking to the goods for the storage and charges, and shall, from time to time, promptly report to the Collector any and all damaged or perishable articles that may be found or stored in said stores, and all gunpowder, fire crackers and explosive substances sent to said store, and shall not remove, nor suffer to be removed, any goods, wares or merchandise from said store, without lawful permit, and without the presence of the custom officer in charge, or, in case of such removal, shall pay to the proper collecting officer at the port the value of the merchandise so removed, and five thousand dollars as liquidated damages for each removal, then this obligation is to be void; otherwise, in full force and virtue.

Sealed and delivered in presence of

[SEAL.]
[SEAL.]

SEIZED OR UNCLAIMED GOODS MAY BE STORED IN THIS CLASS.

Unclaimed and seized goods may be stored in this class of stores, on the order of the Collector; and the proprietor or occupant shall look to the goods for the storage and charges, at the usual and customary rates, and shall be liable for the safe-keeping of the merchandise as for other storage.

STORES IN CHARGE OF OFFICERS.

These stores shall be placed in charge of an officer of the customs, under the separate and different locks of the custom house and the owner or occupant acting as agent for the importers warehousing their merchandise in such stores. Should the amount of business at any one store require, in the judgment of the Collector, the services of more than one officer, the owner or occupant shall be required to pay, monthly, such additional sum as will be equivalent to the salary of such officer or officers.

In classes Nos. 2 and 3, an office for the accommodation of the owner or occupant may be allowed, but such office must be separated by a permanent partition from the rest of the store, so that the owner shall have no access to the goods, except in the presence of the officer, who must be allowed such use of the office as may be necessary for him in making his daily return of receipts, deliveries and examinations.

Class 4.

BONDED YARDS AND SHEDS.

For the storage of wood, coal, mahogany, dye-woods, lumber, molasses, sugar in hogsheads and tierces, rail road, pig and bar iron, anchors, chain cables and other articles specially authorized, yards or sheds of suitable construction may be used, to be bonded in the manner hereinbefore prescribed for warehouses of class No. 3.

HOW ENCLOSED AND SECURED.

These yards must be enclosed by substantial fences not less than twelve feet in height, with gates provided with suitable bars and other fastenings, so as to admit of being secured by customs locks, and must be used exclusively for the storage of the above named merchandise, duly entered for warehousing by the owner or occupant, or for the purpose of general storage of warehoused goods; the purpose to be set forth in the application, and the bond to be taken accordingly, as in case of the warehouses of the second and third classes. The sheds must be substantially constructed, with or without flooring or roofing, as the Treasury Department and the Collector may require; and when required, the roof or exterior shall be covered with slate or metal. The doors and other openings must be provided with suitable fastenings, and be secured by the different and separate locks of the occupant and the customs; and the occupant shall provide a proper room for the use of the officer in charge.

SEIZED AND UNCLAIMED GOODS IN THIS CLASS.

Collectors of the customs may order unclaimed and seized merchandise of the description authorized to be deposited in sheds or yards, to be placed in such sheds or yards, under the same regulations and conditions as are provided for the deposit of unclaimed or seized goods in warehouses of class No. 3.

BONDED CELLARS.

The owner or lessee of a store occupied for general business purposes may use the cellar or vault of such store, under the conditions hereinafter prescribed, as a bonded warehouse of class No. 2, for the storage of wines and distilled spirits only, and exclusively of his own importation.

The entire cellar or vault shall be appropriated to this purpose, and shall have no opening or entrance except the one from the street, on which the separate and different locks of the customs and the owner or proprietor of the cellar shall be placed; and a bond shall be entered into by the owner according to the foregoing form for stores of class 2.

One officer may have in charge as many cellars as, in the judgment of the Collector, he can superintend efficiently, not exceeding six. A sum equivalent to the salary of the officer in charge shall be paid monthly to the Collector, by the owner or occupant.

Where a single officer has charge of more than one warehouse of the second class, or more than one cellar or vault, the amount to be contributed by each will be agreed on by the owners or occupants, and the Collector; and the agreement shall be in writing, and filed with the bonds.

APPLICATIONS TO BOND STORES, ETC.

Whenever it is desired to have any building constituted a private bonded warehouse of the second and third classes, the owner or occupant shall make application in writing to the Collector, or other chief revenue officer of the port, describing the premises, the location and capacity of the same, and setting forth the purpose for which such building is proposed to be used, whether for the storage of merchandise imported or consigned to himself exclusively, or for the general storage of merchandise in bond. This application, to entitle it to consideration, must be accompanied by a certificate, signed by the proper officers of two or more insurance companies, that the building offered is a first class fire proof store, according to the classification of insurance offices at that port.

Applications for bonding yards and sheds as warehouses of the fourth class will be made in a similar manner, and under like regulations.

STORES, HOW SECURED.

The stores described in the second and third classes will be required, previous to their being used for the storage of bonded goods, to have such fastenings on the doors and windows as the Collector may deem requisite for the security of the property. The store must be separated from adjoining buildings by a brick or stone wall, in which no door or other opening will be permitted, and must have a party wall above the roof.

ADDITIONAL FASTENINGS.

After stores have been approved and placed under customs lock, the Collector will retain the right of ordering additional fastenings, to be provided by, and at the expense of the owners or occupants having charge of the premises.

WAREHOUSES MAY BE DISCONTINUED.

Should the owner or occupant of any store, cellar or yard neglect or refuse to pay to the Collector the sum required by these instructions for the use of an officer or officers, as the case may be, or fail or refuse to comply with any law regulating the storage of merchandise, or any rules or regulations issued by the Treasury Department or by the Collector for the safety of the goods stored, the Collector shall refuse permission to deposit goods in such store, and report the facts at once to the Department for its further action.

BONDS MAY BE RENEWED.

The proprietors or occupants of stores Nos. 2, 3 and 4, on ten days' notice from the Collector, may be required to renew their bonds; and if they fail to do so, no more goods shall be sent to their stores, and those within the same shall be withdrawn, at their expense.

STORES, HOW SURRENDERED.

The proprietor or occupant of a bonded warehouse shall have the right to relinquish the business at any time, on notice to the Collector and the owners of the merchandise deposited therein, and paying the expense of its removal to other stores.

TRANSFER OF MERCHANDISE FROM ONE WAREHOUSE TO ANOTHER.

Merchandise duly deposited in a warehouse under bond, and entitled to remain therein, may be transferred to another warehouse, on the request of the importer or owner thereof; or when an importer may obtain the privilege of using a store or cellar of class 2, and may desire to transfer thereto such merchandise imported by or consigned to him, it may be done on his written request to the Collector; but such transfers shall, in all cases, be at the risk and expense of the party requesting it, and under the supervision of an officer of the customs.

GOODS REMAINING IN STORE OVER FIVE DAYS.

In all cases where merchandise shall be suffered by the importer, owner or agent thereof, to remain in warehouse for a period of five days after the payment of the legal duties and charges thereon, and the issuing of the permit for the delivery thereof, the Collector will permit no more merchandise to be deposited in such store while any such goods shall so remain, and will report the case to the Secretary of the Treasury, that he may discontinue the store as a bonded warehouse, or adopt such other course to enforce the warehousing regulations as he may deem the law and facts to require.

NO FIRE OR LIGHTS PERMITTED.

No fire must be permitted in any warehouse, except in the business office attached thereto; and where lights are required, lanterns must be used, such as are used in naval vessels, and known as magazine lanterns.

THE OFFICERS IN CHARGE OF WAREHOUSES.

All bonded warehouses, whether public or private, as well as the stores occupied by the appraisers, where there are such, will be placed by the Collector in the custody of officers designated for that purpose, to be known as assistant storekeepers, who will always keep the keys thereof in their own possession, and personally superintend the opening and closing of the doors and windows. They will be required to be in constant attendance at the stores from seven o'clock, A. M., to sunset from April 1 to October 1, and for the residue of the year, from eight o'clock, A.M., to sunset, except at the time necessary for their meals, not over one hour at noon, when the stores will be closed.

They will not suffer any goods to be received, delivered, sampled, packed or re-packed, except in their presence, or the presence of some person designated as an assistant by the Collector.

QUANTITIES IN BULK TO BE ASCERTAINED AT EXPENSE OF OWNER.

When goods are withdrawn from warehouses in quantities less than the entire importation, the expense of weighing, guaging or measuring must be paid by the owner, importer or agent, if it be necessary to weigh, guage or measure such portion in order to ascertain the dutiable value.

SAMPLING. PACKING AND RE-PACKING.

All merchandise in public or private bonded warehouses may be examined at any time during the business hours of the port by the importer, consignee or agent, who shall have liberty to take samples of his goods in quantities according to the usage of the port; make all needful repairs of packages, and to re-pack the same, provided the original contents are placed in the new package, and the original marks and numbers placed thereon; provided, that no samples shall be taken, nor shall any goods be exhibited or examined, unless under the immediate supervision of an inspector of the customs, and by order of the importer, owner, or consignee, at his expense; nor shall any package be repaired, or goods re-packed, without a written order from the Collector of the port.

UNCLAIMED GOODS SENT TO STORE.

All the goods unclaimed by the owner or consignee at the expiration of the period allowed by law for the discharge of the vessel in which the same may have been imported, shall be sent by the Collector to the stores owned or leased by the Confederate States, class 1, if there be any at the port. If there be no such stores, then said goods shall be deposited in such private bonded warehouses as may be specially designated for that purpose by the Collector, with the approval of the Secretary of the Treasury, the Collector paying to the proprietors, in case the goods are sold as unclaimed, their charges for storage and labor at the usual rates, and charging the same on the proceeds, in pursuance of law.

RIGHT TO BOND UNCLAIMED GOODS.

The owner or consignee of any goods thus sent as unclaimed may, at any time thereafter, within the period provided by law, be allowed the privileges herein granted to bonded merchandise, on making due entry thereof for warehousing.

NO DELIVERY WITHOUT PERMIT.

No goods are to be delivered from these stores, unless on a permit signed by the Collector and naval officer, and endorsed by the clerk in charge of the general storage books at the custom house. Permits for unclaimed goods in private bonded warehouses, with all the foregoing requirements, will not be acted on until all the charges on them due the warehouse proprietor have likewise been paid.

CHARGES FOR STORAGE, ETC.

ON GOODS ENTERED FOR WAREHOUSING.

The rates of storage, labor and other expenses on goods entered for warehousing and deposited in stores of class 3 or 4 are determined by agreement between the party storing and the proprietor of the warehouse, and are not subject to the control of the Collector, as it is optional with the importer to select the warehouse in which to deposit bonded merchandise.

ON UNCLAIMED GOODS.

All charges for labor, storage and other expenses on unclaimed goods deposited in warehouse by order of the Collector, shall not exceed, in any case, the regular rates for such objects at the port in question. In cases where differences of opinion shall arise as to the correctness of the charges so made, the decision of the president of the chamber of commerce or the board of trade, in ports where such bodies exits, or if there be no such officers, the decision of the Collector or chief revenue officer of the port shall be binding on both parties.

CHARGES, ETC., TO BE PAID BEFORE DELIVERY.

The Collector shall give no permit to withdraw such goods without payment of the legal duties and charges so assessed, and if sold, shall cause the storage and charges to be paid out of the proceeds of the sale.

SALES OF UNCLAIMED AND OTHER MERCHANDISE.

All merchandise duly bonded, and so remaining in public store for the space of three years from the date of importation; all merchandise in respect to which there is a failure or neglect to pay the duties within the time prescribed by law, and so remaining in public store for a period of one year, shall be sold at public auction, in some public or private warehouse, within thirty days after the expiration of the several periods before mentioned, respectively.

DISPOSITION OF PERISHABLE GOODS AND EXPLOSIVE SUBSTANCES.

No perishable goods, gunpowder, fire-crackers, or other explosive substances can be deposited in warehouse; and, if not immediately entered for export or transportation for export, from the vessel in which imported, as hereinafter provided for, or entered for consumption, and the duties paid within the time prescribed by law for the unlading of the vessel, will be sold forthwith, the Collector giving public notice for three days before the sale, and disposing of and accounting for the proceeds as in the case of sales of other unclaimed goods.

DISPOSITION OF GOODS DEPRECIATING IN VALUE.

Any unclaimed goods, wares and merchandise deposited in public warehouse, which, in the opinion of the Collector, may, from depreciation in value, damage, leakage or other cause, prove insufficient, on the sale thereof, to pay the duties, storage and other charges, if suffered to remain in the store for the period allowed by law, will be sold at public auction, on giving public notice of not less than six nor more than ten days, as the Collector may determine under the circumstances of the case, and the proceeds disposed of and accounted for as in other cases of unclaimed goods.

GOODS CARTED FROM VESSEL TO WAREHOUSE TO BE IN CUSTODY OF COLLECTOR, THE CARTAGE, DRAYAGE OR LIGHTERAGE OF GOODS IN BOND, ETC.

All goods in bond, whether passing from the vessel or other conveyance in which imported to the warehouse, or from one vessel or conveyance to another vessel or conveyance, or from the warehouse on permits for exportation; all unclaimed goods, and all goods ordered to the appraisers' store for examination, will be carted, drayed or lightered by responsible cartmen, draymen or lightermen, who, while performing their duty, will be known as custom house cartmen, draymen or lightermen, and be under the control and direction of the inspector of the vessel, or assistant store keeper of the store, as the case may be, from which the goods are sent; it being intended that bonded goods or goods ordered for examination shall at all times be in the custody of the government or its authorized agents. Such persons shall also be subject, while so employed, to the orders of the Collector, and will be held to a strict compliance with all the warehouse rules and regulations.

CARTMEN, ETC., WILL TAKE TICKETS OF MERCHANDISE, ETC.

Cartmen, etc., will in all cases require of the officers, whether at the vessel or warehouse, a ticket descriptive of the merchandise delivered to them, and designating the store, vessel or other place to which it is to be taken; which ticket they will return to the officer from whom the merchandise was received, duly receipted by the officer to whom such merchandise may have been delivered, and will be held liable for the safe conveyance of all merchandise delivered to them, and for the good condition of all delivered by them.

TRANSFER OF MERCHANDISE IN BOND.

The frequency of requests by purchasers of bonded goods, which they do not desire to withdraw from warehouse immediately, to have them transferred from the importer's name to their own on the warehouse records at the custom house, in order to obtain a more perfect and secure control of the property, and the warehousing laws and regulations, by requiring all withdrawals to be made by the importer, consignee or agent, or some persons duly authorized by him on the withdrawal entry, not permitting transfers of this character, induces me to suggest that the object of such transfers may be obtained by having the property transferred on the books of the proprietor of the warehouse in which the goods are stored; for as under the warehousing system all bonded merchandise deposited in warehouse are in the joint custody of the Government and the importer, the warehouse proprietor being the importer's agent for this purpose, a transfer of goods sold, to the name of the purchaser, by an order from the vendor on the warehouse proprietor for that purpose, will effectually place the merchandise in the purchaser's possession, subject it to his control and render it at his risk and expense; for by virtue of this transfer the warehouse proprietor, as joint custodian with the Government of the goods, becomes the agent of the purchaser, responsible to him for the safety of the merchandise and its proper delivery after the Government's control is relinquished by the issue and presentation of a permit.

Transfers of this character are not necessarily limited to first purchasers, but may be continued on all changes of ownership until the maturity of the warehousing bond.

ENTRY OF GOODS IN BOND.

Importers of merchandise of every description, except such as are perishable or explosive, being entitled to the privileges of the warehousing system, provision is made by the regulations for the several forms of entries by which these privileges are obtained.

These entries are of two classes—Simple and Combined.

The Simple forms are—

1. Entry for warehousing.
2. Entry for withdrawal from warehouse for consumption.
3. Entry for withdrawal from warehouse for transportation.
4. Entry for withdrawal from warehouse for exportation.
5. Entry for withdrawal from warehouse for inland transportation and exportation to adjacent foreign territory.

Combinations of these simple forms have been established, to facilitate business transactions, by avoiding the delay, as well as the expense, attending the deposit of goods in bonded warehouses, when such are intended, at the time of importation, for destinations other than the port of original entry; and such are known as:

1. Warehouse and transportation entry.
2. Warehouse and exportation entry.

This system, while permitting merchandise to remain under bond for three years from the date of the original importation, authorizing the transfer of the same in bond, from one port to another within the Confederacy, on transportation entries, provides for the restoration of goods so transported to the custody of the revenue officers of the Government at the port of destination, with all the privileges appertaining thereto at the port of original entry, re-deposit in warehouse, and subsequent withdrawal by entries known as—

1. Re-warehousing entry.
2. Re-warehouse withdrawal entry for consumption.
3. Re-warehouse withdrawal entry for transportation.

4. Re-warehouse withdrawal entry for exportation.

Also, by combinations of these simple forms, known as—
1. Re-warehousing and withdrawal entry for consumption.
2. Re-warehouse entry for immediate exportation.

FORM OF ENTRIES, ETC.

The following are the forms of the several entries under the Warehouse System, and the explanations and regulations applicable thereto:

ENTRY FOR WAREHOUSING.

The entry of goods for warehousing shall be in the following form, and must be verified by oath or affirmation, as in an entry of merchandise for immediate payment of duties:

FORM OF ENTRY.

Warehouse Entry.

Custom House,

Port of   186

Entry of merchandise imported on the   by
, in the
master, from

MARKS.	NUMBERS.	PACKAGES AND CONTENTS.	QUANTITY.	PER CENT.	PER CENT.	PER CENT.	PER CENT.	PER CENT.	TOTAL.	DUTIABLE VALUE OF EACH PACKAGE.

The dutiable value of each package of dry goods, hardware or other package goods, must in all cases be stated on this entry, when the invoice will permit its being done; and in case of deduction for damage or other causes, it must be adjusted on each package separately, that this entry may always be a true basis for withdrawal entries, either for consumption, transportation or exportation, and also for the warehouse accounts. The owner or importer will exercise the option given to him by law, by designating upon the entry the warehouse in which he desires the merchandise shall be deposited, in the following form:

Sir:—I request that the merchandise now entered by me to be warehoused, as described in the within entry, per
from   may be deposited in bonded warehouse No.   street; and I do hereby constitute and appoint the proprietor of said warehouse as my agent, for me and in my name, to have the joint custody of such goods, and possession of the key to said premises allowed to the importer, under the provisions of the warehousing acts and the regulations of the Secretary of the Treasury made in pursuance thereof.

(Signed,)   A. B.
To Collector of Customs, at

QUANTITY TO BE ENTERED.

Any portion of an invoice, not less than an entire package, or, if the merchandise be in bulk, not less than one ton in weight, may be entered for warehousing, if the importer desire, and the remainder for immediate payment of duties; in which case, the two entries must be made simultaneously.

RESTRICTION TO WAREHOUSING.

Under this form may be entered all imported merchandise, except such as are of a perishable or explosive nature; provided the importation is accompanied with an invoice. If no invoice has been received, or an invoice without the certificates required by law, the goods must be sent to store as unclaimed, unless entered for consumption by appraisement, or for immediate exportation, conformable to treasury regulations.

BOND.

The entry having been examined by the proper officer in the Collector's office, and the duty estimated thereon, it will be transmitted to the naval officer, with the invoice or invoices, for examination and estimate of the duties by that officer; which being done, the Collector will take a bond, with satisfactory security, in double the amount of such estimated duties.

PERMIT AND GOODS TO BE EXAMINED.

The bond having been executed, the Collector will issue a permit to the inspector (which order must be countersigned by the naval officer, where there is one) to send the goods to the warehouse named therein, with the exception of such as may be designated for examination, which will be sent to the appraisers' stores; such order must also indicate what goods are to be weighed, gauged or measured; and such weighing, gauging or measuring is in all cases to be done before the deposit of the goods in warehouse, or their removal to the appraisers' stores.

MAY PAY DUTY ON WHOLE OR PART BEFORE GOING INTO STORE.

On completion of entry for warehouse, should the importer desire to take the whole or any portion of his property from the vessel, and pay the duties before the same go into store, he shall be at liberty to do so by paying the duty on withdrawal entry for consumption, and one-half storage for one month, and giving penal bond as required by the 4th section of act of 28th May, 1830.

EXAMINED GOODS TRANSFERED TO WAREHOUSE.

When the packages designated by the Collector on the invoice, and ordered to the appraisers' stores, shall have been reported as examined, the Collector shall direct the storekeeper to cause such packages to be removed from the appraisers' stores to the warehouse where the remainder of the goods described in the entry have been deposited. The expense of such removal shall be borne by the importer.

ENTRY TO BE ADJUSTED BEFORE WITHDRAWAL.

The appraisers having reported on the invoice, the weigher, gauger or measurer having made his return of the quantity, the damage, if any, having been ascertained, and the dutiable value of the merchandise and duties finally determined, the importer, consignee or agent may, at any time within three years from the date of importation, withdraw from warehouse any quantity of the same, not less than an entire case or package, or not less than one ton in weight, if the merchandise be in bulk; but it is to be distinctly understood that no merchandise can be entered for exportation or for transportation from one port to another in the Confederate States, and withdrawn from warehouse on such entry, until all the examinations and returns have been made, and the dutiable value and duties definitely fixed.

PENAL DUTY TO BE PAID BEFORE WITHDRAWAL.

If, on examination by the appraisers, the merchandise be found to be undervalued in the entry, and additional duty incurred, such additional duty must be paid before any withdrawal entry of the merchandise from warehouse for consumption, transportation or export can be allowed.

ENTRY FOR WITHDRAWAL FROM WAREHOUSE FOR CONSUMPTION.

The entry for withdrawal of merchandise from warehouse for CONSUMPTION at port of original importation shall be made by the party in whose name the merchandise was warehoused, or by some person duly authorized for the purpose by him; and in either case shall be signed by the party making the withdrawal. This entry shall exhibit the marks and numbers of the packages, the description and quantity of the goods, and the dutiable value of the same. On presentation to the proper officer in the Collector's office, it shall be compared with the record on the warehouse books of the original warehouse entry, and, if found correct, be properly entered therein, the warehouse bond number endorsed thereon, and the amount of duties payable estimated. From the Collector's office it shall then be taken by the importer to the naval office, where a similar comparison will be made with the warehouse records of that office, and the estimate of duties verified and endorsed upon the duplicate entry. The amount of duties thus ascertained having been paid, a permit will be issued for the delivery of the goods. The entry shall be in the following form, and shall be made in duplicate:

FORM OF ENTRY.

Withdrawal Entry for Consumption at Port of Original Importation.

Entry of merchandise intended to be withdrawn from warehouse by   , which was imported into this district on the   , 186 , by   , in the   ,   master, from   .

MARKS	NUMBERS.	PACKAGES AND CONTENTS.	QUANTITY.	PER CENT.	PER CENT.	PER CENT.	PER CENT.	PER CENT.	TOTAL.	DUTIABLE VALUE OF EACH PACKAGE.

[To be signed by the importer.]

No oath will be required on this entry. If merchandise be withdrawn by any other than original importer, the following certificate must be placed thereon:

FORM.

I authorize   to withdraw from warehouse the goods described in this entry.

[To be signed by the importer.]

Merchandise in bulk, liquors, sugars, molasses, cocoa, pepper and other articles bought and sold by weight, when withdrawn for export or transportation, must be entered for such destination at the actual quantities on which duties were estimated at the time of arrival in the Confederate States; and to secure this, weighers, measurers, and gaugers will be required to mark on each package its contents as determined by them on its entry for warehouse. On these quantities the duties on export and transportation entries will be estimated. Goods withdrawn for consumption may be taken at average valuations, care being had that on the last withdrawal the entire balance of duty be collected.

Should the final withdrawal entry be for export or transportation, and there be any difference between the actual duty and the amount to close the sum due on the warehouse entry, the excess, if any, shall be refunded on the last withdrawal for consumption, and the deficiency, if any, collected on amendment to said entry.

WITHDRAWAL ENTRY FOR TRANSPORTATION.

The entry *for Transportation* from one port to another in the Confederate States shall be made and signed as required in case of entry for consumption, and shall be in the form following:

FORM OF TRANSPORTATION ENTRY FROM ONE PORT TO ANOTHER IN THE CONFEDERATE STATES.

Entry of merchandise intended to be withdrawn from warehouse by   , for transportation to   , which was imported into this district on the   , 186 , by   , in the   ,   master, from   .

CUSTOM HOUSE, , 186 .

MARKS.	NUMBERS.	PACKAGES AND CONTENTS.	QUANTITY.	PER CENT.	PER CENT.	PER CENT.	PER CENT.	PER CENT.	TOTAL.	DUTIABLE VALUE OF EACH PACKAGE.

This entry shall be made in triplicate, and when withdrawn by other than the original importer, the same authority must be required as in case of entry for consumption. And in addition to the particulars required in that case, this entry shall exhibit the name of the consignee, and the name of vessel by which the goods are to be transported; or if the transportation be by land, or partly by land and partly by water, the particular rail road or other route shall be designated, which route shall be in accordance with the regulations hereinafter provided. The party making the entry shall also present a copy of so much of the original invoice as relates to the merchandise, if package goods, described in such entry, or if other than package goods, a copy of the whole invoice. This copy must be a literal copy of the original, and if in a foreign language, must be a translated copy, and contain all the particulars set forth in that document. The entry having been compared with the record of the original warehouse entry, as provided in case of entry for consumption, entered in the appropriate column in the warehouse account, and the warehouse bond number endorsed thereon, and having also been compared and entered in the books of the naval officer, and the duties payable estimated, and the following oath taken by the party making entry, the Collector will take a bond, in a penal sum equal to double the invoice or appraised value of the goods, with sufficient surety or sureties:

FORM OF OATH.

I do solemnly, sincerely and truly swear that the goods, wares and merchandise described in the within entry, now delivered by me to the Collector of the customs for the port of   , are truly intended to be transported in bond by me to the port of   , and delivered to the Collector of said port, according to the provisions of the warehousing laws, and the regulations of the Secretary of the Treasury: So help me God.

Sworn to this   day of   , 18 , before me.

            , Collector.

TIME OF TRANSPORTATION BOND.

If the port to which the merchandise is to be transported be not more than one hundred miles distant by the route proposed, the time inserted in the bond shall be twenty days; if over one hundred, and less than two hundred and fifty miles, thirty days; if over two hundred and fifty, and less than five hundred miles, sixty days; and if over five hundred miles, ninety days; but if the distance be over two hundred and fifty miles, the Collector may, at the instance of the party, allow thirty additional days.

Nine months will be allowed for transportation of merchandise in bond between the Atlantic and Pacific ports around Cape Horn, and four months by other routes between those ports. If the transportation within the time prescribed is retarded by accident, or other unavoidable cause, on regular protest and due proof of the accident or other unavoidable cause, the Collector may receive said goods, or any part thereof, within a reasonable time thereafter.

The bond having been executed, the Collector will then issue an order, countersigned by the naval officer, for the delivery of the goods to the party making entry for transportation:

To enable the proper entry for re-warehousing to be made, the Collector of the port where the goods are withdrawn will transmit to the Collector of the port for which they may be destined, the triplicate copy of the transportation entry, with a copy of the invoice attached.

GOODS TO BE SEALED, MARKED AND SAMPLED.

Wines and distilled spirits, in casks of all sizes, must have the number of bung or other holes legibly branded on the exterior, and sealed, to prevent alteration or adulteration in the transit.

Goods in bulk, and other articles which cannot be sealed, must be examined before delivery for transportation by the Collector, and the weight, gauge, or measure specified on the entry and on the triplicate copy thereof. Before delivery from warehouse, whenever practicable, each package will also be legibly marked, "Port of   , in bond for   ;" and samples will be taken of each package of liquors, except when in bottles, not exceeding eight ounces in quantity, and will be so marked as to insure identity, and be deposited with the store-keeper of the store, subject to the order of the Collector.

ENTRY FOR RE-WAREHOUSING.

On the arrival of any goods, transported in bond, at the port of destination, they must immediately be entered for re-warehousing, the entry for which purpose shall be in the form following; such entry, in all cases, being a copy of the withdrawal entry at the port of last withdrawal:

RE-WAREHOUSING ENTRY.

Entry of merchandise intended to be re-warehoused by   , which was imported into the port of   , on the   day of   , 18   , and withdrawn from warehouse at port of   on the   day of   18   , for transportation to this district.   , 186   .

MARKS.	NUMBERS.	PACKAGES AND CONTENTS.	QUANTITY.	PER CENT.	PER CENT.	PER CENT.	PER CENT.	PER CENT.	TOTAL.	DUTIABLE VALUE OF EACH PACKAGE.

(To be signed.)

This entry shall be verified by the oath or affirmation of the party to whom the goods are consigned, and in the form following, viz.:

FORM OF OATH.

DISTRICT OF   .

I,   , do solemnly, sincerely and truly swear, that the goods described in the entry now delivered by me to the Collector of this district are the identical goods mentioned in a transportation entry made at the custom house at   , by   on the   day of   , 186   , and that said goods are the same in quality, quantity, value and package, wastage and damage excepted, as at the time of original importation: So help me God.

Sworn to this   day of   , 186   , before me.

                                        , Collector.

This oath or affirmation having been taken and the place of deposit designated, a bond, with satisfactory security, in a penal sum, equal to double the amount of the duties, shall be executed.

The Collector will thereupon issue a permit, as in the case of goods entered for warehouse at the port of original importation, directing the goods to be deposited in the warehouse designated.

If the Collector is satisfied that the goods so deposited and examined are the identical goods described in the entry and invoice received by him from the Collector at the port of withdrawal, and were correctly appraised, he will immediately furnish the party making entry with a certificate, countersigned by the naval officer, where there is one, of the delivery in the form annexed, and will also transmit a duplicate of such certificate to the Collector at the port of withdrawal.

FORM OF CERTIFICATE OF DELIVERY OF GOODS TO CANCEL TRANSPORTATION BOND.

District of   ,
Port of   ,   , 186

We hereby certify that the merchandise marked and numbered as follows, withdrawn from warehouse at the port of   , on the   day of   , by   , has been duly delivered to the proper officer of the customs at this port.

[Here describe the merchandise.]

, Collector.

, Naval Officer.

Goods transported under bond from one port of the Confederate States to another, and arriving in advance of the transportation papers, are to be treated as unclaimed goods, and sent to the bonded warehouses provided for the reception of that class of merchandise, until entry is made, when the goods may be transferred to such bonded store as the consignee may designate.

If, however, the consignee should desire to pay the duties and get possession of his goods immediately on arrival, an entry may be made in the following form, to be verified by oath or affirmation:

FORM OF ENTRY.

Re-warehousing and Withdrawal Entry for Consumption.

Entry of merchandise to be re-warehoused and withdrawn by   , which was brought into this district by   from the port of   , on the   , 186 , having been originally imported into   by   , in the   from   on the   day of   18   .

MARKS.	NUMBERS.	PACKAGES AND CONTENTS.	QUANTITY.	PER CENT.	PER CENT.	PER CENT.	PER CENT.	PER CENT.	TOTAL.	DUTIABLE VALUE OF EACH PACKAGE.

(To be signed.)

The value and duty as assessed at the port of original importation, and so stated in the triplicate copy of transportation entry forwarded to port of destination, will, in all cases, be the value and duty to be charged on the re-warehouse entry; and said triplicate copy will in all cases be attached to the re-warehouse entry, or, if withdrawn immediately on arrival, to re-warehouse withdrawal entry, as the vouchers and authority for the assessment of duty. Should there, however, on the examination, be found any clerical error in the entry or invoice, it shall be forthwith corrected, entry allowed, and the fact reported to the Collector at the port of withdrawal.

But should any difference in valuation or classification be reported by the appraisers, the case will be reported to the Department, as hereinbefore provided, and the Collector at the port of withdrawal duly notified of the fact, and the entry, in the meantime, will be suspended.

In this case, no re-warehouse bond will be required; but the duties which shall be the amount certified as payable on the triplicate entry having been paid, and a penal bond taken, as provided in the 4th section act 28th May, 1830, the Collector will issue a permit for the delivery of the goods, except the packages ordered for examination, which will be sent to the appraisers' store.

EXAMINATION BY APPRAISERS, ETC.

The same examination shall be had by the appraisers of the goods in this case as in case of entry for actual re-warehousing;

and on their report that the goods agree with the entry, and are correctly classified and valued, a permit shall issue for the delivery of the examined packages, and a certificate in duplicate be issued to cancel the bond at the port of withdrawal.

RE WAREHOUSE WITHDRAWAL FOR EXPORT.

Should the consignee of any merchandise transported under bond desire to export the same immediately on arrival at port of destination, he will give notice of the same to the Collector in writing, who will direct the storekeeper to assume the custody of the goods, wherever they may be, until the necessary entry is completed, and permit issues. Should there be any delay in the preparation of those papers, the goods will be sent by the Collector to such warehouse as he may select. The entry will be made in the form annexed:

Form of Entry.

Re-warehouse Entry for Immediate Exportation.

Entry of merchandise brought into this district by   , from   , and now to be exported by   , on board the   , for   , which was imported into the port of   , on   , 186   , having been originally imported into   , by   , in the   , from   , on the   day of   , 18   .

MARKS.	NUMBERS.	PACKAGES AND CONTENTS.	QUANTITY.	PER CENT.	PER CENT.	PER CENT.	PER CENT.	PER CENT.	TOTAL.	DUTIABLE VALUE OF EACH PACKAGE.

[To be signed by the exporter.]

The entry having been verified by the oath or affirmation of the consignee, as provided in case of entry for re-warehousing, and also by the oath or affirmation of the exporter, in the following form, viz:

Form of Oath.

District of

I do solemnly, sincerely and truly swear, that the goods, wares and merchandise described in the within entry, now delivered by me to the Collector of the customs for the port of   , are truly intended to be exported by me to the port of   , without the limits of the Confederate States, and are not intended to be re-landed within the limits of the Confederate States. I further swear that, to the best of my knowledge and belief, the said goods, wares and merchandise are the same in quality, quantity, value and package, wastage and damage excepted, as at the time of importation. So help me God.

Sworn to this   day of   , 186 , before me.

, Collector.

And the export bond having been executed, the Collector will issue a permit, to be countersigned by the naval officer, in the annexed form, viz:

Form of Permit.

District of   ,
Port of   , 186 .

To the Storekeeper of the Port:

You are directed to deliver to the surveyor for exportation on board the   , for   , [here describe the merchandise,] brought into this district by   from   .

, Collector.

, Naval Officer.

At the same time that this order is given to the store keeper, a copy of the enry shall also be transmitted to the surveyor for the due shipment or lading of the goods.

The direction to the surveyor upon this entry shall be as follows:

FORM OF ORDER.

PORT OF   , 186 .

TO THE SURVEYOR:

You will direct an inspector to examine the goods described in this entry, and, if found to agree exactly therewith, to superintend the lading thereof on board the   , for   , of which, when completed, you will grant a certificate.

, Collector.

, Naval Officer.

The return of the inspector upon this entry shall be as follows:

FORM OF RETURN.

PORT OF   186 .

I,   , have examined the goods described in the within entry, and finding them to agree therewith, they were laden under my supervision on board the   , for

, Inspector.

BOND.

No bond other than the export bond will be required; and in this case, as well as in that of payment of duties, the certificate already prescribed for the cancellation of the transportation bond will be furnished to the party making entry, immediately on the receipt of the necessary evidence that the merchandise described in the transportation entry has been delivered; and a duplicate of the same will also be forwarded to the Collector, or other proper officer, at the port of withdrawal.

THIS ENTRY ONLY IN CERTAIN CASES.

This form of entry will only be allowed on articles in bulk: woods, liquors that are branded and sealed, cases corded and sealed, sugar, molasses, coal, iron, and other heavy and bulky goods, when the identification can be readily made by the inspecting officer. All other articles must be re-warehoused, as previously provided for, and examined by the appraisers, before an export entry can be allowed.

The merchandise must in all cases be actually delivered to the officer of the customs at the port where landed or unladen, whether entered for re-warehousing, payment of duties, or immediate exportation.

Should merchandise, after having been re-warehoused, be withdrawn for consumption, transportation or exportation, the entries shall be according to the forms annexed—all the regulations as to oaths, bonds, examinations, etc., to be complied with, as herein provided for entries at first and second ports.

Form of Entry.

Re-warehouse Withdrawal Entry for Consumption.

Entry of merchandise intended to be drawn from warehouse for consumption by   , which was brought into this district on the   day of   , 186 , by   , from the port of   , having been originally imported into   by   , in the   , from   , on the   day of   , 186 .

MARKS.	NUMBERS.	PACKAGES AND CONTENTS.	QUANTITY.	PER CENT.	PER CENT.	PER CENT.	PER CENT.	PER CENT.	TOTAL.	DUTIABLE VALUE OF EACH PACKAGE.

(To be signed.)

Form of Entry.

Re-warehouse Withdrawal Entry for Transportation in the Confederate States.

Entry of merchandise intended to be withdrawn from warehouse by   , for transportation to   , which was brought into this district on the   186 , by   , from the port of   , the same having been originally imported into the district of   , on the   day of   , 18   , in the   , from   .

MARKS	NUMBERS.	PACKAGES AND CONTENTS.	QUANTITY.	PER CENT.	PER CENT.	PER CENT.	PER CENT.	PER CENT.	TOTAL.	DUTIABLE VALUE OF EACH PACKAGE.

(To be signed.)

Form of Entry.

Re-warehouse Withdrawal Entry for Exportation.

Entry of merchandise withdrawn from warehouse by   , and to be exported by   , in the   master, for   , which was brought into this district on the   186 , from the port of   , the same having been originally imported into the district of   , on the   day of   , 186 , in the   , from   .

MARKS.	NUMBERS.	PACKAGES AND CONTENTS.	QUANTITY.	PER CENT.	PER CENT.	PER CENT.	PER CENT.	PER CENT.	TOTAL.	DUTIABLE VALUE OF EACH PACKAGE.

(To be signed.)

If the merchandise be withdrawn, in either of these cases, by any other than the party by whom brought into the district, the same authority is required as in case of withdrawal at port of original importation.

WAREHOUSE AND TRANSPORTATION ENTRY.

On the arrival from any foreign port of any goods destined for immediate transportation to other ports in the Confederate States, the warehousing and transportation may be combined in one entry, the oaths to be the same as prescribed in the warehouse entry. The forms of entry shall be as follows, the foregoing regulations as to examinations being in all respects complied with:

FORM OF ENTRY.

Warehouse Entry and Transportation in the Confederate States.

Entry of merchandise imported by   ,
in ship   ,   master,
from   for warehouse
and for transportation in bond to   ,

MARKS.	NUMBERS.	PACKAGES AND CONTENTS.	QUANTITY.	PER CENT.	PER CENT.	PER CENT.	PER CENT.	PER CENT.	TOTAL.	DUTIABLE VALUE OF EACH PACKAGE.

This entry must be made in triplicate, in accordance with the rules already prescribed, stating, in addition, the date and time of transportation bond, and the triplicate forwarded to place of destination, as in case of withdrawal from warehouse for transportation in the Confederate States. The entry having been verified by the oath or affirmation of the importer, and the transportation route having been designated, and all other requirements complied with, the Collector will take a bond, in a penal sum, equal to double the invoice or appraised value of the goods.

TO BE SENT TO STORE, EXAMINED, ETC.

On the execution of the bond, the Collector will issue a permit, to be countersigned by the naval officer, directing the goods to be sent to the warehouse designated by the importer, while the requisite examinations are being made by the appraisers, and until the dutiable value shall have been determined; which having been done, a permit shall be issued for the delivery of the goods to the importer for transportation, and the same proceeding shall be had as heretofore provided in case of goods withdrawn from warehouse for transportation; especial care being taken that the triplicate entry is transmitted to the second port in season to anticipate the arrival of the goods.

IMPORT VESSEL MAY BE MADE WAREHOUSE DURING EXAMINATION.

The same permits are to be used as when the warehouse and

transportation entries are made separately. In case of warehouse and transportation entries, the importing vessel may be considered the warehouse, without charge, during the time the examination is being made by the appraisers, and from which deliveries may be made for transportation; but should the examination be delayed beyond the time allowed by law for the goods to remain on board, they must be sent to such bonded warehouse as the importer may select, until the examination is completed, under the usual warehouse permit; and when delivered for transportation, the delivery to take place under the permit as delivery for transportation. It shall be the duty, and it is required of the appraisers, whenever practicable, that the goods so entered shall be examined on board the vessel in which imported, in order to save the importer the charges for sending the same to store.

BOND MAY BE GIVEN BY IMPORTERS AT INTERIOR PORTS.

In order to facilitate the transmission of merchandise in bond from a port of entry to any interior port of delivery, under the act of 28th March, 1854, the importer of any goods, wares or merchandise, residing at such interior port of delivery, and desiring to have the merchandise transported in bond, may produce his invoice to the Surveyor or designated Collector of the interior port, take the oath or oaths required by law, and execute the transportation bond, with proper sureties, before the Surveyor or Collector of said port, who shall certify on said bond the sufficiency of the sureties, and transmit the bond to the Collector of the port of importation; and the bond so taken shall be as valid and binding as though executed in the office of the Collector where the entry shall be made. The invoice, with the oath attached, may be transmitted by the importer to his agent or attorney at the port where the goods are expected to arrive, who, upon their arrival, shall present the transportation entry, with bill or bills of lading therefor, in the form and setting forth the particulars hereinbefore required; whereupon, the same proceedings shall be had as in other entries for transportation under bond from one port to another in the Confederate States.

EXPORT FROM WAREHOUSE AT PORT OF IMPORTATION.

When goods are withdrawn from warehouse for exportation at port of original importation, the entry shall be in the form following:

FORM OF ENTRY.

Export Entry from Port of Original Importation.

Entry of merchandise intended to be withdrawn from warehouse by   , and to be exported by him in the   , master, for   , which was imported into this district by   in the   , master, from   , on the   day of   , 186 .

MARKS.	NUMBERS.	PACKAGES AND CONTENTS.	QUANTITY.	PER CENT.	PER CENT.	PER CENT.	PER CENT.	PER CENT.	TOTAL.	DUTIABLE VALUE OF EACH PACKAGE.

[To be signed by the exporter.]

If exported by other than the original importer, the same authority will be required as in case of withdrawal for consumption, and the oath to be taken by the exporter shall be in the following form, viz:

FORM OF OATH.

DISTRICT OF   :

I do solemnly, sincerely and truly swear, that the goods, wares and merchandise described in the within entry, now delivered by me to the Collector of the customs for the port of   , are truly intended to be exported by me to the port of   , without the limits of the Confederate States, and are not intended to be re-landed within the limits of Confederate States. I further swear, that, to the best of my knowledge and belief, the said goods, wares and merchandise are the same in quality, quantity, value and package, wastage and damage excepted, as at the time of importation.   So help me God.

Sworn to this   day of   , 186 , before me.

Collector.

The entry having been duly entered in the warehouse accounts, and the oath as above prescribed having been taken, the exporter shall enter into a bond with satisfactory security, in a penal sum equal to double the amount of the estimated duties on the goods, to produce the proofs required by the 81st section of the act of March 2d, 1799, of the landing of the same beyond the limits of the Confederate States.

The bond having been duly executed, a permit will be issued, signed by the Collector and countersigned by the naval officer, where there is one, directing the storekeeper to deliver the goods to the surveyor.

The entry shall at the same time be transmitted to the surveyor, with directions to cause the merchandise described therein to be laden for exportation, indicating such as is to be weighed, measured or gauged.

The return of the officer under whose inspection the goods are shipped shall be in the form annexed:

FORM OF RETURN.

PORT OF   ,   , 186 .

I,   , have examined the goods described in the within entry, and finding them to agree therewith, they were laden under my supervision on board the   ,   master, for   .

Inspector.

WAREHOUSE AND EXPORTATION ENTRY.

When any goods, wares or merchandise are imported into any port in the Confederate States, and the intent is shown by invoice and manifest, bill of lading or other evidence that the same are to be exported immediately by sea beyond the limits of the Confederate States, an entry for warehouse and exportation may be made in the following form:

FORM OF ENTRY.

Warehouse and Exportation Entry.

Entry of merchandise imported for warehouse by   ,
in the   ,   master, from   , on the   day of   , 18   , and to be immediately exported by   , in the
         ,   master, for

DATE.	IMPORT VESSEL.	WHERE FROM.	TO WHAT PLACE EXPORTED.	DESCRIPTION OF GOODS.	PER CENT.	PER CENT.	PER CENT.	PER CENT.	PER CENT.	TOTAL.

EXPORT BOND TO BE GIVEN.

No bond other than the export bond shall be required for this entry; which bond having been duly executed by the party making entry, the Collector, together with the naval officer, shall issue a permit addressed to the inspector of the vessel by which said goods were imported, directing him to send said goods to the vessel in which they are to be exported, the import vessel being considered the warehouse.

The same order to surveyor to ship, and same return from said officer of shipment, required on this as on the usual export entry.

RESTRICTIONS AS TO USING THIS FORM OF ENTRY.

This entry for warehouse and exportation will only be permitted when an opportunity exists for immediate export. If the goods cannot be re-shipped immediately on arrival, they must go to a bonded warehouse as unclaimed, and remain until an opportunity offers, when entry in this form can be made.

EXPORT BOND, HOW CANCELLED.

For the discharge of export bonds, the exporter must produce, within one year if the shipment be to any port of Europe or America, and within two years if to any port of Asia or Africa, a certificate under the hand of the consignee at the foreign port, describing the articles exported, and declaring that the same have been received by him from on board the vessel, specifying the name and nation of the vessel from which they were so received; which certificate shall be authenticated by the consul or agent of the Confederate States residing at said port; or, in the absence of such officer, by two American merchants residing at such port; or, if there be no American merchants resident there, then, by two respectable foreign merchants; which certificate shall be confirmed by the oaths or affirmations of the master and mate, or other principal officers of the vessel, to be taken before the consul or commercial agent of the Confederate States, if there be one; and if not, before some other person authorized by the laws of the country to administer the same. The forms of these certificates shall be as follows:

Certificate of a Consignee, declaring the Delivery of Merchandise at a Foreign Port.

I,   , of the (town or city) of   , merchant, do hereby certify that the goods or merchandise hereinafter described have been landed in this (city, town or port,) between the   and   days of   , from on board the   , of   , whereof   is at present master, viz: [here describe the merchandise,] which, according to the bill of lading for the same, were shipped on board the   , at the port of   , in the Confederate States of

America, on or about the   day of   , and consigned to me (me, or to us,) by   , of   aforesaid, merchant, (or by the master of said   ,)

Given under (my or our) hands, at the (city) of   , this   day of   , 186 .

Oath or affirmation of the principal officers of a vessel, confirming the Landing of Merchandise at a Foreign Port.

PORT OF

We,   , master, and   , mate, of   lately arrived from the port of   , in the Confederate States of America, do solemnly (swear or affirm) that the goods or merchandise enumerated and described in the preceding certificate, dated the   day of   , and signed by   , of the city of   , merchant, were actually delivered at the said port, from on board the   , within the time specified in the said certificate.

Sworn (or affirmed) at the city of   , before me, this   day of   , in the year   .

Verification of the Delivery of Merchandise at a Foreign Port, to be executed by a Consul or Agent of the Confederate States.

I,   (consul or agent) of the Confederate States of America, at the city of   , do declare that the facts set forth in the preceding certificate, subscribed by   , of the said city, merchant, and dated the   day of   , are (to my knowledge just and true; or, are in my opinion just and true, and deserving of full faith and credit.)

In testimony whereof, I have hereunto sub-
[SEAL.]   scribed my name, and affixed the seal of my office, at   , this   day of   186 .

Consul.

Verification of the delivery of Merchandise, to be executed by American or Foreign Merchants, as the case may require.

We,   , residing in the city of
                , do declare that the facts stated in the preceding certificate, signed by   , of the said city, merchant, on the   day of   , are (to our knowledge just and true; or, are in our opinion just and true, and worthy of full faith and credit.) We also declare that there is (no consul or other public agent for the Confederate States of America, or American merchants, as the case may require,) now residing at this place.

Dated this   day of   , at the city of   .

(Signatures.)

PRINTING OF SILKS IN BOND—PONGEES AND OTHER PLAIN WHITE.

Silks in bond may be withdrawn from warehouse to be colored, printed, stained, dyed, painted, or stamped, the collector taking a deposit in money equal to the amount of duties ascertained to be payable ; which deposit shall be refunded if the goods aforesaid shall be returned to the warehouse re-packed in the original condition, and according to original marks and numbers, within sixty days from date of delivery thereof. Each package shall, before the same be delivered from warehouse, be opened and examined by the proper officer of the customs, and the contents thereof measured or weighed, and the quality thereof ascertained, and a sample of each piece thereof reserved at the custom house, and a particular account or register of such examination shall be entered on the books of the custom house. On the return of said goods, if the Collector shall be satisfied that the contents of each package are the identical goods imported and registered as aforesaid, and not changed or altered, except by being colored, dyed, stamped, stained, painted or printed, as aforesaid, he shall thereupon refund the deposit as aforesaid, and said goods shall be entitled to the same privileges as if in original condition, as per 4th section act 22d May, 1824.

The form of entry for delivery of silks for this purpose shall be as follows:

WITHDRAWAL OF SILKS FOR DYEING, ETC.

Entry of silks intended to be withdrawn from warehouse for dyeing, coloring, printing, painting, or stamping, under the provisions of the act of 22d May, 1824, and Treasury instructions, which were imported into this district on the day of   18 , in the
master, from   .

DATE.	DESCRIPTION OF MERCHANDISE.	DUTY.	PER CENT.	DUTY.	PER CENT.	TOTAL.	DUTIABLE VALUE OF EACH PACKAGE.

(To be signed.)

DEPOSIT FOR DUTY.

On the same estimate of duties being made as required in withdrawal entries for payment of duties, and the goods being duly entered on the books as withdrawn for printing, etc., the party making entry will deposit with the Collector a sum equivalent to the duties thus estimated. Whereupon, a permit will issue in the following form, to be countersigned by the naval officer:

FORM No. 147.
DISTRICT OF
Custom House,

To THE WAREHOUSE SUPERINTENDENT:

You will have the following described silks withdrawn from warehouse by   , in order to be printed, painted, stamped, dyed or colored, and which were imported by   in the   , from viz :

[Here describe the merchandise.]

sampled and weighed, or measured and examined, as required by the act of 22d May, 1824, and Treasury instructions, and deliver the same to   , to be returned to the warehouse from whence withdrawn within sixty days from this date.

Collector.

Naval Officer.

On the return of the goods within the time specified, they shall be examined by the warehouse superintendent, and if found to agree with the samples retained, he shall issue a certificate in the following form :

District of
Custom House,

I do hereby certify that the following described goods, returned to warehouse by   are the same goods as withdrawn by   on the   day of   , 18   , to be printed, painted, stamped, dyed or colored.

[Here describe the merchandise.]

I also certify the said goods are in the same condition as when withdrawn, except by being printed, painted, stamped, dyed or colored.

Warehouse Superintendent.

On the presentation of this certificate, the deposit shall be refunded and the withdrawal entry cancelled.

Goods withdrawn under this entry and permit will be considered in the accounts as still in warehouse, the entry and deposit being made only to secure the return of the goods. If the goods are not returned within the period specified in the entry, the same will pass into the accounts as a regular withdrawal entry for consumption, and the deposit will go into the accounts as duties received.

INLAND EXPORTATION OF GOODS IN BOND TO PORTS AND PLACES IN MEXICO.

Merchandise in the original packages, duly entered and bonded, may be withdrawn at any time within three years from the date of importation, for immediate exportation to Chihuahua, in Mexico, either by the route of the Arkansas river, through Van Buren, or by the route of the Missouri river, through Independence.

Merchandise duly entered and bonded, or re-warehoused under bond at point Isabel, in the collection district of Brazos de Santiago, may be withdrawn from warehouse at any time within three years from the date of importation, for immediate exportation to ports and places in Mexico, by land or water, or partly by land and partly by water, by the following routes, viz.: 1st, directly by water, to ports and places in Mexico lying on the sea-coast or Rio Grande; 2d, by land or water, under warehouse transportation bond, to Brownsville, Rio Grande City, Roma and Loredo; thence by water to places in Mexico lying on the Rio Grande. Merchandise transported in bond from Point Isabel to Brownsville, Rio Grande City, Roma, and Loredo, may be re-warehoused thereat, only in first-class fire-proof stores, according to the classification of the insurance companies at these places, previously approved by the Department and bonded.

Entries of Goods in bond at Point Isabel may be made for transporting to and re-warehousing at Brownsville, Rio Grande City, Roma and Loredo, on like bonds as are provided in the regulations for the transportation and re-warehousing at interior ports of delivery. Merchandise entered for exportation in bond at Point Isabel for Mexico may, at the option of the owner, be withdrawn at Rio Grande City, Roma, Loredo, or Brownsville, for consumption, on due entry thereof and payment of the proper duties and charges to the Deputy Collector, at either of those points at which the merchandise may be; prompt returns of such entries and duties collected to be made by the Deputy to the Collector at Point Isabel, that the proper endorsements may be made on the entries and bonds at that port.

Merchandise duly entered and bonded at any port of the Confederate States may be withdrawn for immediate exportation in bond to San Fernando, Paso del Norte, and Chihuahua, and be transported by water to the port of Lavaca, in the collection district of Saluria, Texas, and be transhipped thence inland to San Antonio, and from the latter place to the before mentioned destinations in Mexico, either by way of Eagle Pass, de Presidio del Norte, and San Elizario, all on the Rio Grande. On the arrival of such goods at the port of Lavaca, they need not be re-warehoused, but must be landed by permission and under inspection of the surveyor of that port.

In consideration of the long inland transportation and the risk of injury and defacing of the marks on the packages, thereby rendering the identification difficult, if not impossible, the packages must be corded, and a lead seal attached thereto, at the expense of the exporter, under the direction of the storekeeper, before leaving the warehouse.

Each package shall also be marked, under direction of the storekeeper, and before the goods are delivered from the warehouse, with these words: "Port of   , in bond for   ," [naming the port or place of destination in Mexico.]

The entry for withdrawal from warehouse for exportation inland to ports and places in Mexico, by land or water, or partly by land and partly by water, shall be in the following form, and shall set forth particularly the route and mode of conveyance by which the merchandise is to be exported—naming always the last customs station at which inspection is to be made, and from which the goods are to be exported:

Withdrawal Entry for Transportation and Exportation in Bond to Mexico.

Entry of merchandise to be withdrawn from warehouse, by   , which was imported by   , into this district, in the   ,   master, from   , and to be transported to   , and thence exported to   , in Mexico, by way of   .

MARKS	NUMBERS.	PACKAGES AND CONTENTS.	QUANTITY.	PER CENT.	PER CENT.	PER CENT.	PER CENT.	PER CENT.	TOTAL.	DUTIABLE VALUE OF EACH PACKAGE.

This entry shall be verified by the oath or affirmation of the exporter, and he shall enter into bond, in a penal sum equal to double the value of the goods, with security satisfactory to the Collector.

The bond having been duly executed, a permit will be issued, signed by the Collector, and countersigned by the naval officer, if any, directing the storekeeper to deliver the goods to the surveyor.

The Collector will hand one of the entries to the surveyor, with directions thereon to superintend the lading thereof on board the conveyance for exportation to Mexico.

Upon the receipt of this order, the surveyor will designate an inspector for the discharge of this duty, who shall carefully examine the packages, and if they agree in all particulars with the description in the entry, he shall make return of such examination.

INLAND MANIFESTS.

The manifest shall contain a description of the marks, numbers, packages, or quantities, by whom shipped, to whom consigned, and the route by which the merchandise is to be transported, and shall be certified by the officer of the customs superintending the shipment, and shall be delivered by the master, owner, conductor or driver of the vehicle to the customs officer at the first station for inspection on the route; and after packages shall have been duly examined, and if it is found that they have remained unbroken and conform to the manifest and triplicate entry, the inspector shall certify the fact on the triplicate entry.

The surveyor at Lavaca and the officers of inspection at the points named on the several designated routes inland to Mexico, must each keep a record, in which will be duly noted all the particulars of the merchandise and transportation contained in the manifest or entry.

EXAMINATIONS ON THE WAY.

Having entered and verified the statement of the entry thus passed inspection, the inspecting officer will endorse on the manifest a permit for the party to proceed on the designated route to the next station, where the like examination, certificates, entry on the record, and permit will be made; and the inspector at the last port will endorse on the manifest that the merchandise has been examined and found correct, and exported to   , its destination in Mexico; and having made the proper entry in his record, will forward the manifest to the Treasury Department with his semi-annual report. He will also endorse the proper certificate on the triplicate entry, with a permit to export the merchandise described therein to its destination in Mexico.

PROOF TO CANCEL BOND.

The proof of due landing at the port of destination in Mexico will be a certificate of the Confederate States consul or agent, which will be in the following form:

FORM.

I,   , consul or agent of the Confederate States of America, residing at   , in   , do hereby certify that I have duly examined the packages of merchandise described in the within entry and invoice, and am fully satisfied that the goods have arrived in this place in the original packages as imported, without any change or alteration, and have been exported from the Confederate States in good faith, to be disposed of and consumed in a foreign country.

 In testimony whereof, I have hereunto set my hand and affixed my official seal, this   day of   , A. D.
[L. S.]   186   , and of the independence of the Confederate States of America the   .

               Consul of C. S.

If there be no consul or agent of the Confederate States residing at the place, then the certificate may be made by the consul of a nation in amity with the Confederate States; and if there be no such consul there, then by two reputable merchants at said place.

 This certificate will be endorsed on the triplicate entry; and on the production of the entry to the Collector of the customs at the port of withdrawal, with proper certificates thereon, showing a full compliance with the bond within the time therein limited, the same will be cancelled; and if not so produced, the bond will be enforced without delay.

 By the law authorizing the exportation of merchandise in bond by certain routes in Mexico, it is provided that no goods, wares or merchandise exported out of the limits of the Confederate States, according to the provisions of that act, shall be voluntarily landed or brought into the Confederate States; and that, on being so landed or brought into the Confederate States, they shall be forfeited; and that the same proceedings shall be had for their condemnation and distribution of proceeds as in other cases of forfeiture of goods illegally imported; and every person concerned in the voluntary landing or bringing such goods into the Confederate States, shall be liable to a penalty of four hundred dollars.

PROTESTS AND APPEALS.

PROTESTS AGAINST PAYMENT OF DUTIES.

The Treasury Department having authority to refund duties paid in excess only in cases where the duties *have been illegally exacted;* and the Supreme Court having decided that where no protest (stating specially the ground of objection) is made, the duties *are not* illegally exacted, in the legal sense of the term, it becomes necessary for importers in cases where they regard the rate of duty or the value on which such duty is assessed erroneous, and from a desire to obtain possession of their goods are obliged to pay the duty, to file with the Collector at the time of paying such a written protest against the exaction, in order to reserve the legal right to a refundment of the amount or excess paid, should the questions at issue on investigation be decided in their favor.

Form of Protest.

The following is a suitable form of protest, in which all the reasons to sustain the importer's position against the exaction should be explicitly set forth; as on the trial of such cases before the courts it has been decided that the applicant must confine his claim to the grounds declared in the protest, and is debarred from introducing other or new objections.

Form.

New Orleans,   186

Sir:

I hereby protest against the payment of duty at the rate of   per cent., charged on (describe the goods) imported by me in the   from   and described in an entry made by me on   186   numbered   claiming that under existing laws said goods are only liable to duty at the rate of   per cent., (or are exempt from duty, as the case may be,) for the following reasons, viz:

(Here state clearly and explicitly all the grounds relied upon to sustain the claim.)

I pay the amount exacted in order to obtain possession of the goods—claim to have the same (or excess) refunded, and reserve my right of appeal to the judicial tribunals.

(Signed,) A. B.
To
    Collector of customs.

Should the protest be against the payment of duty on an erroneous valuation, the above must be altered to conform to the facts.

Protests against the payment of duty must be made in duplicate, and delivered to the cashier of the custom house *at the time of paying the duty*.

General protests against the exaction of duties are not admissible, the law requiring a protest to be made to the Collector of the customs in writing, subscribed by the importer or his duly authorized agent, at or before the payment of the duties, setting forth DISTINCTLY and SPECIFICALLY his objections to the payment of the duties demanded. A general protest, it has been decided by the Department, in conformity with judicial decisions, made on any one importation, cannot be taken as extending and applying to future importations of a similar character.

No return of alleged EXCESS OF DUTIES can be made, arising from the rate at which Collectors estimate the values of FOREIGN CURRENCIES, unless the duties are paid under due and sufficient protest.

NOTICE OF DISSATISFACTION OR PROTEST, AND APPEAL FROM COLLECTOR'S DECISIONS UNDER 4th SECTION OF ACT 21st MAY, 1861.

The 4th section of the Tariff Act of 21st May, 1861, renders the decision of the Collector at the port of importation and entry, as to the liability of importations to duty, final and conclusive, unless the owner, importer, consignee or agent shall, within ten days after entry, give notice to the Collector, in writing, of his dissatisfaction with such decision, etc.; and shall, within thirty days after the date of such decision, appeal therefrom to the Secretary of the Treasury. It is therefore incumbent upon importers, when dissatisfied with the rate of duty assessed by the Collector on their importations, in order to obtain redress, to avail themselves of the rights granted by this act by conforming strictly to its provisions, thus:

If the merchandise be entered for consumption and the duty paid, the *protest* against the payment of the duties before explained will be sufficient for the notice to the Collector of dissatisfaction, required by the act.

If the duty is not paid or the entry is for warehousing, a notice corresponding in form with the protest protesting against the *assessment* of the duties will be sufficient.

In addition to this notice, should the Collector fail to alter his decision, the importer must appeal to the Secretary of the Treasury, by representing clearly to that officer all the facts of the case, and questions at issue. This appeal may be in the following form, viz:

FORM OF APPEAL.

New Orleans, 186

SIR:

Availing myself of the privilege granted by the fourth section of the act of 21st May, 1861, I have the honor to appeal to you from the decision of the Collector of customs of the port of   assessing duty at the rate of   per cent. on the following goods imported by me in the   from   and entered for (here state the kind of entry) on   186   , numbered   viz:
(here describe the goods)
          claiming the said goods are, under existing laws, liable to duty at the rate of   per cent., (or are entitled to free entry, as the case may be,) for the following reasons:

(Here state clearly all the reasons relied upon, and the objections to the Collector's ruling.)

I have complied with the requirements of the act, by notifying the Collector of my dissatisfaction with his decision, and submitting the case for your consideration, solicit the relief to which I feel entitled under the laws.

    (Signed,)   A. B.
Hon.
    Secretary of the Treasury.

TIME OF MAKING APPEALS, ETC.

To prevent misapprehension as to the time in which notice or protest of dissatisfaction may be made to the Collector, and an appeal taken to the Treasury Department from his decision, under the fourth section of the Tariff Act of 21st May, 1861, it has been decided that the Treasury Department can entertain no case of appeal from the Collector's decision as to the rate of duty on imports in which the notice or protest shall not have been made before the expiration of *ten days from and after the final liquidation* of duties, and the appeal taken within *thirty days* from and after the date of the final liquidation of duties; which must be held to be the *final decision* of the Collector as to the rate and amount of duties to be exacted in this case.

MANNER OF TRANSACTING BUSINESS AT THE CUSTOM HOUSE.

While the routine of business at the custom houses in the several ports is not strictly uniform, the following is given as that more generally practiced in the principal ports:

ENTRY OF MERCHANDISE FOR CONSUMPTION, HOW MADE, AND PROCEEDINGS CONNECTED THEREWITH.

Entries for consumption on arrival—or *impost entries*, as this class is usually styled—are made by the importer preparing, in duplicate, an entry in the form below, by describing therein the goods by the marks, numbers, description of package, contents, and value as stated in the invoice, adding all dutiable charges, and in every case a charge for commission at the usual rate. In addition to the value being stated in the general column, the importer will carry out the value of each description of goods paying a different rate of duty under the appropriate head of 25, 20, 15, 10 and 5 per cent, etc., as the case may be, adding each column, to show the gross amount subject to the different rates, thus:

PRO FORMA ENTRY.

Entry of merchandise imported into the port of New Orleans, by John Doe, in the ship "Confederate," Pride, master, from Bordeaux:

Marks and Numbers.	Description of Merchandise.	Quantity.	Invoice Value.	Rate Per Cent.			Dutiable Value.	Rate of Duty.	Duty.
				25	20	15			
J D 15.....	One hundred and fifty cases empty bottles. Charges............	300 doz.	Francs, 486. 20.	....	....	6506	$71	15 p.ct	
D 21@30...	Ten casks wines....... Charges............	600 galls	373.32	373.32	....	....	58	20 p.ct	
J D 11@20.	Ten barrels prunes... Charges............		301.45 6.75	....	308.20	....	96	15 p.ct	
			1187.52 23.75	373.32 7.47	308.20 6.16	506. 10.12			
	Commission 2 per cent	....	Frs. 1,211.27	380.79	314.36	516.12			
			$225.25				$225		

New Orleans, September 10, 1861.

The importer will not estimate and extend the duty on the entry, as this is the proper duty of the clerk at the custom house.

The entry, thus prepared, together with the invoice and bill of lading, will be delivered to the entry clerk (or the officer discharging that duty) in the Collector's office, who will examine the entry by the invoice and bill of lading, stamp or certify the invoice estimate, and extend the duties and make out the permit, and return all these documents to the importer, who will then take them to the invoice clerk to be recorded and numbered for identification; from thence he will proceed to the naval office and deliver the papers to the entry clerk there, who will examine the entry by the invoice and bill of lading, as in the Collector's office, test the correctness of the permit and the calculation of the duties, and, if correct, checking both with his initials, return the papers to the importer, with the exception of the duplicate entry, which is retained for the files of the naval office.

The importer then proceeds to the Deputy Collector and takes the appropriate oath endorsed on the entry, the Deputy Collector, ordering the packages for examination on the invoice, entry and permit, signs the invoice and retains it, returning the entry and permit to the importer. The importer, if he wishes to obtain possession of his goods under the penal bond, authorized by the act of 28th May, 1830, will proceed to the bond desk and execute the bond, or, if he has given a six months bond, as provided for by treasury regulations, will have the value of his entry endorsed on such bond by the bond clerk; he will then go to the cashier's desk and pay the duty and fees; from thence he takes the entry and permit to the naval officer, or his deputy, who will check the amount of duties, sign the permit and return the papers; he will then return to the Deputy Collector, who will sign the permit, deliver it to him, and retain the entry.

In some custom houses this order is changed, by simply requiring the importer, after having the estimated duties examined by the entry clerk of the naval office, to proceed directly to the bond desk, from that to the cashier and deputy naval officer, and then to the Deputy Collector, where the oath is administered and documents retained, except the permit, which is signed and delivered. This is the practice at New Orleans, and avoids the trouble of applying twice to the Deputy Collector.

The importer will then send the permit to the importing vessel, unless some of the articles are to be weighed, gauged, or measured, in which case he will take it first to the surveyor's office, for record and endorsement.

In sending permits to the importing vessel, great care should be taken that they are left only with the customs officer in charge, as leaving such with other persons and in improper hands is the fruitful source of errors, delays and annoyances in obtaining goods after entry.

On all permits where the examination of the goods is not to be made by the appraisers on the levee or wharf, a portion of merchandise is ordered to be sent to the public or appraiser's stores for appraisement.

The invoice, or other document in lieu thereof, deposited by the importer at time of entry, is sent by the Collector to the appraisers, to enable them to examine and appraise the goods ordered for that purpose; while at the appraisers' office the computations and extensions of the invoice are examined and tested by clerks charged with that duty. After the examination of the merchandise, the appraisers report, on the invoice, a description of the packages and goods examined and the result of their appraisement, and return the invoice to the invoice clerk in the Collector's office. Here the invoice is again placed with the entry, and both pass to the liquidating clerks for the final adjustment of the duties. By the report of the appraisers, as to value and damage, and the weigher's, gauger's, or measurer's return, as to quantity, all allowances for deficiency, damage, or excessive rate of duty, or additions for increase in value, excess in quantity, or rate of duty, are made, and the duty finally determined. This liquidation is examined and verified by clerks in the naval office and the entry returned to the Collector's office, where, if the liquidation shows that the ascertained duty is either in excess or less than the estimated duty originally paid, the entry is deposited with the cashier for either the collection or refunding of the difference between the estimated and and ascertained amount.

DELIVERY OF THE GOODS ORDERED FOR APPRAISEMENT.

The packages sent to the appraisers for examination are obtained by the importer by application to the permit or order clerk in the Collector's office, who, if the invoice has been returned by the appraisers and the entry liquidated without showing an additional amount of duty to be collected, will furnish the applicant with an order on the storekeeper in charge of the appraiser's stores, for the delivery of the packages. Should, however, the liquidation of the entry show an additional amount of duty to be paid, the importer will be first directed to the cashier's desk for the entry and payment of the additional amount. After payment, the entry, properly stamped and checked to exhibit that fact, will be delivered to him by the cashier. He will then present it to the deputy naval officer and returning to the order desk, receive an order for the delivery of the goods, which, on being delivered to the deputy Collector, together with the entry, will be signed by that officer, who will retain the entry. This order the importer will then hand to the storekeeper or clerk having charge of the general storage books in the Collector's office, for endorsement; after which, on its presentation to the storekeeper at the appraisers' stores, the examined packages will be delivered.

In some offices, the delivery orders are made out and enclosed in the entries on which sums are to be collected at the time they are deposited with the cashier. In these cases, the entry, after being checked in the naval office, will be taken to the deputy Collector, without going to the order desk.

APPLICATIONS FOR DAMAGE ALLOWANCE.

Should the importer ascertain that the merchandise entered, or which he desires to enter, has been damaged on the voyage of importation, he must, in order to obtain an abatement of the duties in consequence of such damage, make an application for an examination and estimate of the damage within ten working days after the landing of the merchandise. This application is made by obtaining at the Collector's office a blank of the proper form, *(see form under heading of custom house blanks,)* describing therein, carefully and accurately, the goods alleged to be damaged, together with the entered value, signing and taking the oath or affirmation before the Deputy Collector, and depositing the application with him. In these applications care should be taken to state where the goods are stored or may be found, for the information of the examining officer, as this will ensure more promptness in the execution of the warrant issued on the application.

Examinations for damage are made by the appraisers, conformable with the regulations on this subject, explained under that heading; and the merchandise should be so arranged by the importer, as to enable the examination to be thoroughly as well as expeditiously made.

ENTRY FOR CONSUMPTION BY APPRAISEMENT WITHOUT INVOICE.

In cases where no invoice has been received, and the importer desires to enter the goods, it is necessary for him to present an application in writing, to the Collector, for the issue of an order for the appraisement of the merchandise. (A form of this application will be found under the heading of custom house blanks.)

This application, together with the bill of lading, will be handed to the permit or order clerk, who will prepare the order for appraisement, and an order on the inspector or storekeeper, as the case may be, to send the goods to the appraiser's store; these he will deliver to the importer, who having first paid the fees at the cashier's desk, will present the documents to the Deputy Collector, when the oath on the application will be administered, and the order for the goods signed and returned to the importer, while the remaining papers are retained. The importer will send the order for the goods to the vessel or store, as the case may be, and after the goods have been examined, and the appraisement order, with the appraiser's report thereon, returned to the Collector's office, he will obtain the appraisement from the invoice or order clerk, and presenting it to the Deputy Collector and obtaining thereon his written permission to enter, he will proceed to make an entry in the same manner as required for the consumption entry, substituting the appraisement for the invoice, and giving bond to produce an invoice.

Where imports have been entered by appraisement, in the absence of an invoice, and the value in the invoice afterwards produced is less than that found by the appraisers on the entry, no allowance by return of duties can be made for the difference. But if the invoice shows a value greater than that ascertained by the appraisement, the Confederate States will be entitled to duties on such excess of value.

WAREHOUSE ENTRIES.

The manner of making entries for warehousing is the same as that for consumption, with the exception that the warehouse bond is executed at the bond desk instead of the penal bond, and paying duties to the cashier. *See explanation under Warehouse System.*

Warehouse and transportation entries are made in triplicate, one of which, with a copy of the invoice, is left with the warehouse clerk; otherwise, the routine is the same as the entry for warehousing. *More full particulars will be obtained by referring to the explanation this class of entry in the Warehouse System.*

Entries for withdrawal from warehouse are made by describing the goods to be withdrawn on the entry of the proper form, (made in duplicate,) and delivering it to the warehouse clerk in the Collector's office, who will compare it with the warehouse records, transcribe therefrom to the entry the amounts of value and duty, and make the delivery permit; these documents will then be taken to a similar clerk in the naval office, who will verify the amounts of value and duty by a comparison with his records, and return the original entry and permit. Duty will then be paid to the cashier, or bond given at the bond desk according to the class of entry made, and the entry and permit presented to the deputy naval officer and Deputy Collector for completion and signature.

Withdrawal entries for exportation are made in triplicate, one copy of which, after passing the Collector's and naval office, is deposited with the surveyor.

Further explanations in reference to entries for warehousing or withdrawal are not deemed necessary, as the subject has been explained in detail in the article explanatory of the Warehousing System.

ENTRANCE AND CLEARANCE OF VESSELS.

ENTRY OF VESSELS FROM FOREIGN PORTS.

It is necessary that the manifests (three copies) of vessels from foreign ports should be made out before arrival, in order to be presented to the boarding officer upon arrival. They should include *everything* on board; and, after stating the cargo laden at the port of departure, if there should be any return cargo, it should then be added under that head. If there are any surplus stores, these should then be particularized; and finally, the passengers' names, individually, with the numbers of packages of baggage belonging to each—the whole to be signed by the master.

Where there are passengers, a separate list, besides the names on each manifest, including the names, ages, sex, occupation, country to which they severally belong, and of which they intend to become inhabitants, and if any have died on the passage, will also be necessary.

If any part of the cargo is to be landed at a different port than the first one of entry, it must be so stated in the manifest, as otherwise that privilege will be lost, and the cargo required to be landed at the first port of entry.

ENTRY AT THE CUSTOM HOUSE.

On making entry of a vessel at the custom house, the master will deliver to the clerk at the entrance desk in the Collector's office, duplicate manifests of the entire cargo, together with the passenger list and register, if a vessel of the Confederate States; and this clerk, having prepared the proper oaths and endorsed the amount of fees, light money, hospital dues, etc., on the original manifest, will return both to the master, who will proceed to the cashier's desk, pay the fees and light dues, etc., and from thence to the deputy naval officer, where he will leave the duplicate manifest, and then take the original and passenger list to the Deputy Collector, who will administer the oath, and, retaining the documents, complete the entrance.

Masters of vessels from foreign ports will obtain permits to land chronometers, etc., at the permit desk, and present them to the Deputy Collector for signature at the time of entering the vessel.

Notice of the time in which he desires to discharge cargo will also be given by the master, at the time of entering his vessel.

ENTRANCE OF VESSELS, COASTWISE.

Nothing further is required than to present to the entrance clerk in the Collector's office the manifest, endorsed with the clearance from the custom house at the port of departure, and the register or enrolment, (if a vessel of the Confederate States,) the payment of the fees and light money to the cashier, having the amount checked in the naval office, and the final delivery of the manifest to the Deputy Collector.

CLEARANCES.

CLEARANCE OF VESSELS FOR FOREIGN PORTS.

Every shipper must clear his goods at the custom house *before* the vessel can clear. From these shippers' clearances the vessel's manifest is to be made, after the same form, and including all the particulars therein contained. If there is any change of owner or master, notice thereof should be given, at least the day previous, in order that the register may be endorsed, or a new one issued.

Inquiry should also be made, a day or two previous to clearing, (in case of vessels last from foreign ports,) whether the return of the inward cargo corresponds with the manifest, as delays may otherwise occur in settling discrepancies, which to adjust may and do frequently detain vessels from clearing, when the hurry is great, and consignees are anxious to get their vessels to sea.

If there is any cargo brought in the vessel, not to be landed, a permit must be obtained to retain the same on board, several days before clearing, as the officer discharging the vessel cannot make his return without it; and, without *his* return, the vessel cannot be cleared.

CLEARANCE AT CUSTOM HOUSE.

In order to clear his vessel for a foreign port at the custom house, the master will present duplicate manifests of the outward cargo to the manifest clerk in the Collector's office, who will check the same as evidence that the inward cargo has been correctly accounted for. The master will then take both manifests to the clearance clerk in the Collector's office, who will prepare all the papers needed, such as certificate of clearance, bill of health, etc., and on the original manifest endorse the fees chargeable, and deliver these documents to the master, who will pay to the cashier the fees, have the same checked and papers signed by the deputy naval officer, and present the documents to the Deputy Collector, who will administer the oath, retain one manifest, and sign and deliver the other papers. With these the master (if it be a vessel of the Confederate States) will return to the clearance clerk and obtain the register deposited at the time of entrance.

In case of a *foreign* vessel, all that the master requires, in addition to the manifest, is a clearance and bill of health, upon presenting which to the consul of his nation, he will receive all other necessary papers.

In case any part of the cargo consists of goods subject to inspection, by the laws of the Confederate States, a certificate of inspections must be produced, previous to clearance.

Before clearance, the shippers or consignors of the cargo must deliver a manifest of their portion of the cargo, under oath, setting forth the kind, quantity and value of each article, and the foreign port where intended to be landed, and pay all export duties.

CLEARANCE OF VESSELS COASTWISE.

Duplicate manifests, made out from the bills of lading, (number of packages in each bill of lading being stated in *writing*,) with the shippers and consignees, and their places of residence, and the presentation of these documents to the clearance clerk, cashier, deputy naval officer and Deputy Collector, (as in case of clearance for foreign ports,) is all that is required.

UNLADING OF CARGOES.—TIME WITHIN WHICH VESSELS MUST DISCHARGE.

Vessels of 300 tons burden or less, arriving from a foreign port, are allowed fifteen working days from the time within which the report of the master is required to be made to the Collector, for the discharge of her cargo; or if she exceed 300 tons burden, she is allowed twenty working days for that purpose. All merchandise found on board at the expiration of these periods, not reported for some other district or a foreign port or place, must be taken possession of by the Collector. But with consent of the owner or consignee of such merchandise, or with consent of the owner or master of the vessel, the remaining cargo may be so taken possession of after five day's notice to the Collector.

VESSELS LADEN WITH SALT OR COAL.

The foregoing limitation does not apply to vessels laden with salt or coal, requiring a longer time to discharge their cargoes, which the Collector is authorized to grant; the wages of the inspector in charge to be paid by the master or owner of the vessel, for each day's service in excess of such limitation; and if, by reason of the delivery of the cargo in several districts, the limitation is exceeded, the compensation of the inspector in charge is to be so paid for every day's excess; and before clearance shall be granted to such vessel, the inspector must render an account to the Collector of all sums so paid to him, or so due and payable, by the owner or master.

STEAM VESSELS.

Merchandise imported in steam vessels, appearing by bill of lading to be deliverable immediately after entry of the vessel, may be taken possession of by the Collector and deposited in bonded warehouse. But if it does not appear by the bill of lading that the merchandise is so deliverable, the Collector may take possession thereof and deposit the same in bonded warehouse, at the request of the owner, master or consignee of the vessel, on three day's notice, after entry of the vessel, to the Collector.

MISCELLANEOUS VALUABLE INFORMATION,

EXTRACTED FROM TREASURY REGULATIONS, ETC.

CUSTOM HOUSE BLANKS.

The various blank forms of entries will be found in the warehouse system and explanation of consumption entries. The following are also some of the blanks in general use:

FORM OF APPLICATION FOR DAMAGE ALLOWANCE.

TO THE COLLECTOR OF CUSTOMS:

SIR: An order to ascertain and estimate the damage (here specify the merchandise and its entered value) on   ,
imported by   , in the   ,
whereof   is master, from   ,
is respectfully requested.

PORT OF   , '8   .

(Signed,)

FORM OF OATH OF APPLICANT.

I,   , of the firm of   , do solemnly   , that I have personally inspected and examined the merchandise described in the foregoing application to the Collector of the customs; that the same has sustained damage on the voyage of importation, and has not been landed ten days from the vessel in which the importation was made: So help me God.

Sworn to, this   , before me,

(Signed,)

FORM OF APPLICATION FOR APPRAISEMENT WITHOUT INVOICE.

TO THE COLLECTOR OF CUSTOMS,

       Port of   ,

SIR: The undersigned would respectfully request you to issue an order to appraise and estimate the value of the packages marked and numbered as follows, for which no invoice has been received:

MARKS AND NUMBERS.	DESCRIPTION OF PACKAGES AND CONTENTS.

 Said goods were imported by   , in the   , whereof   is master, from

        186

  (Signed,)

 I,   do solemnly swear that I have received no invoice of the goods described in the foregoing application to the Collector of the customs, the cause being

And that if at any time hereafter I receive an invoice thereof, I shall immediately produce the same to the Collector of this port. So help me God.

 Sworn to before me, this   186 .

      Collector.

Form of Inward Manifest of Cargo.

Report and manifest of the cargo laden on board of the   , whereof   is master, which cargo was taken on board at   , burden   tons, built at   , and owned by   , merchants at   , as per register granted at   , the   day of   , and bound for   .

MARKS.	NO. INCLUSIVE.	PACKAGES AND CONTENTS.	BY WHOM SHIPPED.	TO WHOM CONSIGNED, OR IF TO ORDER.	PLACE OF CONSIGNEE'S RESIDENCE.	PORTS OF DESTINATION.

Form of Outward Manifest.

Report and manifest of the cargo laden at the port of   , on board the   ,   master, bound for   port.

MARKS.	NUMBERS.	PACKAGES OR ARTICLES IN BULK.	CONTENTS or QUANTITIES.	VALUE AT THE PORT OF EXPORTATION.

FORM OF CLEARANCE OF VESSEL WITH CARGO TO A FOREIGN PORT.

DISTRICT OF   , PORT OF

These are to certify all whom it doth concern, that   , master or commander of the   , burden   tons, or thereabouts, mounted with   guns, navigated with   men,   built, and bound for   , having on board   , hath here entered and cleared his said vessel according to law.

Given under our hands and seals, at the custom house of   , this   day of 18   .

    (Signed,)
    (Signed,)

FORM OF CERTIFICATE OF PAYMENT OF LIGHT MONEY,

Attached by Collector to Register, Enrolment or License of Vessels in the Coasting Trade.

CUSTOM HOUSE,

    Collector's Office,   186 .

This is to certify, that the   called the   , whereof   is at present master, measuring   tons, trading regularly between ports of the Confederate States, has this day paid at this office light money, amounting to   dollars, as provided by the act of 16th March, 1861.

                                    Collector.

FORM OF A CUSTOM HOUSE POWER OF ATTORNEY.

Know all men by these presents, that   do make, constitute and appoint   to be   true and lawful attorney for   and in   name and behalf, to receive and to enter at the custom house, in the District of goods, wares and merchandise

for   and in   name to sign, seal, and execute and deliver any bond or bonds which may be required for securing the duties on any such goods, wares and merchandise; and also for   and in   name to sign, seal, execute and deliver any bond or bonds requisite for obtaining the debenture on such goods, wares or merchandise, when exported for or by   , to receive and give receipts for the amount of said debenture , and generally to transact all business in which   or may be interested at the said custom house, in relation to the said importation or consignment,

with power also an attorney or attorneys to make and substitute, hereby ratifying and confirming all that shall or may be lawfully done by virtue hereof. This power shall remain in full force until revoked by a written notice, given to the Collector.

Witness   hand and seal , the   day of   , A. D. one thousand eight hundred and

Sealed and delivered in the presence of us,

Be it known, that on the day of the date hereof, before me, , notary public, personally appeared

and acknowledged the foregoing letter of attorney as and for act and deed. In witness whereof, I have hereunto set my hand and affixed my notarial seal, the   day of   , 186 .

Form of Power of Substitution.

Know all men by these presents, that I,   , by virtue of the power of attorney executed by   to me, bearing date the day of   , 186 , do substitute and appoint to do, perform and execute every act or thing which I might or could do, in, by and under the aforesaid power.

In witness whereof, I have hereunto set my hand and seal, this   day of   , 186 .

In the presence of

ADMEASUREMENT OF VESSELS FOR TONNAGE, ETC.

RULE OF ADMEASUREMENT OF DOUBLE DECKED VESSELS.

The officer measuring shall, if the ship or vessel be double decked, take the length thereof, from the fore part of the main stem to the after part of the stern post, above the upper deck; the breadth thereof, at the broadest part above the main wales, half of which breadth shall be accounted the depth of such vessel, and shall then deduct from the length three-fifths of the breadth; multiply the remainder by the breadth, and the product by the depth, and shall divide this last product by ninety-five, the quotient whereof shall be deemed the true contents or tonnage of such ship or vessel.

OF SINGLE DECKED VESSELS.

If a ship or vessel be single decked, the said surveyor, or other person, shall take the length and breadth as above directed in respect to a double decked ship or vessel, shall deduct from the said length three-fifths of the breadth, and, taking the depth from the under side of the deck plank to the ceiling in the hold, shall multiply and divide, as aforesaid, and the quotient shall be deemed the tonnage of such ship or vessel.

RULE FOR ADMEASUREMENT OF COAL IN FLAT BOATS.

Take the length outside, allow one foot for break of bow, take breadth at the bow, midship and aft, take depth about four feet six inches from the side, so as to clear the floor beams, which will indicate the true depth by the sounding rod; if sounding is wet, ascertain the top level by the eye; multiply the length calculated by the average breadth, and the sum total by the average depth, and divide the grand total by FOUR, which gives the quantity in barrels. The grand total gives the quantity in bushels.

LIST OF FEES.

The following is the list of fees required by law to be paid at the several custom houses, and no other fees shall be received than those here specially enumerated:

For admeasuring every vessel, in order to the enrolment, or licensing and recording the same, if of 5 tons and less than 20	$0 50
Of 20 and not over 70	0 75
Over 70 and not over 100	1 00
Over 100 tons	1 50
For certificate of enrolment	50
Endorsement on certificate of enrolment	20
License, and granting the same, including bond, if not over 20 tons	25
Above 20 and not over 100	50
Over 100 tons	1 00
Endorsement on a license	20
Certifying manifest, and granting permit for licensed vessels to go from district to district, under 50 tons,	25
Over 50 tons	50
Receiving certified manifest, and granting permit on arrival of such vessel, if under 50 tons	25
Over fifty tons	50
For certifying manifest, and granting permission to registered vessels to go from district to district	1 50
Receiving certified manifest, and granting permit on	

arrival of such registered vessel..................	1 50
Granting permit to a vessel not belonging to a citizen of the Confederate States, to go from district to district, and receiving manifest...................	2 00
Receiving manifest, and granting permit to unload for last mentioned vessel, on arrival at one district from another...	2 00
Granting permit for vessel carrying on fishery to trade at a foreign port...............................	25
Report and entry of foreign goods imported in such vessel	25
Entry of vessel of 100 tons and more...............	2 50
Clearance of vessels of 100 tons and more..........	2 50
Entry of vessels under 100 tons....................	1 50
Clearance of ditto................................	1 50
Post entry..	2 00
Permit to land or deliver goods....................	20
Bond taken officially..........c...................	40
Permit to load goods for exportation entitled to drawback	30
Debenture or other official certificate..............	20
Bill of health.....................................	20
Official documents, except register, required by any merchant, owner or master of any vessel not before enumerated.......................................	20
Admeasurement, and certifying vessels of 100 tons and under ....1 cent per ton.	
Over 100 and not over 200........................	1 50
Over 200...	2 00
Other services to be performed by the surveyor, in vessels of 100 tons and more, having on board merchandise subject to duty........................	3 00
For like services in vessels under 100 tons, having similar merchandise.............................	1 50
All vessels not having merchandise subject to duty...	66⅔
Protection....,...................................	25

Crew list	25
Certificate of registry and bond	2 25
Endorsement on register	1 00
General permit to ship, to land passengers' baggage	20

Weighing: $1\frac{7}{8}$ cent per 112 pounds.
Gauging: casks, 12 cents each; cases and baskets, $4\frac{1}{2}$ cents each. Ale, porter, etc., $1\frac{1}{2}$ cent per dozen bottles.
Measuring: coal, 90 per 100 bushels; chalk, brimstone, etc., 90 cents per 100 bushels; salt, 75 cents per 100 bushels; potatoes, seeds, grain and all other measurable articles, 45 cents per 100 bushels. Marble, mahogany, cedar wood, etc., the actual expense incurred.

} When invoice does not contain the weight measure or gauge of merchandise, required to be weigh'd, measured or gaug'd and when goods are with drawn from warehouse in less quantity than the entire importation.

For recording all bills of sale, mortgages, hypothecations, or conveyance of vessels, under act of July 29, 1850	50
For recording all certificates for recording and cancelling any such conveyances	50
For furnishing a certificate setting forth the names of the owners of any registered or enrolled vessel, the parts or proportions owned by each, and also the material facts of any existing bill of sale, mortgage, hypothecation, or other incumbrance, the date, amount of such incumbrance, and from and to whom made	1 00
For furnishing copies of such records, for each bill of sale, mortgage, or other conveyance	50

The term, "or other official certificate," will embrace every certificate requiring the Collector's official signature in the regular transaction of the business of the custom house, including his certificate to an oath or invoice.

The term, "permit to land goods," is intended to include all permits to land, whether for immediate delivery or otherwise, all permits to warehouse or public store, or delivery therefrom, all permits to transfer goods from one store to another when required by owner or importer, and all permits or orders to appraise without invoice.

The term, "permit for exportation," is intended to apply to all permits for export or transport from vessel or warehouse.

PERSONS AUTHORIZED TO MAKE ENTRIES, ETC.

Entries are to be received when made by the owner or owners, consignee or consignees, such ownership or consignment to be shown by the invoice and bill of lading.

In case of the absence or sickness of the owner or consignee, an agent authorized by a duly authenticated *power of attorney* will be permitted to make entry in the name of such owner or consignee.

When the owner resides in the Confederate States, but is sick or absent from the port, and entry is made by the importer, consignee or agent, such entry can not be received unless the *invoice* presented is verified by the oath of the owner; or the importer, consignee or agent executes a bond in a penal sum equal to the amount of the duties assessable on the merchandise, to produce, within four months, the invoice duly verified by the oath of said owner.

When the invoice and bill of lading is made to order, or to the order of a banker through whose credit the merchandise may have been purchased, the party presenting the bill of lading and invoice and taking the owner's oath, will be regarded as the owner of the merchandise, and as such be permitted to make entry in his own name.

This provision will not authorize entries by parties who may become sub-purchasers on or after arrival, as such, under the laws, have not the authority to enter the goods. In such cases, the entry must be made by the *original* importer or consignee.

The transfer of a bill of lading by endorsement is not sufficient to constitute the assignee an agent, or to authorize him to enter.

The assignee of a bill of lading or invoice, however, will be considered the owner when taking the owner's oath that the goods were purchased abroad and imported for him; and as such may be permitted to enter.

In cases where the bill of lading and invoice is to order, and does not express the name of the owner or consignee, and the invoice is accompanied by the oath of an owner, entry can only be made by the agent of such owner, authorized by a power of attorney.

Entries cannot be allowed on an invoice and bill of lading *to order*, when the invoice is not verified by the owner's oath.

No entry for warehousing can be received unless it is accompanied by an invoice, and the importer designates on said entry the warehouse in which he desires the goods deposited.

Entries for withdrawal from warehouse can only be made by the importer, consignee, agent, or some person authorized by him on the withdrawal entry.

Merchandise shipped by several vessels cannot be embraced in a single invoice and be covered by a single consular certificate. The merchandise shipped by each vessel must be embraced in a distinct invoice, duly verified, if on foreign account, by the oath of the owner, and authenticated by consular certificate.

The invoices presented on entry must be the true and original invoices received, and be made out in the currency of the country or place from which the importation is made.

Invoices of ad valorem or free goods, when made out in a foreign depreciated currency, or a currency the value of which is not fixed by the laws of the Confederate States, must be accompanied by a consular certificate, showing the value of such currency in the Confederate States or Spanish silver dollar.

If this certificate is not produced, the importer will be required to give a bond to produce the same.

The practice of allowing custom house brokers, express agents, and other parties, not the owners or original consignees, to make entries of merchandise in their own names, on the production of bill of lading endorsed by the importer or consignee, is in contravention of the express provisions of law and the decisions of the courts.

Entry must, in all cases, be made by the owner or consignee, who alone is authorized, under our revenue system, to take the prescribed oath, give the requisite bond, and pay the duties; and in cases where, from either of the causes adverted to in the act, the owner or consignee may be unable to attend personally at the custom house, he will be required to be represented by a duly constituted agent or attorney, whose power must be lodged with the Collector, who will make entry and perform all the necessary acts in the owner's name, giving bond for the due production of his oath.

DUTIABLE VALUE OF IMPORTS.

The value upon which duties are to be assessed is established to be:

First. The actual market value or wholesale price of the merchandise in the principal markets of the country from which it was imported into the Confederate States, at the date of exportation, to be ascertained by appraisement.

Second. All costs and charges, except insurance, and including, in every case, a charge for commissions at the usual rates, to be ascertained and added to the value found by appraisement, by the Collector and naval officer, or the Collector alone at ports where there is no naval officer.

These charges are:

First. The expenses of putting up and packing, together with the value of the sack, package, box, crate, hogshead, barrel, bale, cask, can, bottles, jars, vessels and demijohns, and coverings of all kinds.

Second. Commissions must in every case be made a dutiable charge at the usual rates, but never less than 2½ per cent., without the special sanction of the Department, nor less than is stated in the invoice. If it appear on the face of the invoice or entry at less than the usual rate, it must be advanced to that rate for the ascertainment of dutiable value. Where there is a distinct brokerage, or where brokerage is a usual charge at the place of shipment or purchase, that is to be added likewise. Commissions on the amount of *shipping charges* at the foreign port of exportation constitute one of the charges liable to duty under existing laws and instructions.

The following have been decided by the Department to be the usual rates of commissions:

From all places in France, except Paris.......2 per cent.
" Paris.................................3 " "
" Bremen...............................2 " "
" United States........................2½ " "

If from other places the rate is claimed to be less than 2½ per cent., the fact must be established to the satisfaction of the Treasury Department.

Third. Export duty, as on silks from China, storage at the foreign shipping ports, cost of putting cargoes on board ship, including drayage, labor, bill of lading, lighterage, town dues and shipping charges, dock or wharf dues, and all charges to place the articles on shipboard, and fire insurance, if effected for a period prior to the shipment of goods to the Confederate States.

Marine insurance is not to be treated as a dutiable charge.

Freight, or cost of transportation, from the foreign port of exportation, is not a dutiable charge.

DISCOUNTS.

Discounts exhibited on the invoice, and according to the usual and established usage of the trade, may be allowed; but in no case where the invoice value will be reduced thereby below the foreign market value of the merchandise at the date of exportation to the Confederate States.

ENTRY OF THE MANUFACTURES OR PRODUCTIONS OF THE CONFEDERATE STATES EXPORTED AND BROUGHT BACK.

Articles of the growth, production or manufacture of the Confederate States, exported to a foreign country and brought back to the Confederate States in the same condition in which exported, and upon which no drawback or bounty has been allowed, are entitled to entry free of duty, if proved to be of the growth, production or manufacture of the Confederate States, in the manner provided by law, and the regulations of the Treasury Department.

By the 48th section of the general collection act of 2d March, 1799, it is made requisite that the merchandise should have been cleared out on its original exportation from the Confederate States. If it be brought back to the port of original exportation, and was regularly cleared for its foreign destination, the fact will be shown to the satisfaction of the Collector and naval officer, by the records of the customs, and by the oath or affirmation of the person or persons having knowledge of the facts, which oath or affirmation will be in the following form:

DISTRICT OF   , PORT OF   .

I,   , do solemnly, sincerely and truly swear, (or affirm, as the case may be,) that the several articles of merchandise mentioned in the entry hereto annexed, are, to the best of my knowledge and belief, truly and bona fide of the growth, production or manufacture of the Confederate States, (as the case may be,) and that they were truly exported and imported as therein expressed, and that no drawback, bounty or allowance has been paid or admitted thereon, or any part thereof. So help me God.

Sworn to this   day of   .

But when the re-importation is made into a port other than that of the original exportation from the Confederate States, the law requires the production of a certificate, testifying the exportation thereof, from the Collector and naval officer of the port where the exportation was made; which certificate shall be in the following form:

COLLECTOR AND NAVAL OFFICER'S CERTIFICATE.

District of   , Port of

This is to certify, that there were cleared out at this port, on the (insert the day of clearance) in the (insert the denomination and name of the vessel) whereof (insert the name) was master, for (insert the port or place for which cleared) the following articles of merchandise, (here enumerate the number of packages, their denomination, marks and numbers, together with their contents,) on which no drawback, allowance or bounty hath been paid or admitted.

Collector.

Naval officer.

If the foregoing certificate cannot at once be procured, and the proof otherwise required be made, free entry will be permitted, on a bond to produce such certificate being given to the satisfaction of the Collector of the district of re-importation, in a sum equal to what the duties on the merchandise would be, if it were not of the production, growth or manufacture of the Confederate States.

To guard against fraud on the revenue, and insure identity, it is also thought proper to direct that, before admitting any such merchandise to free entry, the Collector shall require, in addition to proof of clearance, the production of a statement, certified by the proper officer of the customs at the foreign port from which the re-importation was made, of the fact that such merchandise was imported into that country from the Confederate States in the condition in which it is returned; the certificate of the foreign customs officer to be authenticated by the consul of the Confederate States.

In cases where the certificate of the custom house officer at the foreign port of shipment required for the free entry of manufactures or productions of the Confederate States exported and brought back, cannot be obtained for the reason of there being no such officer at the foreign port of exportation, a certificate of the foreign recipient of the goods or his representative having a knowledge of the facts, duly authenticated by the consul of the Confederate States, or of a friendly nation, may be admitted in lieu thereof.

DUTIES, ALLOWANCES, DEFICIENCIES, ETC.

The foreign market value of imported merchandise, as ascertained and returned by the appraisers, with costs and charges added, is to be taken as the dutiable value of the same; but under no circumstances can the duty be assessed upon any amount less than the invoice value.

Duties on imports accrue on the arrival of the importing vessel in a port of entry with intent to unlade thereat, and not upon the entry of the cargo at the custom house.

All importations liable by law to duties, are so liable for legal duties unpaid at any time after their entry as before, although, through an erroneous construction of law or Treasury regulations, by Collectors or subordinate officers, or from any other cause, they may have been brought into the Confederate States, or passed the custom house, without the payment of the duties imposed by law.

Dutiable merchandise imported into the Confederate States, and afterwards exported, although it may have paid duty on the first importation, is liable to duty on every subsequent importation into the Confederate States.

The value of foreign goods, at the date of exportation to the Confederate States, is that on which, under the laws, the duty is to be levied; and all attempts to evade the payment of duties on such value, by recourse to alleged purchases at remote periods from that date, and the substitution of any other name for that of the true owner or importer at the time of exportation, are to be held as fraudulent, and dealt with accordingly.

ADDITIONAL DUTY.

The additional duties incurred under the 5th section of the Tariff Act of 1861, must be levied upon the dutiable value of the merchandise, as ascertained by the appraisers, although alleged to have been damaged during the voyage of importation; but when the actual damage shall have been afterwards established by the proper proof, appraised and allowed, the proper proportions of the regular tariff duty, but not the additional duty, assessed as above, are to be abated.

When the ADDITIONAL DUTIES imposed under the 5th section of the Tariff Act of 1861, have been incurred, they must be paid before the delivery of the merchandise for consumption, or withdrawal from warehouse for transportation in bond, or before permission shall be given for lading the merchandise on board the vessel from warehouse for exportation to a foreign port; and in no case can they be returned as a drawback of duties.

Additions to entries of goods, under the 5th section of the Tariff Act of the 21st of May, 1861, on privilege therefor given in the 5th section of the act referred to, is to enable importers of any goods, on making entry of the same, to add to the cost or value given in the invoice, to bring it up to the true market value abroad, and by so doing, exempt the goods from the additional duty imposed by said section. The additions contemplated by the law in such cases must take place at the time of making entry, and cannot be allowed at any subsequent period.

Allowances for deficiency properly reported and ascertained, are to be made in assessing the additional duty incurred, under 5th section act 21st May, 1861.

ALLOWANCES.

When it shall be ascertained by the Collector at whose port the importation is made, that by actual gauge, weighing or measuring, as the case may be, the quantity of merchandise imported is less than the quantity given in the invoice, and the said Collector shall be satisfied from proofs adduced, that the diminution was consequent on leakage, drainage, breakage, shrinkage, evaporation or accidental loss or destruction, during the voyage of importation, and was not caused in whole or in part by the abstraction from the quantity given in the invoice of any portion thereof, with a view to its illegal introduction into the Confederate States, or for any other purpose, he is authorized, in the estimate of duties on the importation, to make allowance for the difference between the invoice and ascertained quantity; it being considered by the Department that the Tariff Act levies duties on imports only; and consequently, that with the restrictions above stated, duties on merchandise are to be exacted on the quantity which arrives in the Confederate States, and not on the quantity shipped at the foreign port.

Where the voyage of importation has terminated, and the full quantity shipped of merchandise, as per invoice, has been landed in the Confederate States, no claim to allowance for deficiency in quantity, subsequently incurred by leakage or otherwise, can be granted.

Lost or missing articles or packages appearing on the invoice, are not allowed for in the estimate of duties, unless shown by satisfactory proof not to have been originally laden on board, or lost or destroyed by accident during the voyage.

Allowances for leakage, etc., in warehouse cannot be made, as dutiable quantity is ascertained at time of importation and entry.

LIQUORS INVOICED AND ENTERED BY THE PACKAGE.

Where wines or other liquors are invoiced and entered by the package without quantity stated in measure, the appraisers will be required to report what quantity the invoice value will cover. On their report, allowance is to be made on liquidation for the difference, if any, between gross and net, if the result is short; but if it be found that the actual quantity bears a value exceeding the value given in the invoice by ten per cent. or more, the goods having been invoiced and entered by the package, the twenty per cent. additional duty, as provided in section 5th of the Tariff Act of 1861, is to be levied on the appraised value.

In all cases, however, where wines and liquors are purchased, invoiced and entered by the gallon, the excess or deficiency of gallons will be ascertained by the gauger before liquidation of duties.

ABATEMENT OF DUTIES FOR DAMAGE DURING THE VOYAGE OF IMPORTATION.

In pursuance of the 52d section of the general collection act of 2d March,1799, no abatement of duties on merchandise, on account of damage occurring during the voyage of importation, can be allowed, unless proof to ascertain such damage shall be lodged in the custom house within ten working days after the landing of such merchandise.

The term "during the voyage" means after the vessel has started from the foreign port of exportation, and during the voyage to, and before her arrival at, her port of destination in the Confederate States.

Where the article was damaged before the voyage commenced, and this damage proceeded from rust, decay, dampness, or other cause, which may have rendered the merchandise unfit to withstand the ordinary risks of importation, no allowance is to be made; the law, in authorizing abatement of duties for damage, having reference to the unforeseen contingency of damage during the voyage of importation.

The proof of damage required to be so lodged with the Collector, will consist of the claim of the importer or his agent for the allowance, in writing, subscribed and sworn to by him, specifying, by marks and numbers, the particular articles or packages which are alleged to be damaged, the character of the goods, and the value at which he has entered them, respectively; and the official examination and appraisement must be confined to the articles and packages so specified, and proved to have received damage during the voyage, except in the case of the discovery of damage in the appraiser's department.

The specification of articles, as above required, must in no case be dispensed with.

No damage is to be allowed in any case, except on merchandise on which damage is duly claimed, proved, and found by the examining officers, on actual inspection, to be a' substantial and actual damage, and incurred during the voyage of importation; and if the articles be contained in a package, the package must be opened, and a strict examination made, in order that the extent of the actual damage may be ascertained, and fictitious or pretended damage detected.

No average allowance for damage is to be made, and damage on the voyage of importation is to be ascertained by reference to the value of the merchandise in the principal markets of the country whence imported, and not according to the home valuation. Auction or forced sales are not regarded as a fair criterion of damage.

Damage on the voyage of importation must be ascertained at the port where the vessel originally enters, and cannot be certified from any other port; and no re-appraisement is authorized by law in case of allowance for damage.

The law authorizes an allowance to be made in the assessment of duties for actual damage occurring during the voyage of importation, properly proved and estimated; and a rigid scrutiny will be made in each case to ascertain, not only the amount of damage, but whether it occurred on the voyage of importation or not.

RELIEF FROM DUTIES ON GOODS INJURED OR DESTROYED WHILE IN BOND.

The 8th section of the warehousing law of the 28th March, 1854, providing for relief from duties in case of the destruction, in whole or in part, of bonded goods while in warehouse, or in transitu, under warehouse transportation bond, from one port to another, or in the appraisers' store undergoing appraisal, it is deemed proper to state that the law proposes relief where actual injury is incurred, or the property is destroyed, in whole or in part, by accidental fire, shipwreck or other like casualty; but does not provide for deterioration from dampness or other like cause, in the warehouse or in transitu under bond.

Application for relief under the 8th section of the act of 28th March, 1854, must be made in writing, under oath or affirmation, by the claimant to the Collector of the port where the alleged injury or destruction, in whole or in part, of the goods, wares and merchandise, by accidental fire, or other like casualty, occurred, setting forth that the same happened while the goods remained in the custody of the officers of the customs, in a public or private warehouse under bond, or in the appraisers' stores undergoing appraisal, or while in transportation under bond, describing the place and manner of the accident, together with the extent of the injury, loss, or destruction, and the precise time when sustained.

This statement must be accompanied by affidavits of two or more credible and disinterested persons, as to the injury, loss, or destruction aforesaid.

On receipt of the foregoing application and statement, the Collector will subjoin thereto an official statement of the officers of the customs connected with the custody of the goods, as to the facts stated by the claimant, together with a statement whether the store or building in question was, at the time of the occurrence, a duly constituted bonded warehouse under the law, or appraiser's store, as the case may be.

The Collector will report the foregoing to the Department, giving his views as to the character of the proof and the validity of the claim, stating the date of maturity, and parties to each bond, the amount due on each, the amount of duties, if any, paid, together with any views or facts connected with the case he may deem useful in enabling the Department to discharge its duty under the law.

When total loss or damage is alleged to have occurred in the course of transportation from one port to another under bond, in pursuance of law and the reguletions of the Department, applications for relief must be made in the following form. In cases of total loss of the vessel or vehicle in which transported, the application must be sustained by the protest of the master or conductor of such vessel or vehicle, the affidavit of the applicant, setting forth that the goods so alleged to be lost were actually on board such vessel or vehicle, and have been totally lost, and no reasonable expectation exists of saving any part thereof, together with the bill of lading, or other receipt for the transportation of said goods. In cases of damage when the goods have arrived at the port of destination, the application of the party must be sustained by evidence as hereinbefore prescribed in cases of loss in warehouse, and must be lodged with the Collector within ten days after the landing of the merchandise, and while the goods are in the possession of the officers of the customs, and due appraisement will be made of the goods so alleged to be damaged, as in the case of damage occurring on voyages of direct importation from foreign ports.

It will be borne in mind, however, that no abatement of duties, satisfaction, or cancellation of the bond will be made under the 8th section of the act of the 28th March, 1854, without the previous sanction of the Treasury Department.

RE-APPRAISEMENT.

If the importer be dissatisfied with the decision of the appraisers, or the officer of the customs acting as appraiser, he may, in pursuance of the provisions of the 17th section of the act of August 30th, 1842, if he have complied with their requirements, give notice in writing, to the Collector, of such dissatisfaction. This notice will be given, in all cases, within twenty-four hours, and may be in the following form:

IMPORTER'S NOTICE TO COLLECTOR, CLAIMING RE-APPRAISEMENT.

186 .

SIR: As I consider the appraisement made by the Confederate States appraisers too high on   , having been imported by   , in the   , from   ,
I have to request that they may be re-appraised pursuant to law, with as little delay as your convenience will permit.

Very respectfully,

To   , Collector of the Customs.

Whereupon, the Collector will select two discreet and experienced merchants, citizens of the Confederate States, familiar with the character and value of the goods in question, to examine and appraise the same, agreeably to the provisions of law. The merchants selected will be notified by the Collector of their appointment, and of the time and place of the re-examination. The importer will likewise be notified of the time and place, but not of the name of the merchants selected to assist in the re-appraisement.

Merchants selected will be sworn to faithfully discharge their duty before entering on the re-appraisement.

The importer or his agent will be allowed to be present, and to offer such explanations and statements as may be pertinent to to the case.

An appraisement legally made by the Confederate States appraisers, and affirmed by merchant appraisers, the duties having been levied and paid accordingly, will not be re-opened upon opinions afterwards expressed by the merchants on testimony not before them when acting as officers of the Confederate States on the appeal.

Importers are concluded by their appeal to merchant appraisers, from afterwards alleging any informality in the proceedings of the Confederate States appraisers on the original appraisement.

COMPENSATION OF MERCHANT APPRAISERS.

The merchant appraiser is entitled, under existing laws, to a compensation of five dollars per diem while so employed, whether one or more cases of appeal have been heard and decided during the day. This expense is to be paid by the party making the appeal: in cases, however, where such party refuses or delays to make the payment, the Collector is authorized, if claimed by the merchant appraiser, to advance the sum due to said merchant appraiser, such payment to be noted on the entry of the merchandise in question, and no permit is thereafter to be issued for the delivery of said merchandise, or any part thereof, for consumption, transportation or exportation, until the Collector shall be reimbursed by the importer for the advance so made.

EXTRACTS.

The provision of the 2d section of the Tariff Act of 21st May, 1861, classifying unenumerated articles by similitude to articles enumerated, being applicable only to dutiable articles, does not authorize the transfer of non-enumerated articles to the free list.

Goods suffered by importers to remain in warehouse five days after the payment of duties, and the issue of the permit for delivery, are to be treated by the Collectors as unclaimed.

Additions to the value of merchandise, where the invoice value is less than the actual market value, in order to avoid the additional duty of 20 per cent., imposed by 5th section of act 21st May, 1861, must be made on the entry at the time the entry is presented at the custom house. The invoice must in no case be altered or defaced.

Dutiable articles purchased by persons visiting foreign countries, for themselves or others, are placed on the same footing as to liability to duty as merchandise imported on formal orders sent abroad by residents of the Confederate States.

Articles imported into the Confederate States, and sent abroad for repairs, are dutiable on re-importation.

Treasury notes issued under act of 16th May and 25th July, 1861, are receivable in payment of all public dues, except export duties.

Goods required to be weighed, gauged or measured, must not be removed from the landing until the quantity is thus ascertained by the proper officer of the customs.

Examinations and appraisements of imported merchandise are required to be made at the first port of entry, at which port, also, the actual quantity must be ascertained by weighing, gauging or measuring.

Invoices of goods subject to ad valorem duty must be made out in the currency of the country from whence they are imported.

CLAIMS FOR REFUNDING.

In all cases where parties allege to have claims for return of duties paid in error, illegal exactions or otherwise, the application must be made direct to the Treasury Department, upon receipt of which, a report of the case, when requisite, will be called for by the Collector, and, upon its examination, the decision of the Department will be rendered.

INFORMATION FOR SHIPMASTERS AND OTHERS.

EQUALIZATION OF FOREIGN VESSELS.

All discriminating duty on the tonnage of foreign vessels, or upon goods imported in such, is abolished; the vessels of all nations are equalized as to rights and privileges in commerce and navigation, with those of the Confederate States, and permitted to engage in the coasting trade, by the act of 26th February, 1861.

LIGHT MONEY.

All vessels entering the seaports of the Confederate States are subject to a duty of five cents per ton, as light dues, by the act of 16th March, 1861.

Vessels in the coasting trade, trading regularly between ports of the Confederate States, are required to pay light dues but once in every three months, by the act of 16th March, 1861.

ABOLISHMENT OF PROHIBITIONS ON IMPORTS.

All prohibitions against the importation of distilled spirits, liquors and sugars, in packages not below certain prescribed capacities, or in vessels of a certain tonnage, are abolished by the act of 5th March, 1861.

REGISTERS.

Vessels, wherever built, owned in not less than one-fourth, and commanded by citizens of the Confederate States, are permitted to be registered as vessels of the Confederate States, by the act of 6th March, 1861.

Previous to the registration of a vessel in part owned by a citizen or citizens of the Confederate States, the consent of a majority in interest of the owners shall be presented to the Collector to whom the application for the register is made, and the former register of the vessel must be surrendered.

Registered vessels must have the name of the vessel and of the port to which they belong painted on the stern, under a penalty of fifty dollars.

CHANGE OF MASTER OF REGISTERED VESSEL.

When the master, or person having command or charge of a ship or vessel, registered pursuant to law, is changed, the owner, or one of the owners, or the new master, of such ship or vessel must report such change to the Collector of the district where the same shall happen, or where the ship or vessel shall first be after the same shall have happened, and must produce to him the certificate of registry of such ship or vessel, and make oath or affirmation showing that such new master is a citizen of the Confederate States, and the manner in which, and the means whereby, he is so a citizen; and if such change is not reported, the master, or person in command, shall forfeit the sum of one hundred dollars.

VESSELS IN THE COASTING TRADE.

The license, issued to a vessel in the coasting trade is granted for one year, and must be renewed within three days of its expiration; or if it expires while the vessel is absent, within three days after her arrival. The penalty for neglect is fifty dollars.

Captains are required to exhibit their papers, when demanded by an officer of the revenue. The penalty for refusal is one hundred dollars.

The name of the vessel must be painted on her stern, with white letters three inches long, on a black ground, under a penalty of twenty dollars.

On the change of the master, or person having the charge or command of any enrolled ship or vessel, the owner, or one of the owners, or the new master of such vessel, shall report said change to the Collector of the district where the change shall happen, or where the vessel shall first be after such change, and produce the enrolment, and shall make oath or affirmation that such new master is a citizen of the Confederate States, and the means whereby he became a citizen; whereupon, the Collector shall endorse on the certificate of enrolment a memorandum of such change, specifying the name of the new master, and subscribe his name thereto.

Every change of master must be reported to the Collector of the port, and endorsed on the license, under a penalty of ten dollars.

The enrolment and license expire whenever there is any change of owner, or alteration is made in the rig or size; and must be reported to the Collector of the port, under the penalty of forfeiture of the vessel.

Whenever a change is made of the master of a licensed vessel, a memorandum of such change is to be endorsed on the license in the same manner as is directed in respect to the enrolment. The new master, or, if he be absent, one of the owners, must, however, make the oath or affirmation.

TRANSFER OF PROPERTY IN VESSELS.

The laws regulating the issuing of register, enrolments and licenses to vessels, provides that when any ship or vessel thus documented is sold in whole or in part to a citizen of the Confederate States, or altered in form or burden or in rigging, by change from one denomination to another, the vessel should be registered, enrolled, or licensed anew by her former name; and in every case of such sale or transfer there should be an instrument of writing in the nature of a bill of sale, which shall recite at length the former certificate of registry, enrollment or license

The recital of the former certificate of registry, etc., is an indispensable requisite in all such transfers, and unless such is contained therein the Collector cannot issue the new papers required.

Bills of sale, transferring property in vessels, should also be recorded in the office of the Collector at the port where the purchaser resides, and at that at which the new register, etc., is to be issued, as the act of July 29, 1850, provides, that no bill of sale, mortgage, hypothecation, or conveyance of any vessel, or part of any vessel of the Confederate States, shall be valid against any person other than the grantors, etc., unless recorded in the office of the Collector of customs where the vessel is registered or enrolled.

WRECKED GOODS.

Goods shipped coastwise, and the vessel wrecked or condemned in a foreign port, or the goods carried to such port, may be brought to the Confederate States and admitted free of duty, on satisfactory evidence of the facts being presented to the Collector, and proof that the articles of foreign origin comprising the cargo had once paid duty in the Confederate States, and that the vessel was bound in good faith on a coasting voyage, with no intention of touching at a foreign port of destination.

MANIFESTS.—For forms of manifests, see custom house blanks.

REPORT AND ENTRANCE.

Vessels must report at the custom house, within twenty-four hours, and enter within forty-eight hours after arrival.

ENTRANCE AND CLEARANCE.—For explanations on these subjects,

see entrance and clearance of vessels in article on "manner of transacting business with the custom house."

TONNAGE MEASUREMENT.—See article on rules for admeasurement of vessels for tonnage.

IMPORTATION.—It is a settled principle of law that goods must be brought into port with intent to land or discharge them, to constitute an importation. The arrival must be voluntary, with intent to land the cargo. Coming into port is *prima facie* evidence of intent to land, unless proof be adduced against it, such as destination declared on manifest for another port, etc.

If a vessel come into a port of entry by distress of weather, or to avoid capture, it is not an importation. If her cargo be afterwards sold for consumption, it becomes liable to duty; but not if exported.

Vessels arriving off a district or port with a cargo, and wishing to take it to some other port on account of advantage in markets, may do so, by the master changing the vessel's destination before delivering a manifest to any officer of the customs.

COMMERCIAL AND PORT RATES AT NEW ORLEANS.

Tariff of Charges, etc., agreed upon and adopted by the New Orleans Chamber of Commerce.

COMMISSIONS ON SALES.

	PER CT.
Sugar, cotton, tobacco, lead, flour and all other productions of the soil	$2\frac{1}{2}$
Domestic manufactures and all foreign merchandise	5
Guarantee of sales on time	$2\frac{1}{2}$
Purchase and shipment of merchandise or produce	$2\frac{1}{2}$
Sales or purchase of stocks or bullion	1
Collecting and remitting dividends	1
Selling vessels or steamboats	$2\frac{1}{2}$
Purchasing vessels or steamboats	5
Procuring freights	5
Collecting freights from foreign ports	$2\frac{1}{2}$
" Coastwise	5
Outfits and disbursements	$2\frac{1}{2}$
Effecting insurance	$\frac{1}{2}$
Adjusting or collecting insurance or other claims without litigation	$2\frac{1}{2}$
With litigation	5
Purchasing or remitting drafts, or receiving or paying money on which no other commission has been charged	1
If bills remitted are guaranteed, in addition	$1\frac{1}{2}$
Bills and notes remitted for collection protested and returned.	1
Landing, custody and re-shipping merchandise or produce from vessels in distress	2
Do. bullion or specie	1

	PER CT.
Adjusting and collecting general average.................	5
Consignments of merchandise withdrawn or re-shipped per order, on account of advances and responsibilities, full commission.	
On the surplus amount of invoices of such consignments, deducting advances and liabilities ......half commission.	
Drawing, endorsing or negotiating foreign bills of exchange,	1½
Do. on domestic bills of exchange......................	1
Receiving, entering and re-shipping merchandise to a foreign port, on amount of invoice............................	1
On amount of advances, charges, and liabilities on same....	2½
For drawing, accepting, negotiating or endorsing notes or drafts, without funds, produce or bills of lading in hand..	2½
On cash advances, in all cases..........................	2½
For entering and bonding merchandise for the interior, on amount of duties, freight and charges, (besides the regular charge for forwarding,).................................	2½
Agency for steamboats, according to special contract.	

The foregoing rates to be exclusive of brokerage and charges actually incurred.

RECEIVING AND FORWARDING MERCHANDISE.

[*Exclusive of Charges actually incurred.*]

	CENTS.
Sugar, molasses and tobacco, per tierce.................	50
Cotton, per bale.......................................	50
Hemp, per bale..	20
Moss, per bale..	10
Provisions or bacon, per hhd...........................	25
Provisions or bacon, per tierce.........................	12½
Pork, beef, lard and tallow, per bbl....................	5
Box pork, per box.....................................	15
Flour, grain and other dry barrels.....................	5
Lard, nails and shot, per keg..........................	2½

	CENTS.
Lead, per pig	1
Corn, wheat, beans, oats and other grain, per bag	3

LIQUIDS.

Pipes and hogsheads	50
Half-pipes and tierces	25
Quarter-casks and barrels	12½
Whiskey	10
Oils, per barrel	12½

SUNDRIES.

Boxes, bales, cases, trunks and other packages dry goods	10@50
Earthen and hardware, per package	25@50
Bar iron and castings, per ton	75
Railroad iron and pig iron, per ton	50
Hollow ware, per ton	$1 50
Soap, candles, wines, etc., per box	5
Coffee, spices, etc., per bag	6
Gunpowder, per keg	25
Salt, per sack	3

RATES OF DOCKAGE ESTABLISHED BY THE NEW ORLEANS DRY-DOCK ASSOCIATION.

SAILING VESSELS.

Tons.	Entrance.	Tons.	Demurrage.	Tons.	Entrance.	Tons.	Demurrage.
Vessels of 50	$64	Vessels of 825 under 850	$8	850	$340	Vessels of 825 under 850	$72
50 under 75	68	850 " " 875	10	875	350	850 " " 875	74
75 " " 100	72	875 " " 900	12	900	360	875 " " 900	76
100 " " 125	76	900 " " 925	14	925	370	900 " " 925	78
125 " " 150	80	925 " " 950	16	950	380	925 " " 950	80
150 " " 175	85	950 " " 975	18	975	390	950 " " 975	82
175 " " 200	90	975 " " 1000	20	1000	400	975 " " 1000	84
200 " " 225	95	1000 " " 1025	22	1025	410	1000 " " 1025	86
225 " " 250	100	1025 " " 1050	24	1050	420	1025 " " 1050	88
250 " " 275	110	1050 " " 1075	26	1075	430	1050 " " 1075	90
275 " " 300	120	1075 " " 1100	28	1100	440	1075 " " 1100	92
300 " " 325	130	1100 " " 1125	30	1125	450	1100 " " 1125	94
325 " " 350	140	1125 " " 1150	32	1150	460	1125 " " 1150	96
350 " " 375	150	1150 " " 1175	34	1175	470	1150 " " 1175	98
375 " " 400	160	1175 " " 1200	36	1200	480	1175 " " 1200	100
400 " " 425	170	1200 " " 1225	38	1225	490	1200 " " 1225	102
425 " " 450	180	1225 " " 1250	40	1250	500	1225 " " 1250	104
450 " " 475	190	1250 " " 1275	42	1275	510	1250 " " 1275	106
475 " " 500	200	1275 " " 1300	44	1300	520	1275 " " 1300	108
500 " " 525	210	1300 " " 1325	46	1325	530	1300 " " 1325	110
525 " " 550	220	1325 " " 1350	48	1350	540	1325 " " 1350	112
550 " " 575	230	1350 " " 1375	50	1375	550	1350 " " 1375	114
575 " " 600	240	1375 " " 1400	52	1400	560	1375 " " 1400	116
600 " " 625	250	1400 " " 1425	54	1425	570	1400 " " 1425	118
625 " " 650	260	1425 " " 1450	56	1450	580	1425 " " 1450	120
650 " " 675	270	1450 " " 1475	58	1475	590	1450 " " 1475	122
675 " " 700	280	1475 " " 1500	60	1500	600	1475 " " 1500	124
700 " " 725	290	1500 " " 1525	62	1525	610	1500 " " 1525	126
725 " " 750	300	1525 " " 1550	64	1550	620	1525 " " 1550	128
750 " " 775	310	1550 " " 1575	66	1575	630	1550 " " 1575	130
775 " " 800	320	1575 " " 1600	68	1600	640	1575 " " 1600	132
800 " " 825	330		70				

STEAMERS.

Tons.	Entrance.	Tons.	Demurrage.	Tons.	Entrance.	Tons.	Demurrage.
Steamers of 50 under 75	$70	Steamers of 825 under 850	$10	850	$425	Steamers of 825 under 850	$74
75 " " 100	75	850 " " 875	12	875	437	850 " " 875	76
100 " " 125	80	875 " " 900	14	900	450	875 " " 900	78
125 " " 150	90	900 " " 925	16	925	463	900 " " 925	80
150 " " 175	102	925 " " 950	18	950	475	925 " " 950	82
175 " " 200	113	950 " " 975	20	975	487	950 " " 975	84
200 " " 225	123	975 " " 1000	22	1000	500	975 " " 1000	86
225 " " 250	133	1000 " " 1025	24	1025	512	1000 " " 1025	88
250 " " 275	144	1025 " " 1050	26	1050	525	1025 " " 1050	90
275 " " 300	156	1050 " " 1075	28	1075	538	1050 " " 1075	92
300 " " 325	168	1075 " " 1100	30	1100	550	1075 " " 1100	94
325 " " 350	176	1100 " " 1125	32	1125	563	1100 " " 1125	96
350 " " 375	182	1125 " " 1150	34	1150	575	1125 " " 1150	98
375 " " 400	188	1150 " " 1175	36	1175	587	1150 " " 1175	100
400 " " 425	196	1175 " " 1200	38	1200	600	1175 " " 1200	102
425 " " 450	205	1200 " " 1225	40	1225	613	1200 " " 1225	104
450 " " 475	220	1225 " " 1250	42	1250	625	1225 " " 1250	106
475 " " 500	238	1250 " " 1275	44	1275	637	1250 " " 1275	108
500 " " 525	250	1275 " " 1300	46	1300	650	1275 " " 1300	110
525 " " 550	263	1300 " " 1325	48	1325	662	1300 " " 1325	112
550 " " 575	275	1325 " " 1350	50	1350	675	1325 " " 1350	114
575 " " 600	285	1350 " " 1375	52	1375	688	1350 " " 1375	116
600 " " 625	300	1375 " " 1400	54	1400	700	1375 " " 1400	118
625 " " 650	312	1400 " " 1425	56	1425	713	1400 " " 1425	120
650 " " 675	325	1425 " " 1450	58	1450	725	1425 " " 1450	122
675 " " 700	337	1450 " " 1475	60	1475	737	1450 " " 1475	124
700 " " 725	350	1475 " " 1500	62	1500	750	1475 " " 1500	126
725 " " 750	363	1500 " " 1525	64	1525	763	1500 " " 1525	128
750 " " 775	375	1525 " " 1550	66	1550	776	1525 " " 1550	130
775 " " 800	387	1550 " " 1575	68	1575	789	1550 " " 1575	132
800 " " 825	400	1575 " " 1600	70	1600	802	1575 " " 1600	134
	413		72				

ALL DOCKAGES CASH.

All vessels and steamers will be allowed, after ten days demurrage in dock, ten per cent. deduction on their demurrage; twenty per cent. after fifteen days, and thirty per cent. after twenty days.

STORAGE AND LABOR PER MONTH.

	Months.	
	1st.	2d, etc.
Cotton and wool, per bale	20 cts.	10
Tobacco, per hhd	50	25
Hemp, per bale not exceeding 300 lbs	10	7
Hemp, per bale not exceeding 450 lbs	15	10
Hemp, per bale not exceeding 600 lbs	20	15
Hemp, per bale not exceeding 800 lbs	25	18
Moss, per bale	10	6
Bagging and rope	5	3
Peltries, per bale	10	7
Hides, each	1½	1
Lead, per pig	1	1
Hollow ware, per ton	1 25	75
Bar iron and castings, per ton	75	50
Rail road iron and pig iron, per ton	50	25
Bacon and provisions, per hhd	25	25
Pork, beef, lard, tallow, etc., per barrel	8	6
Molasses, oil and whiskey, per barrel	10	8
Flour, per barrel	5	4
Lard, per keg	2½	2
Sugar and molasses, per hhd	40	25
Sugar, Havana, per box	12½	10
Corn, wheat, oats and other grain, per bag	4	3
Coffee, spices, etc., per bag	5	3
Salt, per bag	3	2
Candles, soap, wine, fish, raisins, oils, sweatmeats, cigars, etc., per box or basket	4	2
Do. in half boxes	2	1

	Months	
	1st.	2d, etc.
Nails, per keg	3	2
Dry goods, not exceeding 10 feet	15	10
Dry goods, not exceeding 20 feet	20	15
Dry goods, not exceeding 30 feet	25	20
Dry Goods, over 30 feet	40	25
Crockery, per cask or crate	30	20
Crockery, per half cask or half crate	15	10
Hardware, per cask	40	25
Hardware, per tierce	20	15
Hardware, per barrel	10	8
Liquids, per pipe or hhd	40	30
Liquids, per half pipe or tierce	25	18
Liquids, per quarter cask or barrel	10	8
Claret, per cask	20	15
Gunny bags, per bale	10	8
India bagging, per bale	15	10

WEIGHT OF GRAIN PER BUSHEL.

Wheat and rye	60 lbs.
Corn	56 lbs.
Oats	32 lbs.

TARES.

Lard, butter, cheese, tallow	Actual tare.
Stearine, sugar, rice	Actual tare.
Coffee, in bags	2 per cent.

FREIGHTS.

When vessels are chartered, or goods shipped by the ton, and no special agreement respecting the proportion of tonnage which each particular article shall be computed at, the following regulation shall be the standard. The articles, the bulk of which shall compose a ton, to equal a ton of heavy materials, shall, in weight, be as follows:

Coffee, in casks........1568 lbs; in bags......1830 lbs.
Cocoa, in casks ....1120 lbs: in bags......1300 lbs.
Pimento, in casks ...... 950 lbs; in bags......1100 lbs.
Flour.....................................8 barrels of 196 lbs.
Beef, pork, tallow, pickled fish, naval stores ....6 barrels.
Pig and bar iron, lead and other metals or ore, heavy dye-woods. sugar, rice, honey, or other heavy articles ......gross 2240 lbs.
Ship bread, in casks.....672; bags.....784; bulk..... 896 lbs.
Wines, brandy, spirits and liquids generally, reckoning the full capacity of the casks, wine measure.............200 gallons.
Grain, peas and beans, in casks....................22 bushels.
Grain, peas and beans, in bulk ....36 bushels.
Salt, European...................................36 bushels.
Salt, West India..................................31 bushels.
Stone Coal..28 bushels.
Timber, planks, furs, peltries, in bales or boxes, cotton, wool, or other measurement goods.....................40 cubic feet.
Dry hides..1120 lbs.

When molasses is shipped by the hogshead without any special agreement, it shall be taken at 110 gallons, estimated on the full capacity of the cask.

Freights, (and commissions on them,) when in sterling money, shall be settled at $4 84 per pound sterling; and other foreign currency, at the value fixed by Congress.

SCALE OF RATES ADOPTED BY THE ASSOCIATION OF COTTON PRESSES AT NEW ORLEANS.

CHARGES TO SHIPPERS AND SPECULATORS IN COTTON WHEN COMPRESSED.

Drayage to ship ....20 cents per bale.
Ropes to replace iron hoops................. 8 cents per rope.
Additional ropes, when required ....10 cents per rope.
Covering sample holes.......................10 cents per bale.
Labor, if not ordered the day cotton is weighed, 5 cents per bale.
Storage per month, after 5 days..............10 cents per bale.

A charge of 15 cents per bale for the use of the yard for classing and marking will be made to the purchaser on all cotton moved to any other press for compressing.

Upon all cotton returned from the ship, double drayage will be charged to the shipper; and any labor and storage that may be incurred, as per above rates.

Cotton Uncompressed.

Drayage to ship ....25 cents per bale.
Labor, if not ordered the day it is weighed..... 5 cents per bale.
Storage, first month..........................15 cents per bale.
Storage per month thereafter.................10 cents per bale.

Cotton ordered, and the ship is not ready to receive it, whether compressed or uncompressed, will be charged the same rate as if not ordered.

Small Numbers and Speculation Cotton.

Labor and storage, first month ....20 cents per bale.
Storage per month thereafter ....10 cents per bale.

All cotton changing ownership will be charged anew.

RATES OF THE NEW ORLEANS TOW BOATS.

FROM THE LEVEE TO THE BAR.

Vessels under 70 tons will be charged $20; and between 70 and 125 tons, 30 cents per ton.

Vessels of	125 tons and under	150 tons	$ 45
	150	175	48
	175	200	53
	200	225	58
	225	250	63
	250	275	68
	275	300	75
	300	325	83
	325	350	90
	350	375	100
	375	400	110
	400	425	120
	425	450	130
	450	475	140
	475	500	150
	500	525	160
	525	550	170
	550	575	180
	575	600	190
	600	625	203
	625	650	213
	650	675	225
	675	700	235
	700	725	248
	725	750	258
	750	775	270
	775	800	283
	800	825	295
	825	850	310
	850	875	325
	875	900	338

FROM THE LEVEE TO THE BAR. CONTINUED.

Vessels of	900 tons and under		925 tons	$350
	925	..	950	363
	950	..	975	375
	975	..	1000	388
	1000	..	1025	400
	1025	..	1050	415
	1050	..	1075	430
	1075	..	1100	445
	1100	..	1125	460
	1125	..	1150	475
	1150	..	1175	485
	1175	..	1200	498
	1200	..	1225	510
	1225	..	1250	523
	1250	..	1275	535
	1275	..	1300	548
	1300	..	1325	560
	1325	..	1350	573
	1350	..	1375	585
	1375	..	1400	595
	1400	..	1425	608
	1425	..	1450	620
	1450	..	1475	633
	1475	..	1500	645
	1500			658

And for every rate additional, $15 more.

Vessels requiring the aid of two boats on the bar, will be charged for the extra boat as follows:

Under 500 tons.................. $ 50
Of 500 tons, and under 1000..... 75
Of 1000 and upwards,.... 100

VESSELS FROM THE BAR, OR INSIDE THE BAR, TO CITY.

Vessels under 50 tons, $1 per ton.

Vessels of	50 tons and under		60 tons	$ 55
	60	..	70	60
	70	..	80	70

VESSELS FROM THE BAR, OR INSIDE THE BAR TO CITY, CONTINUED.

Vessels of			
80 tons and under	90 tons,	$ 80
90	..	100	90
100	..	125	100
125	..	150	120
150	..	175	140
175	..	200	160
200	..	225	180
225	..	250	200
250	..	275	215
275	..	300	230
300	..	325	245
325	..	350	260
350	..	375	275
375	..	400	293
400	..	425	308
425	..	450	325
450	..	475	340
475	..	500	355
500	..	525	370
525	..	550	385
550	..	575	395
575	..	600	410
600	..	625	423
625	..	650	435
650	..	675	448
675	..	700	460
700	..	725	475
725	..	750	488
750	..	775	500
775	..	800	515
800	..	825	530
825	..	850	545
850	..	875	560
875	..	900	575
900	..	925	590
925	..	950	605
950	..	875	618
975	..	1000	630
1000	..	1025	643

VESSELS FROM THE BAR, OR INSIDE THE BAR TO CITY, CONTINUED.

Vessels of	1025 tons and under	1050 tons,	$ 658
	1050	1075	675
	1075	1100	685
	1100	1125	695
	1125	1150	708
	1150	1175	720
	1175	1200	735
	1200	1225	748
	1225	1250	765
	1250	1275	790
	1275	1300	805
	1300	1325	825
	1325	1350	845
	1350	1375	860
	1375	1400	875
	1400	1425	890
	1425	1450	905
	1450	1475	920
	1475	1500	935
	1500		950

And for every rate additional, $20 more.

All vessels left at the Powder House or at any point below the City for the purpose of discharging Cargo, Passengers, etc., will be charged the same as if towed to the City.

FROM WILDER'S BAYOU TO CITY.

Vessels under 200 tons, 75 cents per ton.

Vessels of	200 tons and under	225 tons,	$155
	225	250	165
	250	275	175
	275	300	190
	300	325	210
	325	350	225
	350	375	240
	375	400	255
	400	425	268
	425	450	283

FROM WILDER'S BAYOU TO CITY, CONTINUED.

Vessels of	450 tons and under	475 tons,	$295
	475	500	310
	500	525	325
	525	550	340
	550	575	355
	575	600	365
	600	625	375
	625	650	385
	650	675	398
	675	700	410
	700	725	420
	725	750	430
	750	775	440
	775	800	455
	800	825	465
	825	850	478
	850	875	490
	875	900	505
	900	925	520
	925	950	535
	950	975	550
	975	1000	565
	1000	1025	580
	1025	1050	593
	1050	1075	605
	1075	1100	620
	1100	1125	638
	1125	1150	650
	1150	1175	665
	1175	1200	680
	1200	1225	698
	1225	1250	715
	1250	1275	730
	1275	1300	745
	1300	1325	760
	1325	1350	773
	1350	1375	785
	1375	1400	798
	1400	1425	810

FROM WILDER'S BAYOU TO CITY, CONTINUED.

Vessels of				
	1425 tons, and under		1450 tons,	$823
	1450	..	1475	833
	1475	..	1500	845
	1500	•		858

And for every rate additional, $15 more.

FROM FORT JACKSON TO CITY.
Vessels under 200 tons, 70 cents per ton.

Vessels of				
	200 tons and under		225 tons,	$150
	225	..	250	160
	250	..	275	170
	275	..	300	180
	300	..	325	190
	325	..	350	200
	350	..	375	213
	375	..	400	225
	400	..	425	235
	425	..	450	248
	450	..	475	263
	475	..	500	275
	500	..	525	288
	525	..	550	300
	550	..	575	310
	575	..	600	325
	600	..	625	335
	625	..	650	345
	650	..	675	355
	675	..	700	365
	700	..	725	375
	725	..	750	385
	750	..	775	395
	775	..	800	405
	800	..	825	415
	825	..	850	425
	850	..	875	435
	875	..	900	448
	900	..	925	460
	925	..	950	473

FROM FORT JACKSON TO CITY, CONTINUED.

Vessels of	950 tons and under		975 tons,	$483
	975	..	1000	495
	1000	..	1025	510
	1025	..	1050	525
	1050	..	1075	538
	1075	..	1100	550
	1100	..	1125	560
	1125	..	1150	570
	1150	..	1175	580
	1175	..	1200	590
	1200	..	1225	600
	1225	..	1250	615
	1250	..	1275	633
	1275	..	1300	648
	1300	..	1325	660
	1325	..	1350	673
	1350	..	1375	685
	1375	..	1400	695
	1400	..	1425	705
	1425	..	1450	715
	1450	..	1475	725
	1475	..	1500	738
	1500			750

And for every rate additional, $12 more

FROM GRAND PRAIRIE TO THE CITY.

Vessels under 200 tons, 58 cents per ton.

Vessels of	200 tons and under		225 tons,	$130
	225	..	250	138
	250	..	275	145
	275	..	300	153
	300	..	325	163
	325	..	350	173
	350	..	375	185
	375	..	400	198
	400	..	425	208
	425	..	450	218
	450	..	475	228

FROM GRAND PRAIRIE TO THE CITY, CONTINUED.

Vessels of.	475 tons and under	500 tons,	$238
	500	..	525	248
	525	..	550	258
	550	..	575	268
	575	..	600	273
	600	..	625	280
	625	..	650	290
	650	..	675	300
	675	..	700	310
	700	..	725	320
	725	..	750	330
	750	..	775	340
	775	..	800	353
	800	..	825	363
	825	..	850	373
	850	..	875	383
	875	..	900	390
	900	..	925	400
	925	..	950	415
	950	..	975	430
	975	..	1000	443
	1000	..	1025	455
	1025	..	1050	465
	1050	..	1075	475
	1075	..	1100	485
	1100	..	1125	495
	1125	..	1150	503
	1150	..	1175	513
	1175	..	1200	523
	1200	..	1225	533
	1225	..	1250	543
	1250	..	1275	553
	1275	..	1300	563
	1300	..	1325	578
	1325	..	1350	595
	1350	..	1375	608
	1375	..	1400	620
	1400	..	1425	638
	1425	..	1450	650

FROM GRAND PRAIRIE TO THE CITY, CONTINUED.

Vessels of 1450 tons and under 1475 tons, $660
    1475   ..   1500   670
    1500   ..   680

And for every rate additional, $10 more.

FROM JOHNSTON'S TO THE CITY.

Vessels under 200 tons, 50 cents per ton.

Vessels of				
	200 tons and under	225 tons,	$105
	225	..	250	113
	250	..	275	123
	275	..	300	135
	300	..	325	145
	325	..	350	155
	350	..	375	168
	375	..	400	178
	400	..	425	188
	425	..	450	195
	450	..	475	205
	475	..	500	215
	500	..	525	223
	525	..	550	230
	550	..	575	238
	575	..	600	245
	600	..	625	253
	625	..	650	260
	650	..	675	268
	675	..	700	275
	700	..	725	285
	725	..	750	293
	750	..	775	300
	775	..	800	308
	800	..	825	315
	825	..	850	323
	850	..	875	330
	875	..	900	338
	900	..	925	345
	925	..	950	355
	950	..	975	365

FROM JOHNSTON'S TO THE CITY, CONTINUED.

Vessels of	975 tons and under	1000 tons,	$378
	1000	1025	388
	1025	1050	398
	1050	1075	405
	1075	1100	413
	1100	1125	420
	1125	1150	428
	1150	1175	435
	1175	1200	445
	1200	1225	455
	1225	1250	463
	1250	1275	473
	1275	1300	483
	1300	1325	495
	1325	1350	510
	1350	1375	523
	1375	1400	533
	1400	1425	545
	1425	1450	555
	1450	1475	568
	1475	1500	578
	1500		588

And for every rate additional, $9 more.

FROM POVERTY POINT TO THE CITY.

Vessels under 200 tons, 45 cents per ton.

Vessels of	200 tons and under	225 tons,	$ 95
	225	250	100
	250	275	105
	275	300	113
	300	325	120
	325	350	128
	350	375	135
	375	400	143
	400	425	150
	425	450	158
	450	475	168
	475	500	178

FROM POVERTY POINT TO THE CITY, CONTINUED.

Vessels of	500 tons and under	525 tons,	$185
	525	..	550	193
	550	..	575	200
	575	..	600	208
	600	..	625	215
	625	..	650	223
	650	..	675	230
	675	..	700	238
	700	..	725	243
	725	..	750	250
	750	..	775	258
	775	..	800	263
	800	..	825	268
	825	..	850	273
	850	..	875	278
	875	..	900	285
	900	..	925	293
	925	..	950	300
	950	..	975	308
	975	..	1000	315
	1000	..	1025	323
	1025	..	1050	333
	1050	..	1075	340
	1075	..	1100	348
	1100	..	1125	355
	1125	..	1150	363
	1150	..	1175	370
	1175	..	1200	378
	1200	..	1225	385
	1225	..	1250	393
	1250	..	1275	400
	1275	..	1300	410
	1300	..	1325	420
	1325	..	1350	430
	1350	..	1375	443
	1375	..	1400	455
	1400	..	1425	465
	1425	..	1450	475

FROM POVERTY POINT TO THE CITY, CONTINUED.

Vessels of 1450 tons and under 1475 tons, $485
　　　　　 1475　　　　..　　　 1500　　　 493
　　　　　 1500　　　　　　　　　　　　　 500

And for every rate additional, $8 more.

FROM M'CALL'S TO THE CITY.

Vessels under 200 tons, 35 cents per ton.

Vessels of	200 tons and under	225 tons,	$ 73
	225	..	250	78
	250	..	275	83
	275	..	300	90
	300	..	325	95
	325	..	350	103
	350	..	375	110
	375	..	400	115
	400	..	425	123
	425	..	450	130
	450	..	475	138
	475	..	500	145
	500	..	525	153
	525	..	550	158
	550	..	575	163
	575	..	600	168
	600	..	625	173
	625	..	650	180
	650	..	675	185
	675	..	700	188
	700	..	725	193
	725	..	750	198
	750	..	775	203
	775	..	800	208
	800	..	825	213
	825	..	850	218
	850	..	875	223
	875	..	900	228

FROM M'CALL'S TO THE CITY. CONTINUED.

Vessels of	900 tons and under	925 tons,	$233
	925	..	950	238
	950	..	975	243
	975	..	1000	248
	1000	..	1025	253
	1025	..	1050	258
	1050	..	1075	263
	1075	..	1100	268
	1100	..	1125	273
	1125	..	1150	278
	1150	..	1175	283
	1175	..	1200	288
	1200	..	1225	293
	1225	..	1250	300
	1250	..	1275	308
	1275	..	1300	315
	1300	..	1325	323
	1325	..	1350	330
	1350	..	1375	338
	1375	..	1400	345
	1400	..	1425	353
	1425	..	1450	360
	1450	..	1475	368
	1475	..	1500	375
	1500			383

And for every rate additional, $7 more.

FROM ENGLISH TURN TO THE CITY.

Vessels under 200 tons, 35 cents per ton.

Vessels of	200 tons and under	225 tons,	$ 70
	225	..	250	73
	250	..	275	75
	275	..	300	78
	300	..	325	80
	325	..	350	83
	350	..	375	85
	375	..	400	88

FROM ENGLISH TURN TO THE CITY, CONTINUED.

Vessels of	400 tons and under		425 tons,	$ 93
	425	..	450	98
	450	..	475	103
	475	..	500	108
	500	..	525	113
	525	..	550	118
	550	..	575	123
	575	..	600	128
	600	..	625	133
	625	..	650	138
	650	..	675	143
	675	..	700	148
	700	..	725	153
	725	..	750	158
	750	..	775	160
	775	..	800	163
	800	..	825	165
	825	..	850	168
	850	..	875	170
	875	..	900	173
	900	..	925	175
	925	..	950	178
	950	..	975	183
	975	..	1000	188
	1000	..	1025	193
	1025	..	1050	198
	1050	..	1075	203
	1075	..	1100	208
	1100	..	1125	213
	1125	..	1150	218
	1150	..	1175	223
	1175	..	1200	228
	1200	..	1225	233
	1225	..	1250	238
	1250	..	1275	245
	1275	..	1300	250
	1300	..	1325	555
	1325	..	1350	263
	1350	..	1375	270

FROM ENGLISH TURN TO THE CITY, CONTINUED.

Vessels of 1375 tons, and under 1400 tons, $275
　　　　　1400　　..　　1425　　283
　　　　　1425　　..　　1450　　290
　　　　　1450　　..　　1475　　298
　　　　　1475　　...　　1500　　303
　　　　　1500　　　　　　　　　308

And for every rate additional, $6 more.

MOVING VESSELS.

FROM POWDER HOUSE TO THE CITY, AND VICE VERSA.

Vessels under 200 tons..............................$20
　"　of　200 and under 400....................$25
　"　 "　400 and upwards......................$30

FROM SLAUGHTER HOUSE POINT, OR BROOKLYN WAREHOUSE TO THE CITY, AND VICE VERSA.

Vessels under 200 tons..............................$10
　"　of　200 tons and upwards..:...............$12

FROM CANAL STREET TO LOWER TOBACCO WAREHOUSES, OR ANY POINT BETWEEN THESE LIMITS, AND VICE VERSA.

For all vessels..$10

The same rate if moved within the limits of 1st and 4th Districts.

FROM ANY POINT BETWEEN CANAL STREET AND LOWER TOBACCO WAREHOUSES TO ANY POINT WITHIN THE LIMITS OF 1ST AND 4TH DISTRICTS, AND VICE VERSA.

Vessels under 200 tons..............................$10
　"　of　200 and upwards.......................$12

FROM CITY TO SHIP YARDS, AND VICE VERSA.

Vessels under 200 tons..............................$12
　"　of　200 tons and upwards..................$15

Steam Boats to be charged as per agreement.

All vessels are to be charged according to their American measurement, and when not so measured, will be charged 30 per cent. additional on their rates, according to their registered tonnage.

A vessel shall be bound to wait thirty-six hours after being towed in over the bar for the boat which towed her in, or for one belonging to the same line, to make up a tow; otherwise she shall be charged full towage from sea to city.

Any vessel, after waiting thirty-six hours for the boat that towed her in, or one of the same line, to make up a tow, may take any other boat that offers, by paying to the boat which towed her in one quarter of the regular upward towage.

All vessels, whilst in tow of any boat, shall be considered at their own risk, and vessels towed astern will be charged the same as if taken alongside, and in proportion to the distance they may be towed, should they be cast off in consequence of bad weather, or for any cause beyond the control of the master of the boat.

Vessels ashore or in distress, requiring the aid of a towboat, will be charged as agreed on by the masters of the vessel and towboat.

In all cases where cargo is put on board of any boat, it is understood to be at the risk of the vessel discharging it, whether as regards damage or loss; neither will any receipt be given by the master or officers of said boat for goods received on board of her; but the captains of the vessels may send such persons on board to take charge of them as they may think proper.

Vessels without rudders, or with rudders so damaged as to be unserviceable, will be charged double the above rates.

All towage down will be payable on the arrival of the vessel at the Pilot's Station, S. W. Pass, or Balize, and no vessel will be put on the bar until the towage is paid.

When a vessel is towed on the bar, and after a fair and unsuccessful trial to get her in, she shall be charged such a price as may be deemed adequate for the service performed.

Signals for steam are to be hoisted at the main; and in all cases where vessels are taken in tow, it shall be considered as an engagement to be towed to the city, at the customary rates of towage, and under the conditions heretofore expressed, unless a special engagement be made to the contrary.

All services rendered for which no provision is made in the foregoing rates will be charged as per agreement between the captains or agents of the boats and masters or agents of the vessels.

RATES FOR PILOTAGE IN AND OUT THE MISSISSIPPI PASSES.

Vessels drawing 10 feet, or less.............. $2 50 per foot.
" over 10 feet, and under 18.... 3 50 "
" 18 feet, and upwards........ 4 50 "

DRAFT.	PER FOOT.	AMOUNT.
4 feet,	$2 50	$10 00
4½	"	11 25
4¾	"	11 87
5	"	12 50
5½	"	12 75
5¾	"	13 37
6	"	15 00
6½	"	16 25
6¾	"	16 87
7	"	17 50
7½	"	18 75
7¾	"	19 37
8	"	20 00
8½	"	21 25
8¾	"	21 87
9	"	22 50
9½	"	23 75
9¾	"	24 37
10	"	25 00
10½	$3 50	36 75
10¾	"	37 62

DRAFT.	PER FOOT.	AMOUNT.
11 feet,	$3 50	$38 50
11½	"	40 25
11¾	"	41 12
12	"	42 00
12½	"	43 75
12¾	"	44 62
13	"	45 50
13½	"	47 25
13¾	"	48 12
14	"	49 00
14½	"	50 75
14¾	"	51 62
15	"	52 50
15½	"	54 25
15¾	"	55 12
16	"	56 00
16½	"	57 75
16¾	"	58 62
17	"	59 50
17½	"	61 25
17¾	"	62 12
18	$4 50	81 00
18½	"	83 25
18¾	"	84 37
19	"	85 50
19½	"	87 75
19¾	"	88 87
20	"	90 00
20½	"	92 25
20¾	"	93 37
21	"	94 50
21½	"	96 75
21¾	"	97 87
22	"	99 00

QUARANTINE CHARGES AT NEW ORLEANS.

The quarantine station is on the Mississippi river, seventy-two miles below the city of New Orleans.

For certificate of health from resident physician and permit to proceed to the City:

Sailing vessels of 1000 tons or over	$30 00
Ships of 1000 tons or less	20 00
Barks	15 00
Brigs	10 00
Schooners	7 50
Steamboats (except tow boats)	5 00
Steamships from Florida, Alabama, Mississippi, or Texas	10 00
Steamships from other ports	20 00

These fees are to be paid to the resident physician at the quarantine station.

PORT WARDEN'S FEES, NEW ORLEANS.

Master and wardens, for inspecting, when called upon, the hatches of vessels arriving from sea, previous to opening, and being present at the opening of the same, holding survey and furnishing certificate	$2 00
For every duplicate of such certificate	1 00
Master and wardens, for survey upon damaged goods brought into port in any ship or vessel, or upon any damaged vessel deemed unfit to proceed to sea, and presenting certificate	2 00
For every duplicate of such certificate	1 00
Wardens, for services as surveyors of damaged goods or vessels, at rate of	2 50 per day.
Master and wardens, for directing sale of damaged goods by public auction, giving notice of sale in newspapers, attendance at sale and certificate to account of sale	10 00

Master and wardens are allowed, in addition to the above, for each vessel arriving in port from sea, whether called upon to perform any service or not.................................... $5 00

Acts of Louisiana, March 15, 1855.

HARBOR MASTER.

A fee of 2 cents per ton is charged by the harbor master to all vessels arriving from sea and coming to the wharf.

NEW ORLEANS LEVEE AND WHARFAGE DUES.

On ships and other decked vessels, and steamships from sea, 1000 tons and under.......... 20 cents per ton.
Excess of tonnage over 1000 tons............. 15   "
On steamships navigating the Gulf of Mexico or the ocean.................................... 15   "
These rates are for the first sixty days, and an extra duty of one-third of these rates for each additional sixty days.
Steamboats, for five days..................... 10 cents per ton.
    "   after five days..................... $5 00 per day.
    "   arriving and departing twice in a week, for each trip.............. 7 cents per ton.
    "   making three trips per week, each trip............................. 5 cents per ton.
Barges, over 100 tons......................... $25 00
Luggers, pirogues and scows, coastwise....... 2 00 each.
Flatboats, 80 feet............................ 8 00
    "   from 80 to 100 feet................ 10 00
    "   100 feet and over.................. 13 00

PORT CHARGES AT MOBILE, ALA.

For Pilotage of Vessels from Sea to Anchorage, and vice versa.

Vessels drawing from 5 to 10 feet........$2 50 per foot.
" " " 10½ " 12 " ....$2 75 " "
" " " 12½ " 14 " ....$3 00 " "
" " over 14 " ....$4 50 " "

There are no regular rates of tonnage from sea to the city, as vessels generally tow from sea to the lower anchorage, and sail up the bay from there to Dog River Bar.

For tonnage from sea to anchorage, } 10 cents per ton.
Vice versa,......................

There are no wharfage charges at the city on vessels, as the cargo pays all such.

Charge for lighterage on cotton down the bay, 35 cents per bale.

Vessels sail or tow to sea, as suits their pleasure.

RATES OF TOWAGE ON DOG RIVER BAR.

For vessels drawing 9 to 9¼ feet over bar and around river, $50 00
" 9¼ to 9½ " " 55 00
" 9½ to 10 " " 60 00
" 10 to 10¼ " " 70 00
" 10¼ to 10½ " " 75 00
" 10½ to 10¾ " " 80 00
" 10¾ to 11 " " 90 00
" 11 to 11¼ " " 100 00
" 8 to 9 through Pass.......... 25 00
" over 9 " 30 00

Towing in around Spanish river...................... 30 00
For use of tow-line.................................. 5 00
" transporting vessels in port...................... 7 50
" " steamboats in port................. 10 00
" " barges and lighters in port............ 5 00
" extra boat....................................... 30 00

For every inch over 11¼ feet, $5 additional.

Should a captain misrepresent the draft of his vessel, and the boat fail to get her over, she will be charged full towage. Vessels of 500 tons and over will be charged 25 per cent. on above rates.

EXPLANATORY.

It was the original object of this work to furnish, as supplementary to the tariff and revenue matter, accurate tables of the port charges and commercial rates established in all the principal ports of the Confederate States; but the difficulty and delay attending the efforts made to obtain such, and the necessity for the early publication of this edition, has rendered the omission of all but those of the ports of New Orleans and Mobile, which were more accessible, unavoidable. It is, however, confidently expected that this valuable information will be obtained, and embraced in a subsequent edition.

www.ingramcontent.com/pod-product-compliance
Lightning Source LLC
Chambersburg PA
CBHW032053230426
43672CB00009B/1579